THE HIDDEN HISTORY OF BURMA

THE
HIDDEN
HISTORY
OF
BURMA

RACE, CAPITALISM,
AND THE CRISIS
OF DEMOCRACY
IN THE 21ST CENTURY

THANT MYINT-U

W. W. NORTON & COMPANY
Independent Publishers Since 1923

For information about permission to reproduce selections from this book, write to
Permissions, W. W. Norton & Company, Inc., 500 Fifth Avenue, New York, NY 10110

For information about special discounts for bulk purchases, please contact
W. W. Norton Special Sales at specialsales@wwnorton.com or 800-233-4830

Manufacturing by Sheridan
Book design by Marysarah Quinn
Production manager: Anna Oler

Library of Congress Cataloging-in-Publication Data

Names: Thant Myint-U, author.
Title: The hidden history of Burma : race, capitalism, and the crisis of democracy in
    the 21st century / Thant Myint-U.
Description: New York : W. W. Norton & Company, Inc., [2020] | Includes
    bibliographical references and index.
Identifiers: LCCN 2019026007 | ISBN 9781324003298 (hardcover) |
    ISBN 9781324003304 (epub)
Subjects: LCSH: Burma—History—1988–
Classification: LCC DS530.65 .T46 2020 | DDC 959.105/3—dc23
LC record available at https://lccn.loc.gov/2019026007

W. W. Norton & Company, Inc., 500 Fifth Avenue, New York, N.Y. 10110
www.wwnorton.com

W. W. Norton & Company Ltd., 15 Carlisle Street, London W1D 3BS

1 2 3 4 5 6 7 8 9 0

For Sofia

CONTENTS

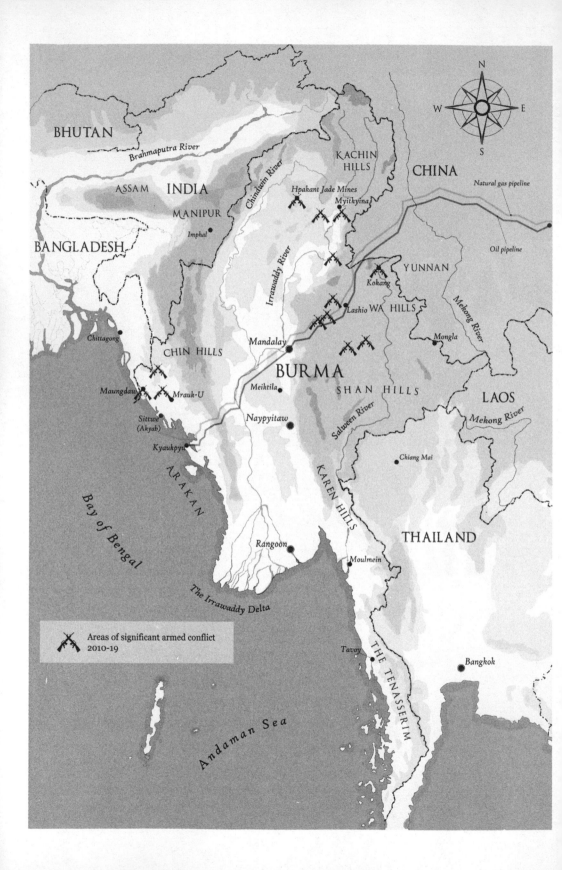

A NOTE ON BURMESE NAMES

BURMA OR MYANMAR? Around a millennium ago, the word "Myanma" first appeared in inscriptions, apparently describing a people living in the valley of the Irrawaddy River and their language. Over the centuries, kings began referring to themselves as Myanma kings, and their kingdom as the *Myanma pyi* (the Myanma country) or *Myanma naing-ngan* (the Myanma conquered lands). By the 17th century, the word was colloquially pronounced "Bama." Both "Myanma" and "Bama" are adjectives.

Around the same time, the first Europeans arrived, and called the country some variant of "Burma": it was "Birmania" to the Portuguese, "Birmanie" to the French. These names are almost certainly derived from "Bama." Under British rule, "Burma" was the country's official English name. The name in Burmese remained *Myanma pyi*.

None of this caused much of a fuss until 1989, when the ruling army junta officially changed the name of the country in English to Myanmar (the final "r" was meant to lengthen the vowel, as it would when spoken in the southeast of England, and not be pronounced). The justification offered was that the name "Myanmar" incorporated all the country's indigenous peoples. This was untrue. Few minorities, if any, would claim that the word historically applied to them. The real reason for the change was that the government of the time was moving in a nativist direction and looking for easy wins to burnish its ethno-nationalist credentials. An equivalent would be Germany insisting on being called "Deutschland" in English, or the Italians insisting on "Italia." Many in the West continued to use "Burma," either out of habit or to show disdain toward the junta dictatorship.

I use "Burma" throughout this book out of habit, because as a Burmese speaker it's awkward to refer to the country using an adjective, because I think "Burma" sounds far better in English, and because of the nativist underpinnings of the name change.

I use "Burmese" to refer either to the ethnic majority people, who speak the Burmese language and are overwhelmingly Buddhist, or to the state. There is no satisfactory term, at least not yet, for referring to all the peoples of the country. I also use older place names, such Arakan rather than Rakhine, for similar reasons.

Other identity-related words are equally, if not more, contentious, none perhaps more so than "Rohingya," a name for a Muslim minority in Arakan. The reasons for this are explored throughout this book.

Burmese personal names also merit some explanation. Most Burmese have only given names. These are traditionally chosen by parents on the advice of monks or astrologers, and often depend on which day of the week the child is born and the corresponding letters in the Burmese alphabet. For example, a child born on a Friday should properly have a name beginning with "th." These names are usually prefixed by a familiar term like "uncle" (U) or "aunt" (Daw). A person may have one name, with the appropriate prefix (U Thant), or several names (Daw Aung San Suu Kyi). None of these names are family or clan names. They are also not fixed: people may use different names in different situations or simply change their entire name whenever they want. It's not uncommon in an obituary to see a list of many names ("Dr. Tun Maung a.k.a. U Ye Htut a.k.a. Johnny"). One former member of parliament styled himself U James Bond.

Some of Burma's minority cultures, such as the Kachin, do have family or clan names, which are placed before their given names, as in the name Maran Brang Seng, where "Maran" is the name of a clan.

Personal names, places names, ethnonyms, even the name of the country, have changed or are changing. Burma is a place where identities are unstable. Much more will be said on issues of identity and its relationship to the country's singular politics and even more bizarre economy in the pages that follow.

THE HIDDEN HISTORY OF BURMA

INTRODUCTION

IN THE EARLY 2010S, Burma was the toast of the world. As the generals appeared to be giving up power, everybody, at least in the West, began to believe that the country was in the midst of an astonishing transformation, from the darkest of dictatorships to a peaceful and prosperous democracy.

Barack Obama, Bill Clinton, Hillary Clinton, Tony Blair, and dozens of other world leaders, past and present, came in quick succession to be part of the celebrated change. Trade embargos were rolled back and billions of dollars in aid promised to make up for lost time. Top businessmen followed, with George Soros at the head of the flock, their private jets crowding Rangoon's little airport, keen to invest in Asia's next frontier market. By 2016, Angelina Jolie, Jackie Chan and other celebrities were added to the mix, as tourism boomed and Nobel laureate Aung San Suu Kyi, freshly released from long years under house arrest, appeared set to finally lead her country.

But by 2018, the mood had turned deathly grim. A new militant outfit, the Arakan Rohingya Salvation Army, had attacked dozens of security posts in the far west of the country, and this had been followed by a fierce

Burmese army response. In the wake of the violence, hundreds of thousands of men, women, and children, nearly all from the Muslim Rohingya minority, fled to neighboring Bangladesh, bringing with them horrific accounts of rape and massacre. Burma now stood accused of genocide and crimes against humanity.

In September 2018, the United Nations Security Council met in New York to discuss possible responses and listened to an impassioned address by the actress Cate Blanchett, who had visited the sprawling Rohingya refugee camps and who became the first film star to speak to the world's highest security organ. New American and European sanctions were imposed, barely two years after the last were lifted, and Aung San Suu Kyi herself came under blistering criticism from once staunch allies in the human rights community for not doing more for the Rohingya. Erstwhile friends, from Bob Geldof to the Dalai Lama and Bishop Desmond Tutu, expressed disappointment at her inaction, and St. Hugh's College, Oxford, which she'd attended, removed her portrait from public display and placed it in storage. The Canadian Museum for Human Rights, not wanting to go that far, kept her portrait in their "Gallery of Honorary Canadians" but dimmed the lights.

Other news was also not good. Peace talks that had since 2012 been a centerpiece of Burma's feted reform process ground nearly to a halt and fighting flared in the northern hills. The economy, in 2014 the fastest-growing in the world, faced worrying headwinds. Investment plunged, business confidence sank, and fears mounted that a banking crisis might be around the corner. In 2016, Burma was on Fodor Guides' list of the world's hottest destinations. By 2018, it was on Fodor's list of top ten places to avoid.

What happened? For decades the story of Burma had been portrayed as a Manichean struggle between the ruling generals and a movement for human rights and a liberal democracy. But the old story and recent developments just didn't add up. Had the world been misreading Burma completely?

Not long ago, few believed that anything in Burma would ever change. The country seemed to be stuck in a time warp, ruled by a thuggish junta that would stay on forever. Then things did change, with political prisoners released, media censorship ended, and Internet restrictions lifted. Opinions pivoted 180 degrees, and many in the West as well as in Asia were quick to embrace the "transition" that seemed to be underway. In 2012, Aung San Suu Kyi became a member of parliament, then in 2015 led her party to a sweeping victory in the country's first free and fair elections in a generation. The word "miracle" was often used to describe what was happening. Whereas before, any idea of progress in Burma had been summarily dismissed, observers now assumed that further progress was inevitable. When discordant news got in the way—a communal riot here, a clash between the army and insurgents there—it was easily swept aside as peripheral to the main story. The story was too good, a much needed tonic at a time when the Arab Spring was giving way to extreme violence. Burma, at least, was a morality tale that seemed to be nearing its rightful conclusion.

Then the morality tale came crashing down.

Burma is a country of about 55 million people, squeezed between China and India but larger than France and Britain combined. More than a dozen rebel armies hold sway over large patches of the eastern uplands, together with hundreds more militias, all fighting the world's oldest civil war. Burma is one of the poorest countries in Asia, with one of the biggest illicit narcotics industries in the world. It is prone to devastating natural disasters (over 120,000 people died in a single day due to a cyclone in 2008) and is predicted to be one of the five nations most negatively impacted by climate change. It's a place where education and health care systems have been starved of funds for decades, a country which isolated itself from the world for a quarter century and then for a generation came under US- and UK-led economic sanctions that were, at the time, the harshest against any country anywhere on the planet (including North Korea).

In a way, Burma resembles parts of Europe and North America in the 19th century, a febrile mix of new freedoms and new nationalisms, unencumbered capitalism, new money and new poverty, fast-growing cities and urban slums, elected governments, excluded peoples, and brutal frontier wars—a mirror of the past, but one turbocharged by Facebook and by a fast-industrializing China next door.

Burma is also a devoutly religious society in which over 85 percent of the population follow neoconservative Theravada Buddhism, a philosophy which could be described as Epicurean but which has, in Burma, created a society whose values are more Stoic. The mother tongue of the majority, Burmese, is as dissimilar to English (or to any other Indo-European language) as possible; it is a language in which words like "national," "ethnic," and "human rights," have unexpected connotations.

On this distant and fragile stage, a twisted drama is being played which features some of the most pressing issues of our day, from exploding inequality, rising ethno-nationalism, and mutating views on race and identity to migration, environmental degradation, and climate change.

Burma was, for the United Nations and the West, the signature democracy project of the 1990s and 2000s. The question of whether democracy (in the sense most in the West would recognize, with competing political parties, a free media, and free elections) was ever really fit for the purpose was never asked, in part because democracy was what "the people" in Burma were demanding and in part because it was the obvious exit from a tyranny that no one could reasonably defend. In the early 2010s, the more the forms of democracy seemed to be taking shape, the more an assumption of progress took hold.

As the path to liberal democracy looked increasingly secure, an additional assumption grew that free markets would soon also take hold, opening the door to global capitalism. But then, as multinational companies queued up to have a look at what they hoped would be a lucrative new market, they saw in Burma a breed of capitalism already in place, well entrenched and intimately tied to China.

It's not impossible that democratic institutions will one day flourish in Burma. And it's far from impossible that global capitalism will defeat its rivals. It may even deliver the goods: growing the Burmese economy by leaps and bounds and reshaping Burma in the image of other Asian societies.

But is the life of the 21st-century Asian consumer really desirable or sustainable? Visiting the air-conditioned new shopping malls of Rangoon, it's clear that there's a desire for a new way of life. It's less clear that the Burmese—as they pose for selfies in front of the escalators and water fountains—are as yet very good at buying things they might not really need. And as Burma, which ranks consistently as one of the most generous countries on earth, integrates itself into the world of the mid-21st century, what is it exactly about this long quarantined nation, with its unique cultures, that needs to be changed, and what should instead be embraced? In an age of reform, few have thought about what it is important to protect.

Burma's story takes place under the long shadow of a particularly brutal and destructive British colonialism, one which first established the modern state as a racial hierarchy. It is a story that has consistently left ordinary Burmese people at the bottom of the heap, as development so far has meant disappearing forests, polluted rivers, contaminated food, rising debt, land confiscation, and most recently the cheap smartphones, Internet access, and Facebook pages on which they see for themselves, and for endless hours a day, the lives they will never have.

Burma is also a warning. Exactly a hundred years ago, modern politics in Burma was born as what we might today call an anti-immigration, anti-globalization movement. The country was gripped by a kind of identity politics. Under British rule, millions of people from the Indian subcontinent settled in the country. Global companies like Burmah Oil (later British Petroleum) extracted enormous sums in profit, paying little in taxes. Populist parties flirted with Fascism and Communism. Then came a long slide into nativism and self-imposed isolation. It was an understandable reaction. But decades on, the cost of withdrawal from the world has been a material and intellectual impoverishment on a scale unmatched in Asia. That cost has included hundreds of thousands of refugees (long before the Rohingya crisis), millions more internally displaced, millions more lives destroyed.

And in today's more open political space, the challenges of inequality and climate change are being met with a cocktail of ethno-nationalism and neoliberalism.

Can the future be different? Is a sharp turn in a fresh direction possible? Or is the recent violence a sign of even worse things to come?

BURMA HAS BEEN molded by big forces and big issues. Its story, the one that will be told in this book, is a story about race, capitalism, and an attempt at democracy. It features people who have plotted, pushed, and pulled to end half a century of army rule and who have been struggling ever since with the deep scars revealed and the energies unleashed. It includes as well the Burmese far from the corridors of power who have borne the brunt of the country's woes, and who have suffered and schemed to improve their lives against impossible odds. And it's about the foreign governments that have also shaped Burma's trajectory, usually in good faith, and sometimes with disastrous consequences. The heroes and villains have not always been whom they seem to be.

This book is mainly about the last fifteen years, from the height of the dictatorship, around the turn of the millennium, to the present day. But the echoes of the more distant past are, if anything, growing stronger. So we start at the beginning.

ONE

NEW WORLD

BURMA IS SHAPED like a kite and extends north to south over 1,300 miles, from icy pine-forested mountains on the marches of Tibet, the highest peaks nearly 20,000 feet high, to scorching hot beaches and little islands in the Andaman Sea. At its center is the Irrawaddy River, brown and muddy, which snakes through teak jungles and sun-baked scrublands before fanning out into a vast, steamy delta and emptying into the Bay of Bengal. To the west and east are uplands of little valleys and increasingly higher hills.

Burma has been home to modern humans since the first migrations out of Africa. There were others before: *Homo erectus* certainly, and probably Denisovans too, eastern cousins of the Neanderthals. Recent discoveries in genetic science are uncovering a fascinating past, with the Irrawaddy basin a hub of Pleistocene settlement, population expansion, and emigration over tens of thousands of years, to places as far afield as Australia and the Americas. Three to four thousand years ago, hunter-gatherer populations gave way to the first farmers, related genetically to the peoples who inhabited what is now southwest China. Two thousand years later, during the Bronze and Iron Ages, fresh migrations from the north brought tongues akin to Tibetan and ancestral to Burmese.

By the first millennium AD Burma was also home to peoples speaking languages related to modern Khmer, Vietnamese, and Mon (a language spoken in southern Burma), whose ancestors may have been the first to grow rice, and who lived along the Yangtze River before spreading across mainland Southeast Asia and into India. There were also people speaking languages similar to modern Thai and Lao. As it is today, Burma was likely always a hodgepodge of very different cultures and communities.

In the valleys, kingdoms came and went. Their people were literate and Buddhist, increasingly of a neoconservative variety. They looked to classical Indian culture for inspiration. In the highlands, on the other hand, there was an array of societies that ruled themselves, practiced animism, and spoke languages that were not written down. Like the Balkans, the Caucasus, and the Himalayan foothills, what's now Burma was a place of many nearly isolated communities, each with its own dialect and way of life, as well as grand civilizations with connections in every direction.

During the middle years of the 18th century, a new dynasty of Burmese-speaking warrior kings emerged from the arid interior, marched south toward the sea, defeated their French-backed and Mon-speaking rivals, and united the valley of the Irrawaddy River. Along the conquered coast they founded a new port and named it Rangoon, meaning "the enemy is vanquished." The elephant-mounted kings then pushed east into the adjacent uplands before taking nearly all of present-day Laos and Thailand, utterly destroying the Siamese capital of Ayutthaya in 1767. Over the next decade their armies repelled no fewer than four Manchu Chinese invasions from the north, defeating elite divisions of Manchu and Mongol cavalry drawn from the distant Russian frontier.

In 1783, at the apex of this newly minted empire, King Bodawpaya, who boasted fifty-three (official) queens and concubines and more than 120 children, founded a new capital, Amarapura, or "the Immortal City."

He and the rest of his dynasty saw themselves as at the head of an all-vanquishing race. They called themselves *Myanma*.

A YEAR LATER, these same Burmese kings conquered the kingdom of Arakan. Arakan is part of a long Indian Ocean coastline, separated from the Irrawaddy valley by a range of low mountains, an incredibly fertile place that's also one of the least hospitable on the planet, prone to earthquakes and devastating cyclones and deluged by up to three feet a month of torrential rain. Arakan today—the state of Rakhine—is the southern two-thirds of this coastline. The northern third, across the Naf River, is today part of Bangladesh.

The area's earliest farmers, perhaps just a handful of people here and there, likely spoke Austroasiatic languages related to Munda (which is now spoken in pockets of central and eastern India). But over the last two thousand years, what's now eastern Bangladesh and Arakan became a kind of frontier. For ancient Indians, speaking an Indo-Aryan tongue, the lands beyond the Meghna River (now in Bangladesh) were a *pandava barjita desh*, a place of utter barbarism where no self-respecting Hindu would go. By medieval times, the Buddhist, Hindu, and later Muslim kingdoms of Bengal had reached the upper end of the coastline. And in the centuries that followed, both Islam and Indo-Aryan languages moved gradually south. These languages are ancestral both to the Bengali of modern Calcutta and Dacca and to the similar dialects of present-day Chittagong and the people who have come to be known as the Rohingya.[1]

Also over the past two millennia, people speaking entirely different Tibeto-Burman languages, some ancestral to both modern Burmese and Arakanese dialects, arrived from the other direction. Burmese chronicles relate long-ago encounters in the region between humans and *bilus*, or ogres.

The region was a frontier between Bengali and Burmese cultures and polities. It was also a civilizational center in its own right. The earliest inscriptions, dating from the first millennium AD, are written in Indo-Aryan Pali and Sanskrit. But by the 15th century, there had developed at Mrauk-U, near today's Sittwe, an impressive kingdom that not only dominated this entire coastline but threatened both their Mughal neighbors to the north and the Burmese to the east.

The kings of this Arakan kingdom spoke an archaic form of Burmese and were Buddhists, but were also cosmopolitans who saw themselves as part of a dynamic Indian Ocean world, taking Bengali–Muslim as well as Burmese–Pali titles, welcoming traders from Lisbon and Amsterdam, recruiting Afghan archers and renegade *ronin* samurai from Nagasaki as their bodyguards, and patronizing at court some of the finest Bengali and Persian poets. They were slavers, too, and together with the Dutch East India Company and Portuguese pirates terrorized the Ganges delta in the 16th and 17th centuries. Many slaves, including Muslims from Bengal, were settled in what is today northern Arakan.

In 1666, invading Mughal armies captured Chittagong, seizing the coastline as far as the Naf River. The British took this territory from the Mughals in 1767.

In 1785, Burmese armies coming from the Irrawaddy valley finished off the rest of this kingdom, setting fire to the capital and carting away the great Mahamuni image, which was believed by the Arakanese to be the most sacred Buddha image of all and a symbol of their sovereignty. Arakan was annexed outright, its centuries-old monarchy destroyed. It had been a cosmopolitan hub. It became Burma's *anauk-taga*, its "western gate."

WITH THIS ANNEXATION of Arakan, the Burmese empire had taken a step toward the Ganges basin—what the Burmese called *Mizzima-desa*, the "Middle Country," the holy land and birthplace of Buddhism. For millennia other parts of modern India, especially Bengal, Orissa, and

South India, were also sources of higher learning, regions from which the Burmese derived their ideals of kingship, art and architecture, mathematics, science, and astronomy. Pali, as the ancient language of the *Mizzima-desa*, was Burma's prestige language, understood by all educated people, as Latin was in pre-20th-century Europe.

Before colonial times, the people to the west were known collectively as *kala*. The word is today portrayed, in foreign media, as a pejorative term for the Rohingya Muslims, but its early use was very different. Its etymology is unclear: it's actually spelled *kula* in Burmese and may be related to the Sanskrit word of the same spelling which means "clan" or "community." The word appears in medieval inscriptions and seems to denote anyone who came from overseas, from India—and "India" in the Burmese imagination was an expansive and somewhat vague place, like "the Indies" of Christopher Columbus.

The Burmese saw the *kala* as a race, a *lu-myo* or "type of person." Indians, Arabs, and Persians, then Portuguese, Armenians, and Dutch, all arrived to trade or offer their services as mercenaries. All appeared similar to Burmese eyes: bearded men (and they were almost all men) from the west. They shared certain ways. To this day, *kala* is part of many Burmese compound words, such as *kala-taing* ("kala-seat") or chair, *kala-ka* ("kala-partition") or curtain, and *kala-pe* ("kala-bean") or chickpea. Europeans generally were *bayingyi-kala*, *bayingyi* being a Burmese corruption of *firangi*, the Persian version of "Franks," which also often referred to all Europeans.

Then came the British. The Burmese viewed the British as another kind of *kala*. England was called Bilat, a Burmese pronunciation of *wilayati*, the Arabic–Mughal word for "province," which first meant Afghanistan, then referred to all lands of the far northwest. It's the same word as "Blighty." The British were the *Bilat-kala*. They were also the *thosaung-kala*, the "sheep-wearing *kala*," after their affinity for woolen clothes. They brought with them their own eccentricities, such as *Bilat-ye* ("British water") or soda.

AT THE TURN of the 19th century, the Burmese began to hear news that the British, through their East India Company, were fast establishing dominion over India. They sent spies who returned with intelligence that the flag of St. George alone now flew along the entire coast from Madras to Calcutta. They sent envoys to the Sikh kingdom of the Punjab, to Nepal, the Marathas in Pune and the Mughals in Delhi, in hopes of an anti-British alliance. It was an offensive strategy. The Burmese had their sights set on Bengal.

By the 1810s, there was a second wave of conquest. This was likely due to a need for people as well as to dreams of fresh imperial glory. The Irrawaddy valley, like most of Southeast Asia, was sparsely populated. Much of the land was forested, filled with tigers, elephants, and pythons. Deadly diseases were a relentless challenge. Land unused became forest very quickly. Human population, rather than land, was the scarce factor of production; people were needed to fight as well as to farm and to manage the irrigation systems on which rice growing depended. There were never enough people. Getting, keeping, and organizing people (to pay taxes or provide military and other services) was a major function of government. Foreign traders were welcomed and encouraged to take local wives, with the strict stipulation that the wife and any children stay behind when they left. When the Siamese capital Ayutthaya was overrun, thousands, including the entire royal court, were deported to the Irrawaddy valley.

The need for manpower may have been particularly acute in the late 1810s and early 1820s. In 1815 Mount Tambora in what is today Indonesia erupted with a force equivalent to 33 billion tons of TNT (about two million times the force of the atomic bomb dropped on Hiroshima).[2] The ash propelled into the stratosphere led to a year of dramatic climate change around the world. In America, the weather in May 1816 turned "backward," with summer frost striking as far south as Virginia. In Europe, as many as 200,000 people died from famine in what became known as the "Year Without Summer."[3] Vacationing near Lake Geneva, Lord Byron, Percy Shelley, and Mary Wollstonecraft Godwin had little choice but to stay indoors, sheltering from the cold and incessant rain. They entertained themselves by reading and writing horror stories. Those stories inspired Mary, later Mary Shelley, to begin work on her first novel, *Frankenstein*.

The same year, unseasonably cold weather led to widespread hunger in China and Tibet. China's Yunnan province, next to Burma, suffered its worst famine in recorded history.[4] At exactly the same time, the first cholera pandemic, originating in Bengal, spread across Eurasia, killing hundreds of thousands of people, including a recorded 30,000 in Bangkok alone.[5] The Irrawaddy valley had already suffered from famine in the early 19th century. The combination of the cholera epidemic and the impact of the Tambora eruption almost certainly placed dramatic new pressure on an already strained demography.

Over the following years, Burmese armies marched westward, seizing first the old kingdom of Manipur, a state in today's India. They then crossed the hills and descended into the valley of the Brahmaputra River, extinguishing another old kingdom, Assam, and depopulating entire regions. Tens of thousands were captured and brought back to the Irrawaddy valley to farm royal lands. The Manipuris remember this period as the "Seven Years of Devastation."

From Arakan, too, the Burmese forced entire communities over the hills to build irrigation works near the capital. Others were corralled into crown service units, which provided other forms of labor to the king. This oppression sent tens of thousands of Arakanese in flight across the border into British-controlled Bengal. A British army officer and diplomat named Hiram Cox was tasked with looking after the refugees. The area, which became known as Cox's Bazar, is exactly where the multitude of Muslim refugees from Arakan are camped today, two hundred years later.

The Burmese soon laid claim to all of southeast Bengal. In official correspondence to the East India Company, they said they understood how the English could have right of possession over all the British Isles but couldn't possibly see how London could have legitimate claims to Dacca and Chittagong.⁶ The Burmese court proclaimed itself the heir of the Arakanese kings who were once sovereign over these same lands. They pursued Arakanese rebels across the Naf River, leading to clashes between British Indian and Burmese forces. In 1823, Burmese forces began moving south from Assam, threatening the little hill principalities of Jaintia and Cachar. Bengal, the richest province of British India, was now in danger of being attacked from two directions.

On February 24, 1824, Lord Amherst, the Governor-General of India, declared war "to humble the overweening pride and arrogance of the Burmese monarch."⁷ The war would be the longest and most expensive in British Indian history, costing the equivalent of nearly $30 billion today. Fifteen thousand British and Indian troops died, along with an unknown but almost certainly higher number of Burmese.

After first repelling Burmese forces in Assam and Arakan, the British made a daring and successful amphibious assault on the port city of Rangoon. Two years of ferocious fighting followed, first around Rangoon and then up the Irrawaddy valley. The same Congreve rockets employed at Fort McHenry in Baltimore in 1812 ("the rockets' red glare") pulverized entrenched Burmese positions, while the first steamship ever used in combat, the *Diana*, destroyed the teak war-boats of the local navy. The Burmese aristocracy was decimated in the attempt to stem the enemy advance, as they led troops on horseback in battle after battle. In May 1826, when the British were within striking distance of the capital, King Bagyidaw sued for peace.

Under the terms of the treaty that followed, the Burmese gave up the kingdoms of Assam, Jaintia, Cachar, Manipur, and Arakan, as well as the eastern shore of the Bay of Bengal near Siam. In the decades to come, the British would turn Assam into the world's tea garden. Assam,

Manipur, Jaintia, and Cachar would become part of independent India. The eastern shore, known as the Tenasserim, and Arakan were kept separate and became the first pieces of a new British Burma.

For the once all-conquering Burmese race, defeat was a shock. All subsequent nationalist thinking harks back to this moment, when the empire was brought to its knees by invaders from the west, as the beginning of an alien interregnum. The late 20th-century military regime would make 1824 the cut-off date in determining who belonged in Burma and who did not, whose ancestors were "natives" and whose came as a result of foreign occupation and therefore were, at best, "guests."

The first Anglo-Burmese war was followed by a second in 1852–53, a relatively short affair that led to the annexation of the Irrawaddy delta and Rangoon. All of Lower Burma was now British, with Rangoon the capital. In the two decades that followed, the Burmese king Mindon tried frantically to modernize what was left of his Upper Burma domain. He built a new city, Mandalay; sent dozens of students to France, Germany, and Italy to study science and engineering; set up the country's first factories; imported steamships; laid telegraph lines; and even invented a Burmese Morse code. And he tried to refashion what was still a kind of feudal system into a proper bureaucracy. Under his son and successor, Thibaw, a faction at the royal court, which included scholars returned from Europe, attempted to go a step further and introduce the beginnings of constitutional government. What they wanted most of all was recognition, from Queen Victoria herself, of Burma's independence.

The British, however, had other plans. In November 1885, secretary of state for India Lord Randolph Churchill (father of Winston) launched a third Burmese war, in the belief that a successful Far Eastern campaign might help the Conservative Party win the upcoming elections. He promised voters in Birmingham, a major manufacturing city near his rural constituency of Woodstock, that free access to markets in Burma, and through Burma to China, would create jobs.

Mandalay was taken easily enough and the king overthrown. But the fierce popular opposition that soon followed, in villages and towns across the Irrawaddy valley, stunned the British. "The people of this country have not, as was by some expected, welcomed us as deliverers from tyranny," wrote one colonial official to another.[8] Years of bloody fighting, summary executions including the crucifixion of Burmese fighters, and a famine caused by Brtitish military operations that left 40,000 dead were needed to break the back of the resistance.

When the dust cleared, there was very little left of the old order. The new overlords abolished Burma's thousand-year monarchy together with all the other storied institutions of state. They exiled the royal family to India. And they smashed the power of the ruling families in the countryside, many with pedigrees extending back centuries. Mandalay was razed to the ground, all except the great city walls and the main palace structures (saved just in time by an intervention in 1905 by Lord Curzon, the Viceroy of India, who wanted to keep intact venues for oriental pomp and circumstance). The British even destroyed memories of the past: just after taking the city, drunken soldiers set fire to the royal library, which contained all official records as well as the genealogies of the ruling class.

In the place of the old order, the British erected entirely new governing structures, ready-made and imported from India. There was no accommodation with Burmese tradition or culture. The modern state of Burma was born as a military occupation.

THE FOCUS OF the new state was essentially to keep the Burmese in check, providing the minimum of services necessary while extracting as much money as possible through taxes and corporate profits. Burma was made a part of India, like Bengal, Madras, and Bombay, and unlike Ceylon (now Sri Lanka), Malaya, Singapore, and Hong Kong, which were all ruled separately, as Crown Colonies. The result was a state divorced from society and a crisis of identity that continues to this day.

This "province of Burma" was divided into three parts. The first part comprised the Irrawaddy basin, the areas ruled by the old kings, plus (important for our later story) Arakan. These districts were ruled directly by British civil servants reporting to a pith-helmeted governor in Rangoon. The second part comprised the upland valleys and surrounding hills, which were ruled indirectly through local princes and chiefs. The mother tongue of these princes and chiefs was not Burmese. In most upland valleys the principal language was Shan, a close cousin of the Thai spoken in today's central Thailand (the word "Shan" is a cognate of "Siam"). The third part comprised the remote mountain regions, which were claimed as part of British Burma but were generally left to themselves. On maps they were labeled "unadministered."

Burmese nationalists would blame the British for following a divide-and-rule policy. The truth was that the British took over a mixed and ever-changing political landscape and fixed boundaries to suit themselves. But by administering areas differently, they set up the fault lines around memory, identity, and aspiration that have vexed all attempts so far at nation-building.

The British stumbled into the Irrawaddy valley to counter and break the power of the Burmese kings. But once ensconced, capitalism dictated policy. Lord Randolph Churchill had suggested that Burma might serve as a back door to China's fabled markets, but China remained largely closed for the time being. The Taiping Rebellion and smaller related rebellions (such as the Muslim Panthay Rebellion in Yunnan, next door) were followed by decades of imperial decline and chaos. The back door would have to wait. So attention turned to the country's natural resources, in particular timber and oil. Burmah Oil, the Irrawaddy Flotilla Company, the Bombay–Burmah Trading Co., Steel Brothers, and other Rangoon-based firms delivered sky-high returns to their shareholders in London and Glasgow. Ports and railways were built to make the export trade as efficient as possible. By the early 20th century, Burma had also become the world's top exporter of rice. Its farming villages, home to the vast majority of the population and never before part of the world economy, were for the first time tightly linked to global markets.

Rangoon was remade as a cosmopolitan business center, with comfortable hotels, clubs, and restaurants to keep happy the few thousand Europeans, Indians, and Chinese who were at the top of the pecking order. A small Burmese elite evolved, which appreciated and mimicked the English style. There were ocean liners (and, from 1933, Imperial Airways flights) to London, well-stocked department stores, brothels and opium dens, churches of every conceivable denomination, literary occasions with visiting writers like Rabindranath Tagore and H. G. Wells, jazz performances at the Gymkhana, and afternoons at the racetrack. All went well for a while.

Indian labor was a crucial part of the mix. There was, as always, a need for people to work the fertile land, as well as a need for people to perform new types of menial labor and become the new Rangoon proletariat. Throughout the colonial period, Burma was richer than the rest of British India. The Burmese were healthier and better fed, enjoyed far higher rates of literacy, and commanded bigger incomes than the average person in India. And so British companies encouraged immigration. Millions came, hoping for a new and better life—not just laborers but businessmen and professionals as well. Most returned to their native countries after making some money, but many stayed on. For a period in the 1920s Rangoon rivaled New York as the biggest immigrant port in the world. Burma was, in the words of Indian-American writer Mira Kamdar, "our first America."[9] By 1931 Indians comprised 7 percent of the country's population of around 14 million, a mix of approximately one million Hindus, Muslims, Sikhs, and others. Most came by ship, except the Muslims from Chittagong who came overland to Arakan. Rangoon became a majority

Indian city. The migration of Indians to Burma was one of the largest human migrations of the 20th century.

J. S. Furnivall called the result a "plural society." He was the first to use the term. Furnivall was a senior civil servant in Burma who, on his retirement in 1923, stayed on to become a distinguished scholar as well as a friend and supporter of many politically active young Burmese. He wrote that in a plural society the constituent ethnic groups interact in the marketplace but otherwise stay separate: "There is division of labor along racial lines, Natives, Chinese, Indians and Europeans all have different functions, and within each major group subsections have particular occupations."[10] He argued that in Burma this plural society worked to serve an "unfettered capitalism far more complete and absolute than in the homogenous western lands." There was, he said, "a total absorption in the exchange and market." Whereas in Western capitalist societies there was "production for life," in Burma there was "life for production."[11]

George Orwell, who was a policeman in Burma in the mid-1920s, put it more simply: "If we are honest, it is true that the British are robbing and pilfering Burma quite shamelessly." Writing a few years later in London, he thought that Burma had indeed developed "to a certain extent" but that the Burmese themselves were now poorer, as wages were not keeping up with the cost of living and the weight of colonial taxation was ever harder to bear. "The reason is that the British government has allowed free entry into Burma for veritable hordes of Indians, who come from a land where they were literally dying of hunger, work for next to nothing and are, as a result, fearsome rivals for the Burmese."[12]

For centuries India had been a source of inspiration. Indians coming to Burma often enjoyed high prestige as bearers of a respected culture. Under colonialism, they were viewed by the Burmese as either exploitative moneylenders and landlords or poverty-stricken workers living in slums, menial servants, and stick-thin seasonal laborers. They alone were now called *kala*, a word that took on increasingly negative connotations.

Europeans, on the other hand, were now referred to as *bo*, which literally means a military officer but became a racial category. *Bo-lo-pyaw*, "to speak like a *bo*," meant to speak English. Formerly grouped together with Indians in Burmese race-thinking, Europeans as rulers became a race apart. And the Burmese themselves, bereft of their monarchy and local hereditary leaders, had few internal gradations left by the early 1900s. Race became the chief cleavage in the new society.

Burma was born as a military occupation and grew up as a racial hierarchy. "Europeans" were accorded the highest rank and for a long time monopolized the uppermost jobs in government. For the British as for the Burmese, "European" was a racial category, never to be confused with Indians. The British in Burma referred to themselves as "European," a category which included all the peoples of the British Isles (Scots were far and away the biggest single group, dominating trade) as well as Burma's smattering of Germans, Swedes, Frenchmen, and other western Europeans. It did not include the significant Jewish community—a mix of Baghdadi and Ashkenazi Jews who felt excluded from "European" society and which in the 1930s numbered over 2,000 in Rangoon alone (the city's population was approximately 400,000). Nor did it include the Armenian community, which had been in the country since the 1600s, whose members also found themselves in a limbo between rulers and "natives."

Lower in status were the Indian, Chinese, and Burmese businessmen, landowners, professionals, and civil servants, who came from the more prosperous sections of their own societies. The Chinese immigration, mainly from Canton and Fujian, was far smaller than the Indian but substantial nonetheless, its leading merchants connecting Rangoon to Singapore and Hong Kong. Some well-to-do Indians, Chinese, and Burmese were schooled in England and were even wealthier than their European counterparts. Still, however rich or well bred, all were excluded on racial grounds from the upper echelons of Rangoon society; membership in the Pegu Club, the city's apex social club, was strictly for whites only. Lowest of all were other non-European peoples, either immigrants from India or people from far-flung regions within Burma, who were seen as belonging to backward or inferior castes and tribes.

In the early 20th century, the British, who already had fairly well-established views of the different peoples of India, made a spirited attempt to analyze their new racial landscape in Burma. Some had strange ideas, which seemed far-fetched even at the time. N. C. MacNamara, in his *Origin and Character of the British People*, tried to make a connection between the Irish and Bronze Age Burmese. The British, he wrote, liked to see the Burmese as "the Irish of the East," and to explain this affinity in character he proposed a prehistoric movement of Asian traders who, attracted to the tin mines of Ireland, settled down, mixed with the "aboriginal Iberian population," and produced the "lazy, rollicking merry Irishmen of caricature." The 1911 census report considered this theory before concluding: "The fact that [the] free-and-easy, jovial disposition [of the Burmese] has been reproduced on the further side of St. George's Channel is the purest chance."

A key part of colonial race thinking was skin color. A detailed examination in 1931 offered an India-wide scale ranging from "the dead black of the Andamanese, the colour of a black-leaded stove before it has been polished" to "the flushed ivory skin of the traditional Kashmiri beauty" which the anthropologist Emil Schmidt compared to "milk just tinged with coffee."[13]

Some, wanting more precision, turned to skull and other measurements. "A brachycephalic mongoloid type" was found to be "the dominant element in Burma," though in the hills was "a second Mongoloid strain characterized by medium stature, longish head and medium nose" that appeared to incorporate "an element of Caucasian stock which penetrated S.E. Asia" in ancient times.[14] A "nasal index" was also employed. Those at the cutting edge of race science even utilized a new "Co-efficient of Racial Likeness" or "C.R.L." to judge the connections between various Burmese types.

Linguistics were also used to determine who was who. In 1786, Sir William Jones, of the Asiatick Society of Bengal, first proposed the existence of an Indo-European language family. One hundred years later, British scholars attempted to sort the many and extremely varied languages found in Burma. They realized that Burmese was closely related to Tibetan; some local languages were incorporated into a "Tibeto-Burman" language family, others were not. In 19th-century censuses, the British tried first to slot Burmese into the caste categories that defined people in India, listing most as "semi-Hindooized aboriginees," before giving up and deciding instead to use language as the basis for racial distinctions. The Tibeto-Burman language family became the Tibeto-Burman race, with a common origin deep in a primordial past.

To some extent, the British were drawing on Burmese antecedents. The Burmese of the old royal court did not think of racial classification in the early 19th-century way, as a scientific endeavor, but they did classify the various *lu-myo* ("kinds of people") they encountered. Almost all populations were placed in one of five overarching categories: Myanma, Shan, Mon, Kala, and Tayok. The first three are peoples in Burma. Kala, before the British conquest, meant Indian and other similar-looking people from the West. "Tayok" is a word likely derived from "Turk," which by the 20th century referred to the Chinese.

From the 1910s the Burma Research Society, a learned body in Rangoon, was producing regular essays on early history and the country's ethnic origins. Scholars, primarily British but also Burmese and others, merged older thinking from the royal court, the extant royal chronicles (which formed the core of Sir Arthur Phayre's seminal *History of Burma*, first published in 1883), linguistics, and the new science of race. The story that emerged told of various tribes—ancestors of the modern races of Burma—appearing at the dawn of time somewhere in the far north, perhaps the Gobi Desert, wandering over mountain passes and finally reaching the Irrawaddy valley or the nearby hills, reaching different stages of civilization, and interacting over the centuries with alien Indians and Chinese.

Colonial officials in the countryside understood that the truth might be a little messier. Those in charge of the 1911 imperial census viewed Burma with dread, as a zone of "racial instability," fretting that the distinctions between races in Burma were "neither definite, nor logical, nor permanent, nor easy to detect . . . they are unstable from generation to generation, the racial designation of a community sometimes changes so rapidly that its elders consider themselves as belonging to one race whilst their descendants claim to belong to another."[15] Census-takers also realized that people in Burma, especially immigrants, tended to make themselves out to be something other than "who they really were." One of the biggest immigrant groups were Pariahs (now usually spelled Paraiyar) from south India, a low caste who came to do menial work, especially in Rangoon. Perhaps not surprisingly, once in Burma, they often listed themselves as belonging to some other, higher, caste or simply as Christian. Many Indians stopped mentioning their old caste altogether and called themselves "Hindustani."

Interracial sex and marriage blurred the lines further and created new tensions. In the Irrawaddy valley in pre-British times, marriage was an informal affair. Men and women who were living together were considered married. If they split up, property was divided equally as a matter of custom. Neither the state nor Buddhist authorities were involved. From the beginnings of British rule, there was a large influx of foreign men: British, Indian, and Chinese. A good number of British men took Burmese mistresses. In 1890 the Chief Commissioner (the highest authority in Burma) issued a confidential circular declaring that this must end; that weekend at the Turf Club, one horse was named CCCC, for "Chief Commissioner's Confidential Circular," and another was named Physiological Necessity. The practice continued.

Burmese women were often unsatisfied with this arrangement, appreciating that only a formal marriage contract offered them adequate protection. Somerset Maugham, on a trip across Burma in 1922, met an Englishman who had two young children with a Burmese woman. The relationship had been an extremely happy one, the Englishman said, until one day she demanded they marry. After a tortuous year of indecision, he refused and she left with the children. He explained his reasoning:

> If I married her I'd have to stay in Burma for the rest of my life. Sooner or later I shall retire and then I want to go back to my old home and live there. I don't want to be buried out here. I want to be buried in an English churchyard. . . . Sometimes I get sick of this hot sunshine and these garish colors. I want grey skies and a soft rain falling and the smell of the country. I want to feel under my feet the grey pavement of an English country town, I want to be able to go and have a row with the butcher because the steak he sent me in yesterday was tough and I want to browse about second-hand bookshops . . .

As D. D. Nanavati, a leading barrister in Bombay, wrote: "I have often heard people when talking of Burma ask with a snigger, 'Oh isn't that the place where you can marry for a month or two?' "[16]

By the early 20th century, Burma had a sizable population of people of recently mixed ancestry, including the highest percentage of "Eurasians" in the empire. Though most were of Scottish and Burmese descent, all were called Anglo-Burman or Anglo-Indian ("Scoto-Burman" was proposed and rejected as too complicated for the census). Their presence, in the tens of thousands by the 1920s, was particularly vexing for British authorities, as some "not handicapped by excessive pigmentation" tended to classify themselves on official forms as "European." The 1931 census offered various ways of determining the truth, suggesting for example that "a Presbyterian born in India or Burma and having a lowly paid occupation and claiming himself to be English (not Scotch) is more likely to be an Anglo-Indian."[17] Up close, British officials knew identity could be a slippery thing.

Though identity was not as straightforward as some might have liked, it seemed clear to more or less everyone that Burma was not India and that the Burmese were not Indians. This was never questioned. That the borders drawn after the Anglo-Burmese wars were somewhat arbitrary was not considered, mainly because so few had any personal experience of places in between, such as Assam, Arakan, and Manipur. Rudyard Kipling visited for all of three days in 1889 and noted on arrival, "And this is Burma, and it will be quite unlike any land you know about . . . not India at all."[18]

With this distinction came the need to classify the many different ethnic communities in Burma as either "indigenous" or not. The 1921 census decided: "Races which are associated particularly closely with Burma, even if the greater part of their people live elsewhere, have been regarded as Indigenous Races, and have been classified in fifteen *Race-groups*" (italics in original). What this meant was that people like the Lisu, who lived mainly in China but who were present in the northern hills of Burma, spoke a language similar to Burmese, and appeared akin to a Burmese racial type, were classed as "indigenous." Tamils, who were of different complexion and physiognomy, were, despite millennia-old connections between south India and Burma, foreigners pure and simple.[19]

In this dichotomy, Burma's Muslims were difficult to pin down. There were several, very different Muslim communities. The Muslims who had originated in the Chinese province of Yunnan were of partly Turkic, Persian, and Central Asian ancestry; they had fled Manchu repression in the mid-19th century and settled in Mandalay and the towns of the northeast. Older communities of Muslims in the middle Irrawaddy valley were descendants of cavalrymen and artillerymen from the Deccan in India who had fought for 17th- and 18th-century Burmese kings and were gifted land in return. The most recent arrivals were the hundreds of thousands of Muslims, nearly all men, who came from across the subcontinent, from Bengal to the Afghan frontier, as part of the broader Indian migration.

Some Muslims, like the descendants of 17th-century Deccani cavalry (and their Burmese wives), had become "Burmese" in all but religion; others had just arrived and had no intention of staying long. Added to the mix, by the 1930s, were tens of thousands of children of recent Muslim immigrant fathers and Burmese mothers, sometimes known collectively as Zerbadi.

Categorizing the Muslims of Arakan—the site of 21st-century violence and the Rohingya exodus—proved particularly troublesome. For millennia people had moved across the Naf River as soldiers, pirates, traders, and slaves. To the north, most people spoke dialects of Bengali and were Muslim; to the south, most people spoke Arakanese, a dialect of Burmese, and were Buddhist. To the north people were darker-complexioned and looked more "Indian" to both British and Burmese eyes, while to the south people had the East Asian appearance of people elsewhere in Burma. But there were also Arakanese Buddhists far to the north of the river, and Muslims speaking either a Bengali dialect or a Burmese dialect well to the south. There were many mixed communities and many people with mixed ancestries.

When the British took Arakan in 1824, much of what is today northern Arakan (now called Rakhine) was depopulated. Arakanese refugees who had fled toward Chittagong during the Burmese occupation came back. Over the late 19th and early 20th centuries, hundreds of thousands of Muslims speaking the Chittagong dialect of Bengali came from north of the border as well. In 1871, Muslims were approximately a fifth of the population in Arakan. By 1911, they were more than a third. In the northern areas they were the majority. At the same time, Burmese from the Irrawaddy valley had settled in the southern part of Arakan, and by 1911 comprised 15 percent of the overall population of Arakan. Racial, linguistic, and religious frontiers, between Arakanese, Burmese, Bengali, and Indian, and between Buddhist and Muslim, intertwined.

The British never used the term "Rohingya." It was the word some

Muslims, especially in the north of Arakan, used to refer to themselves in their own Bengali-related language. It simply meant "of Rohang," their name for Arakan. It implied that Arakan was their home. In the same way, people just across the border, speaking a mutually intelligible Bengali dialect, called themselves Chatgaya, "of Chittagong."

Instead, colonial officials used an array of other terms, including "Chittagonian" and "Arakan Mahomedan" to describe and differentiate the Muslims of the area. Some were classed as "natives," others as "aliens." "Chittagonians," recent arrivals from across the Naf, were considered immigrants. The "Arakan Mahomedans," culturally akin to their Arakanese Buddhist neighbors, were believed to be descended from Muslim communities that had existed since the time of the kings. Officials were never quite sure whether to list them as Burmese or Indian. Identity was again a slippery thing.

Over the decades, violence would erupt in many forms and for different reasons. But the seeds of disagreement over who belonged and who did not were planted solidly, if somewhat absentmindedly, in colonial times.

THE FIRST MODERN Burmese political associations, formed in the 1910s, were content to politely petition the colonial masters. After the First World War came the first mass demonstrations for "home rule," inspired by Gandhi and the Indian National Congress. The British gave Burma, like all Indian provinces, its own semi-elected parliament in 1922, what Orwell called "the mask of democracy," while still making all the important decisions themselves. An older generation of Oxford- and Cambridge-educated Burmese politicians, mainly lawyers, pressed for constitutional reform and attended conferences in London. Younger men dreamed of revolutionary change.

These younger leaders—from small-town backgrounds and products of Rangoon University—read Marx, Lenin, and Sinn Fein. They were drawn to the Irish example of armed insurrection. The British had divided the "natives" of Burma into "martial" and "non-martial" races. The Burmese were classed as "non-martial." This rankled. The young nationalists imagined a Burma restored to its past glory, free of colonial rule, with a new and proud army. They imagined, as well, a society different from the "plural society" in which Indian immigrants played a major part.

The 1911 census had stated that "it is a fundamental article of belief with the majority of Europeans in Burma, that the Burmese race is doomed and is bound to be submerged in a comparatively short time by the hordes of immigrants who arrive by every steamer from India."[20] The actual numbers told a slightly different story, of immigration declining during the early 20th century and Indians barely present in much of the countryside. But no matter. For many young Burmese, going into the modern world, going to Rangoon, meant venturing from their little upriver towns into an alien universe where the British ruled from their exclusive clubs and Indians dominated the marketplace. They would have seen the Shwedagon Pagoda, 400 feet high and clad in solid gold, the most sacred site in Burmese Buddhism, dominating the skyline, described by Kipling as a "beautiful winking wonder" and by Somerset Maugham as a "sudden hope in the dark night." But in the bustling downtown below there was hardly a Burmese face, only a cosmopolitan and capitalist society in which they had become the foreigners.

Seventy years earlier, the Burmese king Mindon told visiting envoy Sir Arthur Phayre, "Our race once reigned in all the countries you hold in India. Now the *kala* have come close up to us."[21] By *kala*, he meant both the British and the Indians. Both were part of a combined threat. British writers at the turn of the century suggested the same: "The [British] expeditions against Burma marked the renewal, after the repose of thousands of years, of the march of the Aryan eastwards."[22]

When the Great Depression hit, commodity prices collapsed and villages found themselves unable to pay taxes or to repay loans to Indian bankers. The bankers, Tamil Chettiyars from Madras, seized millions of acres of land. Work in the cities became scarce and tensions between Burmese and Indians boiled over into violence. In 1930, the first Burmese–Indian riots in Rangoon left hundreds dead.

A younger generation of politicians, men like Aung San, the father of future Nobel laureate Aung San Suu Kyi, banded together in new organizations such as the Dobama Asi-ayone ("We Burmans Association"). They consciously used the more colloquial ethnonym *Bama*, or "Burman," to emphasize a folk identity. They eschewed parliamentary politics. They were attracted to both the far left and the far right. Some formed the first Communist Party. Some used old royal emblems. They called themselves *Thakin*, or "master," a style formerly reserved for the British. All drew from a popular well of antagonism toward both big business and immigrants. Their protest song, the basis of today's national anthem, includes the refrain "*da do-mye, da do-pye*": "this is our land, this is our country." Meaning, it's not yours.

In 1937, the British separated Burma from India, in response to a decades-old Burmese demand. This was India's first and largely forgotten partition. And whereas the second partition, in 1947, created the nation of Pakistan on the basis of religious identity, this first partition created Burma within its modern borders on a basis of racial identity.

Though the British governor was still ultimately in charge, an elected Burmese parliament was given substantial powers, appointing its own government headed by a premier. Nationalist feelings were in full swing. Islam, as the religion of approximately half the Indian immigrants (who then comprised about 7 percent of the country's population but half of Rangoon's), was described in popular pamphlets as a threat to Buddhism. In 1938, a new round of riots between Burmese and Indians targeted Indian Muslims in particular. In 1939, parliament passed the Buddhist Women's Special Marriage and Succession Act, with the aim of protecting Burmese women who married Muslim men.

THE SOCIETY CREATED under British colonialism unwound in stages. In 1942, the Japanese invaded from the east, driving the British back to Assam. Half a million Indians fled. Tens of thousands died trying to reach India on foot. The Japanese also trained a Burma National Army led by young *Thakins*.

Over the next three years, Burma became a giant battlefield involving over a million Japanese, British, Burmese, Indian, African, and Gurkha troops. Nearly every town was flattened by Japanese and Allied bombing. The economy was destroyed. In 1945, the British retook control, but they stayed only a little while. Burmese nationalists were demanding immediate British withdrawal, and with Indian independence in 1947 Burma lost its strategic importance. The cost of rebuilding would be high and the Labour government in London had other preoccupations, not least at home.

On January 4, 1948, Burma became formally independent as a republic outside the Commonwealth. The strident nationalism which gripped the country meant that any remaining imperial connection was suspect and had to be rejected. Independence had to be total and immediate. Months later, Burma collapsed into civil war, with a Communist insurrection against the democratic socialist regime left in power by the British. In Arakan, which now bordered East Pakistan (soon to become Bangladesh), a militant outfit calling itself the Mujahid Party took up arms and called for a separate Muslim homeland. Then the Karen National Union rose in rebellion, demanding a breakaway republic for the Karen ethnic minority. The army, nearly half of which were British-trained Karens (a "martial race"), splintered. By 1949, Burma was a sea of rebels and bandits. At the height of the insurgency that year, Communist and Karen forces came within miles of Rangoon.

Still, a kind of democracy lasted for over a decade. Successive governments tried to win back the country from the rebels while rebuilding the economy, but with only partial success. In the 1950s, CIA-backed Chinese forces loyal to Chiang Kai-shek crossed the border from now Communist China, reigniting heavy fighting. The army grew into a battle-hardened machine.

On March 2, 1962, this battle-hardened machine seized power. Military administrations were then the norm across Asia: South Korea, Thailand, Pakistan, and Indonesia were all under army rule in the 1960s. But Burma's was different: it sealed the country off from the world. The army set up a Revolutionary Council and embarked on what it called a "Burmese Way to Socialism": 400,000 Indians were expelled, all external trade was stopped, and all major businesses were nationalized. This was done partly to placate left-wing aspirations and outflank the Communists. It was also a Cold War strategy, to remove Burma as a chess piece in the spreading wars in Indochina. And it was a direct reaction to worries first aroused in colonial times about an exploitative global capitalism and an identity under threat.

By the 1970s, Burma had become a much simpler place, without luxury, stripped of its once cosmopolitan crowd, without landlords and fat cats— only farmers, soldiers, marauding bands, and the decaying buildings of empire, perhaps like Britain under the early Anglo-Saxons. But its political DNA still contained the ideas first formed in the days of Victorian Empire. They would mutate and find new life at the turn of the 21st century.

TWO

CHANGING LANES

I FIRST VISITED BURMA in December 1974. I was eight years old and living in Harrison, on the outskirts of New York, with my maternal grandparents, parents, and three younger sisters. My grandfather, U Thant, had been Secretary-General of the United Nations in the 1960s and had just died from cancer. My parents were flying his body back for interment in Rangoon and at my grandmother's urging I was brought along too. I missed my fourth-grade classes and instead, over the few weeks between Thanksgiving and Christmas, experienced firsthand a dictatorship in action.

The plan had been for a simple burial. But feelings were high against the military regime. The man at the head of government was General Ne Win. A tough-talking one-time postal clerk, Ne Win was trained by the Japanese during the war and had commanded the Burmese army since independence. Ne Win was an enigmatic figure. He was a playboy who counted British royalty among his friends, traveling often to Europe, sometimes for months at a time, hosting dinners at a rented house in Wimbledon, shopping in Geneva, and consulting a psychiatrist, Dr. Hans

Hoff, in Vienna. But he was also an army boss who set the country on a decidedly authoritarian and puritanical path, directing ruthless counterinsurgency campaigns, jailing any opposition, silencing a once-flourishing press, and banning a slew of entertainments he had once enjoyed himself, from beauty pageants to horse racing.

Ne Win also ruined Burmese education. Whatever the evils of colonialism, the British had left behind in Rangoon one of the best universities in Asia, as well as dozens of excellent English-language schools. With the end of academic freedom and the flight of many distinguished scholars, Rangoon University became a shell of its former self. The schools were nationalized, foreign teachers sent packing, and the teaching of English prohibited except in the higher grades. For decades, investment in education hovered close to zero. There are many reasons for Burma's ills today, but the hollowing out of the education system alone explains much.

U Thant, who had been a high official in a previous, elected government, was seen as a symbol of a different, more liberal Burma. In Rangoon, people lined the streets from the airport and thousands more came to pay their respects at the old racetrack grounds where his coffin, draped in a UN flag, was kept for four days, under a special tent erected for the occasion.

On the day of the actual burial, a throng of Buddhist monks and students, angry with the government for not giving U Thant a state funeral, seized the coffin and drove it by truck to Rangoon University. There they demanded that a fitting tomb be built, as a public monument. A tense standoff followed. The university became the site of protest and fiery speeches denouncing army rule. After days of attempted mediation by my family, troops stormed the university, recovered my grandfather's remains, and buried them under six feet of concrete near the foot of the Shwedagon Pagoda. Riots broke out and in the crackdown that followed an unknown number of people, likely hundreds, were killed or thrown into prison. We were told to leave the country.

As I was eight, I had only a vague idea of what was happening. I remember the *longyi-* or sarong-clad crowds at the racetrack and the university, the look of Rangoon at the height of Ne Win's "Burmese Way to Socialism," the lush, unkempt gardens and derelict Raj-era buildings, the rickety 1950s' Chevrolets and Buicks, the utter lack of TV, the damp heat and the smell of sandalwood, betel nut, and diesel in the air, the feeling that violence could happen at any moment.

A few years later, we moved to Bangkok, and often went to Rangoon on holiday. Bangkok was then, as today, a gritty, sprawling city brimming with commercial vigor, a city I experienced as a teenager to the sounds of Laura Branigan, Rush, and the Eurhythmics. Just an hour away on Burma Airways was a different world, entirely becalmed, waiting for new life.

The official ideology was a half-baked mélange of socialist, nationalist, and Buddhist ideas. For a while it seemed that the socialist agenda might dominate. The army allowed only a single new political party to exist, the Burma Socialist Programme Party, listened to advice from Marxist intellectuals, and took control of most economic life in the interests of the "workers and peasants." By the 1980s, the Revolutionary Council under General Ne Win gave way to a one-party constitutional set-up under President Ne Win. Burma looked like a Soviet-bloc socialist state.

But by the 1980s, the socialist experiment was not working. In the 1950s and 1960s, Burma's economy had been more or less on a par with Thailand's and not far behind South Korea's. Rangoon was no less modern than Singapore and ahead of Bangkok. By the 1980s, Burma had fallen far behind. It was a much more equal society than in colonial times, but there was a growing sense that the country could do much better. The government began to adjust. Foreign aid was resumed after a hiatus of twenty years. Tourists were allowed back, though only for seven days. Private businesses crept back into the picture. For good measure, driving was changed from the left to the right side of the road.

At the same time, the seeds of a new nationalism were being planted.

By the 1980s, the army had cleared the Irrawaddy valley of rebel forces, but in the remote hills brutal fighting was still the norm. The hills were home to different ethnic communities considered "native." Stalin defined a nation as a "historically constituted, stable community of people, formed on the basis of a common language, territory, economic life, and psychological make-up manifested in a common culture"; the Burmese socialists took this concept and merged it with colonial-era scholarship to produce the idea of Burma as a collective of native races or nationalities. They used the word *taing-yintha*, which originally meant "native" in the sense of native medicine or crafts. Now it meant a constituent component of the nation itself.[1]

There was no appetite for racial instability. Identities were fixed, and all races were seen as ancient, unchanging, sons of the soil. Their "unity" was all-important. The army's goal was to defeat the insurgencies and integrate the *taing-yintha* into a unified, socialist state—though the socialist part would soon peel away.

If some belonged, that meant others didn't. Many Indians had left during the Second World War or at independence. In the early years of Ne Win's rule, 400,000 more were compelled to leave. Those who remained, mainly the very poor, kept their heads down. In 1967, anti-Chinese riots had led to an exodus of ethnic Chinese as well, many to the Bay Area in California. In the far northeast were other Chinese who had been settled there for centuries, but those areas were controlled by Communist rebels, so for now they remained out of sight. That left one area of ambiguity: Arakan.

Arakanese nationalism is akin to Burmese nationalism. It's centered on an ethnic identity (Arakanese), intimately linked to neoconservative Theravada Buddhism, and is characterized by a fear of being overwhelmed both by modernity and by outsiders. The difference is that, in the case of the Arakanese, the outsiders are both the *kala* "Bengalis" on the one side and the "Burmese" on the other. It's an identity tied to memories of the old Mrauk-U kingdom as well as a reaction against the more recent influx of Bengali-speaking Muslims under British rule.

When the Japanese invaded in 1942 and civil administration broke down, thousands were butchered, with the Japanese arming the Buddhist Arakanese and the British arming the Muslim "Chittagonians" (as "V Force"). After the war, as Indian independence and partition loomed, local Muslim leaders calling themselves Rohingya ("of Arakan") toyed with the idea of northern Rakhine joining the soon-to-be-created Pakistan (of which East Bengal, now Bangladesh, became a part); when rebuffed by Mohammed Ali Jinnah, the founding father of Pakistan, they demanded instead an autonomous state within Burma. The Mujahid Party and successor insurgencies waxed and waned over the following decades.

Under Ne Win, Arakan became a backwater within a backwater. The traumas of the Second World War were never healed. Muslims and Buddhists lived side by side without any real accounting for the bloodshed of the 1940s. At the same time, racial frontiers simplified. There were the Burmese and the Arakanese, and in the nearby hills small Christian and Buddhist minorities, such as the Mro. In addition, there was a largely undifferentiated population of Muslims. Whereas in British times some Muslims had been seen (or viewed themselves) as "Arakanese Mohammedans"—scions of families present since the days of the old Mrauk-U kingdom—and others as colonial-era Chittagonian immigrants, these identities were now fused. Many of the Chittagonians had left, and those who stayed intermarried with those who had always seen Arakan as home. They came to speak the local dialect of Bengali, very close to but not quite the same as Chittagonian. To the Burmese and Arakanese they were all *kala* or "Bengali." Few, if any, had heard the term "Rohingya." And for decades, the Muslims of northern Arakan had no power to describe themselves.

Power was no longer in the hands of British overlords but in the hands of new outsiders, army generals, nearly all Burmese from the Irrawaddy valley. The border with East Pakistan, later Bangladesh, was porous—

whatever the truth, there was certainly a perception of unimpeded illegal immigration. The Rohingya Solidarity Organization harried government forces. In 1971, during the violence surrounding the birth of Bangladesh and the Indo-Pakistani War, millions of people from East Pakistan fled to India, and an unknown number may have fled to Burma, specifically to Arakan. In 1978, an army operation named Naga-min or "Dragon King," aimed at rooting out "illegal immigrants," prompted the flight of nearly 200,000 people to Bangladesh.

In 1982, a new citizenship law was enacted. There is a common perception that the Rohingya were stripped of their citizenship by this law. That's not true. Under the previous law, enacted in 1948, more or less anyone who was living in Burma at the time could register to become a citizen. Under the new law, *taing-yintha* natives were automatically citizens, and others, for example Indian immigrants, who had become citizens under the older, more liberal law were still citizens. Complicating the picture, though, were many undocumented people who were not considered native, like most Muslims in Arakan. If they or their ancestors had arrived in British times (the "Chittagonians"), they could become naturalized as "guest" citizens. Their descendants by the third generation would be considered full citizens. Thus, by today, seventy years and three generations after independence, citizenship should be equal for everyone except actual and recent illegal immigrants. But that's all in theory. Practice was and is different, and discriminatory.

Membership in a native race—being a *taing-yintha*—was not the only basis for citizenship, but it was the best and easiest. Blood now defined belonging. By the late 1980s, enthusiasm for socialism was fading fast. The door was opening to a new vision of the future.

A TURNING POINT came in 1988. I was back in the United States, in my last year at university. A couple of family acquaintances, Tin Maung Win and Ye Kyaw Thu, had recently established the Committee for the Restoration of Democracy in Burma, known as the CRDB. They were in their forties and their fathers had held senior positions in government before the military takeover. We met over dinner at an all-you-can-eat seafood restaurant in Arlington, Virginia. They told me their desire to see a return to elected government, through a revolution, an armed revolution if need be. The CRDB would play only a marginal role in the dramatic events to come, but for me their ideas were electrifying, instilling a sense that anything was possible, that Burma could be remade.

That summer, I was interning at a UN-related think tank in Geneva (the Independent Bureau) and spending a long weekend near Locarno at the home of Sir Peter and Lady Smithers. Sir Peter had been a friend of Ian Fleming and an inspiration for the character of James Bond. The home was in the Japanese style and built against a mountainside overlooking the little Italian villages far below. Sir Peter had the habit of wearing a kimono and listening to the BBC World Service news over a small short-wave radio on his veranda. We listened together to the news of growing protests in Burma, a stunning announcement by General Ne Win that he would resign, and his even more shocking suggestion that a return to a multiparty system of government be considered. His underlings accepted his resignation but voted in an emergency meeting against any moves toward democracy.

Rangoon erupted. Students organized anti-government demonstrations. Dozens were killed but the momentum for change only increased. On August 8, 1988, the protesters called for a nationwide general strike to bring down the Ne Win dictatorship. Hundreds died in early confrontations with the security forces. But by late August, hundreds of thousands of people were taking to the streets daily, emboldened by the thought that the regime was on its final legs. Everywhere were banners calling for democracy. One by one, government ministries, then the state media, and even the police joined the protests. Civil administration buckled across Burma. For a few days the country seemed on the edge of revolution.

I didn't want to miss my chance to be part of the big change, so I quit my internship and flew to Bangkok. On the very morning I was meant to continue on to Rangoon, the Rangoon airport was shut down by a general strike. Two weeks later, as the protests turned violent and the newly emerged leaders could not agree among themselves on next steps, the army reasserted control. Students and ordinary workers resisted the crackdown. Thousands may have been shot dead. This was the end of what became known as the 1988 Uprising. The uprising failed, but the old socialist state was formally abolished. The army—through a junta named the State Law and Order Restoration Council, or SLORC—now took direct control.

I was marooned in Bangkok. Within days, a tide of young Burmese, around my age, began arriving at jungle camps controlled by ethnic minority rebels all along the Burma–Thailand border. A few dozen became a few hundred, then swelled by December to over 10,000. Over the following year I raised money from the Burmese diaspora and brought food and medical supplies. I was at the founding meeting of the All Burma Students' Democratic Front, or ABSDF. The goal was revolution.

After the first few months of extreme anger and a desire to see change at any cost, my thoughts diverged from those of the ABSDF and other would-be revolutionaries. The idea of an armed insurrection seemed far-fetched. However, I still wanted a strong response from the Western democracies and so, over the next couple of years, in Washington and London, I helped organize the first Burmese advocacy campaigns, encouraging US congressmen and UK members of Parliament to support the nascent democracy movement, impose economic sanctions, and shame and ostracize the new junta to the maximum extent possible.

IN RANGOON, the National League for Democracy, or NLD, had been formed, with Aung San Suu Kyi, then forty-three years old, at the helm. She was the daughter of assassinated independence hero Aung San, photogenic, charismatic, Oxford-educated, and recently returned from a life abroad. She seemed the perfect antidote to years of austerity and isolationism.

Aung San Suu Kyi came to prominence in Burma in 1988. Until then she had been living overseas, having left the country as a child in the 1950s when her mother was appointed ambassador to India. She went to school in Delhi and university at Oxford, where she followed her mother's advice to read politics, philosophy, and economics (PPE), abandoning her own wish to study English literature.

After a short stint at the UN, Aung San Suu Kyi married a British scholar of Tibet, moved with him to Bhutan (where he tutored the future king), then settled back in Oxford, where she and her husband enjoyed a quiet, bookish life and raised two sons. When the anti-military protests began in 1988 she was, by pure chance, in Rangoon, looking after her ailing mother. She gave her first public speech, calling for unity and siding firmly with those seeking democracy. She injected an air of youth and vigor into an opposition patchwork then comprised mainly of green students, ex-army officers, and elderly left-wing intellectuals. Even though the uprising had been crushed, the army came to fear her, for her popularity and her willingness to speak her mind. She became a legend.

Or, more properly, the continuation of a legend. Her father and namesake, General Aung San, was a no-nonsense, single-minded product of the late 1930s, turning alternatively to Communism and Fascism for inspiration, but settling on a simple, unwavering commitment to an independent Burma at all costs. He founded a militia (the Burma National Army) that first sided with the Japanese and then turned against them just in time, joining the Allies in the spring of 1945. His battalions would form the nucleus of the future Burmese army. When the British prepared to quit Burma, he was there to take charge.

He was then all of thirty-three years old and, in his final months, seemed to have mellowed considerably, no more the samurai sword-carrying, shaven-headed warrior but a charming, quick-witted politician, parleying with Clement Attlee and Labour government ministers in London. He embraced a socialist vision of the future, one in which all of Burma's many different ethnic communities might have a place. But then, just months before the actual handover of power, he (along with most of his cabinet) was assassinated by a jealous rival.

Aung San's life became the country's founding story—of a man who devoted himself unswervingly to his country's struggle for independence and who was able almost single-handedly (so goes the story) to bring down the might of the British Empire. The auxiliary to the story was that if only he had lived, things would have been different: the civil wars avoided, prosperity ensured, Burma today standing proud in the family of nations, an alternate reality that could have been if things had gone otherwise on that fateful day in July 1947.

With the emergence of Aung San Suu Kyi, people began to believe that the story could be replayed, this time with a happy ending.

In the West, Aung San Suu Kyi was for more than two decades seen as a fighter for liberal democracy and human rights, a strikingly attractive icon of "universal" values in a distant corner of the world. But her starting point was always a more local context. In the 1980s, before her first foray into politics, she wrote several academic papers about the nationalist movement and "the progressive attempts of the Burmese people to reassert their racial and cultural identity."[2] She argued that, in the early 20th century, the threat of Burmese "racial survival came not so much from the British as from the Indians and Chinese who were the more immediate targets of twentieth-century nationalism. Not only did these immigrants acquire a stranglehold on the Burmese economy, they also set up homes with Burmese women, striking at the very roots of Burmese manhood and racial purity."[3]

She also placed first and foremost the idea of personal courage and determination triggering social change. There is a link to Buddhist ideas of courage and determination, ideas normally meant for an inner journey; for her, what was important was the effect of an individual's pursuit on society. At a book festival years later, in 2012, she mentioned her lack of admiration for the character of Ulysses in Tennyson's poem and her preference for Jean Valjean in *Les Miserables*, the difference being the latter's struggle against the odds to improve not only himself but the world around him.[4]

Aung San Suu Kyi saw her father as someone who had been on "a pilgrimage in quest of truth and perfection." He wanted, she wrote on the eve of her political career, to "carry his country with him in that quest." He trusted "the people" and "the people reciprocated by giving him their full understanding and placing their united strength behind his endeavors."[5] She wrote of those "rare moments in history" when the "leaders of a people" understand "the people's aspirations" and there "is an inner harmony and a climactic release of spiritual and physical vigor." During her father's short period of leadership, "the people of Burma" were "filled with hope and purposeful energy" and the memory of this now constituted "a reservoir of strength and pride" from which to draw.[6]

In 1988, she talked of a "second struggle for independence." There would be a new version of 1947—determination, the forging of national unity, defeat of foes who would part on good terms, but in this 21st-century version the hero survives and leads the nation to a brighter tomorrow. She spoke about democracy: less about specific institutions or ways of government, more about the idea of power returning "to the people" via an elected leader. She spoke about discipline and a willingness to stick to principles through thick and thin. The ends could never justify the means.

Sacrifice was important, too. All Buddhists in Burma know the story of Gautama Siddhartha, the prince who shed his princely existence for a greater pursuit. Buddhist monks leave their families and worldly possessions in their journey toward higher goals. The idea of giving up material comforts in service of a spiritual quest is a strong one. And in Aung San Suu Kyi, the Burmese saw the daughter of their national hero denying herself what everyone assumed would have been a pleasant life with her family in England, not for a personal spiritual quest, but to help her fellow countrymen. When her husband was dying from cancer in 1998, she declined to visit him for fear of not being able to return. This special sacrifice made ordinary Burmese believe even more that she was the only one steadfast and selfless enough to take down the military dictatorship.

The junta—now without Ne Win and headed by a new generation of generals—fretted that she might soon lead another uprising. In July 1989, they placed her under house arrest. In 1990, they held promised elections, but when the NLD won handily, they declared that power could not be transferred until a new constitution was written. Thousands more were detained or jailed. The following year, Aung San Suu Kyi was awarded the Nobel Peace Prize. Draconian martial law restrictions would remain in place for years, banning, for example, gatherings of more than five people.

Around this time, the junta ended the Burmese Way to Socialism. A couple of years before, an army officer had told me, "What we really want is to go from being a left-wing isolated dictatorship to a right-wing pro-American dictatorship." The 1988 uprising hadn't brought about democracy, but it did bring about a new military regime and an end to socialist hibernation. Opportunities for private businesses were opened up for the first time since the early 1960s, allowing foreign trade and investment after decades of autarkic policies, and eagerly welcoming foreign tourists (by extending visas to "twenty-eight days renewable"). Black market smugglers were rebranded "national entrepreneurs" in state media. Pent-up desires to reboot the economy and make money were springing to life.

Nativism was at the same time also springing to life. The junta officially changed the name of the country in English from Burma to a variant of its ancient Burmese-language ethnonym, Myanmar. It was something that would lead to endless confusion and debate in the years to come. The junta claimed to be ending a colonial legacy. But as "Myanma" refers only to the majority Burmese people, not to the Shan, the Karen, or others, the move also signaled the revival of a nationalism centered squarely on a Burmese–Buddhist racial and cultural core.

Continuing in this vein, the old Mandalay palace was rebuilt (in a shoddy way, with the original teak beams resurrected in painted concrete). Buddhist stupas were regilded and the official press regularly carried photos of generals prostrating themselves before elderly saffron-clad monks. As if to further shore up their ethno-nationalist credentials, an operation in 1992 against the Rohingya Solidarity Organization insurgency triggered yet another flight of 200,000 or so Muslims from Arakan. By this time, the conventional wisdom in Rangoon was that northern Arakan had been deluged over the past twenty years or so with illegal immigrants from Bangladesh, swamping whatever Muslim population had been there before. Few, if any, in the incipient democracy movement thought much about these people's rights. The Iranian foreign minister, Ali Akbar Velayati, however, called on the UN to halt what he called "the genocide of Burmese Muslims by the military government."[7]

Sixty-year-old Senior General Than Shwe took over the junta just after the 1992 Rohingya exodus. Stout and square-jawed, Than Shwe was not the creator of the military dictatorship but a product of it. He was born at the tail end of British rule, in a village just south of Mandalay, a parched region with slender streams that turned to sand during the hot weather, soaring toddy palms, and little golden pagodas. He would have been a child during the war—seeing the troops of a dozen nations, perhaps even American GIs—and a teenager when the country became first independent, then toppled into anarchy. In 1953, at the height of the civil war, he trained to be an officer. His trainers were men trained by the Japanese Imperial Army. He would remain in the army for nearly half a century.

Life in the Burmese army in the 1950s and 1960s, even for an officer, was harsh. It meant months if not years at a time in disease-ridden jungles, surviving with few supplies, and fighting foes often better equipped. In 1958, Than Shwe was assigned to the Psychological Warfare Unit in the War Office. He attended a special course in the Soviet Union and then became a psy-ops officer attached to different brigades.

After General Ne Win's takeover in 1962, Than Shwe taught for a while at the newly established Central Political College, imbibing the Burmese Way to Socialism. By the 1980s, he was a battalion commander and part of an unsuccessful attempt (Operation Min Yan Aung, or "King Conqueror of the Enemy") to capture the stronghold of the insurgent Communists, up in the mountains on the Chinese border.[8] He is described by former colleagues as the kind of man who kept his head down and didn't make a fuss, a dependable organization man who watched and waited, always careful of his next move.

By the time of the 1988 uprising, he was already a general, a vice minister of defense, and a member of the ruling party's central executive committee—one of several fifty-something-year-old officers in the shadow of the dictator Ne Win. By 1992, Than Shwe had made it to the top of the pecking order as the new chairman of the State Law and Order Restoration Council.

Than Shwe promised a new direction. As one of his first acts, he quietly allowed the UN to repatriate the Rohingya refugees. Other changes followed, though not quite the ones Aung San Suu Kyi and the West were hoping for. Foreign investment was prioritized and 1995 branded "Visit Burma Year." The army was transformed from a ragtag force of around 150,000 light infantry to a far larger and more modern force of perhaps over 300,000 men, supplied with new tanks and other armored vehicles, a growing navy and air force, little compunction in mobilizing forced labor, and a voracious appetite for land.

Than Shwe was trying to follow the well-worn path of an Asian strongman: allow no political dissent and focus on an exports-based industrialization. This path led some countries, like South Korea, to development and democracy. The same path led others, like China and Vietnam, to economic growth without political liberalization. Wherever it might have led, it was a path denied to the Burmese.

SHORTLY AFTER the failed 1988 uprising, the United States cut off all aid to Burma and downgraded relations. In 1990, George Bush nominated Frederick Vreeland, a former clandestine agent of the Central Intelligence Agency and the son of *Vogue* magazine editor-in-chief Diana Vreeland, to be his ambassador in Rangoon, but the appointment was never confirmed. By then, Senator Daniel Moynihan and other members of Congress were taking a hard line against the junta and looking for ways to show their displeasure.

Within a few years, "boycott Burma" campaigns mushroomed across the US. Divestment campaigns against apartheid in South Africa had proved successful, leaving campus organizations in search of new targets. Burma seemed a fitting replacement. By the mid-1990s, these campaigns became Internet campaigns and Burma became one of the very first causes to gain traction over the World Wide Web. The few American companies that had ventured into Burma, including Pepsi, Levi's, Wal-Mart, Reebok, and Eddie Bauer, pulled out by the mid-1990s, most citing public opinion as the reason.[9]

US senator John McCain visited Rangoon in June 1995 and met spymaster General Khin Nyunt, who made him watch a gory video of protesters in 1988 beheading suspected government informants. His wife, Cindy, had to leave the room. McCain was furious. "These are very bad people," he said. He pushed for sanctions.[10]

Aung San Suu Kyi was released just weeks later. Madeleine Albright visited in September of the same year, after attending the UN Conference on Women in Beijing, and brought with her a poster from the conference signed by Hillary Clinton as well as a letter from President Bill Clinton to

Aung San Suu Kyi. About the generals, Albright said, "I think they might have been surprised that I wasn't a little bit friendlier, and that I delivered a pretty tough message."

An Associated Press clip of the visit shows Albright, then US ambassador to the UN, sitting across the table from khaki-clad generals, everybody stony-faced, then meeting Aung San Suu Kyi, this time everyone all smiles, before cutting to a scene of the ambassador at a random Burmese village, the villagers, men, women, and children, laughing and smearing sandalwood paste (a traditional sun-block) on Albright, who asks, "Is it good?", to which they reply, *"Hla-de"* ("You're beautiful"). This was the image of Burma that was being carved in stone: wicked generals, a faultless icon, and an innocent people waiting for salvation.

The image of Burma in the UK and the US had always been an unusual one. In the 19th century, before the British expeditionary force snuffed out what remained of the Mandalay kingdom, Burma was presented as a naturally rich country of tremendous potential held back by a despotic and singularly inept regime. During colonial rule, the theme was summed up by the title of a well-known book about the country, *A People at School*: Burma was a country of pleasant people, cheerful and politically unsophisticated, in need of extensive tutelage before any possibility of self-government could even be considered. Herbert Hoover, who made a fortune in Burma as a mining engineer, said the Burmese were the only "truly happy people in all of Asia."

In 1993 Than Shwe convened a national convention to draw up a new constitution. The National League for Democracy was invited to join, but with only a minority of places, even though they had won a majority of constituencies in the 1990 elections. The generals saw this as a compromise. Shortly after Aung San Suu Kyi was released, Than Shwe and the other top generals met with her over dinner. There was hope of dialogue, and Aung San Suu Kyi showed signs of wanting to find a middle ground. She spoke at every opportunity of not seeing the army ("my father's army") as the enemy. But after the Albright visit, the NLD took a harder line, buoyed by the solid backing they believed they now had from the world's sole superpower. In November 1995, they boycotted the National Convention. A day later, they were expelled.

"Please use your liberty to promote ours," Aung San Suu Kyi wrote two years later in an op-ed in the *New York Times*.[11] The Clinton administration responded by banning all new investment in Burma. At the time, the US was Burma's biggest investor. By then, Aung San Suu Kyi was back under house arrest. In 2000, Bill Clinton awarded her the Presidential Medal of Freedom in absentia, warning that the generals would be "outcasts" until they ended tyranny in their "land of inherent promise." Of Aung San Suu Kyi he said, "her struggle continues and her spirit still inspires us."

The net result was a stalemate. The democracy movement was in tatters, facing severe repression, with hundreds of activists in prison. But the growing and almost messianic status of Aung San Suu Kyi at home, now coupled with the vociferous support of top political figures in Washington, meant that the generals' political agenda could not easily move forward either.

Change, though, *was* happening in Burma, though it was coming from an entirely different direction. The epicenter was not Rangoon but the far-flung hills along the China frontier, areas that colonial mapmakers had marked "unadministered."

ON APRIL 16, 1989, the Communist Party of Burma, for decades the country's biggest insurgent organization, imploded.

Forty years earlier, the Communists, mainly middle-class Burmese Marxist intellectuals from Rangoon, had managed to mobilize the support of millions. In 1948, they attempted to seize power through a nationwide insurrection, but they failed and became a guerrilla insurgency. In the late 1960s, when they were on their last legs, a heavily armed Communist force crossed the border from China—with the direct support of the Chinese military and with hundreds of Chinese "volunteers" at the helm—and established a "liberated zone" for the Burma Communist Party in the far northeast. By the 1980s the Communists, wiped out elsewhere, held only these mountain strongholds, remote places that were home not to the Burmese Buddhist majority but to culturally distinct peoples like the Kachin and the Wa. These upland peoples, who now made up nearly all their armed force, were used as cannon fodder. China, once an enthusiastic supporter but now moving in a reformist direction under Deng Xiaoping, cut off military aid.

The Communists were still, however, a force to be reckoned with, controlling 20,000 or so well-armed troops and a territory the size of Wales or Massachusetts along the Burma–China border. Harsh taxes on local villagers were imposed to make up for the lost support from Beijing. When some commanders turned to the lucrative drug trade, the party leadership threatened "stern measures." These commanders mutinied, overthrowing the party leadership.

The mutineers (key figures in the dramas to come) stormed the party headquarters, taking control of the armory, burning Communist literature, and smashing portraits of Marx, Engels, Lenin, and Mao Zedong. The Marxist intellectuals who had headed the party, mainly men in their seventies, fled to China. The 20,000 members of the rank and file split up. The Communist insurgency was no more, but in its place were four formidable replacement armies, all uncertain of what to do next.

This took place over the same months in which the junta in Rangoon, after crushing pro-democracy demonstrations, was trying desperately to survive. The government's coffers were empty. The generals first turned to Thailand and secured lucrative deals to sell timber, allowing Thai firms linked to that country's military to clear-cut forests in the southeast. But the key to the junta's survival would be a historic understanding reached with the ex-Communist armies. This understanding was the kernel of the Burma to come.

The broker was a Kokang Chinese man named Lo Hsing-han. Kokang is a small mountainous region along the border, whose people are ethnic Chinese claiming descent from a Ming dynasty loyalist who fled the Manchu conquest in the 1600s and the assortment of freebooters who accompanied him. In the 1960s and 1970s, the Kokang Chinese provided the mule trains that carried opium to heroin refineries in the Golden Triangle, the area straddling Burma, Thailand, and Laos. Lo had his own militia and was a Golden Triangle kingpin.

In 1989, Lo Hsing-han teamed up with General Khin Nyunt, the junta spymaster who would irritate John McCain. Khin Nyunt convinced his junta colleagues that a deal with the ex-communist armies was vital for the army regime's future success. There were other insurgencies to deal with, the democracy movement was still gaining steam, and the West was making threatening noises. Domestic and international pressure would only heat up. Lo arranged the talks. Both sides agreed to a ceasefire. Both agreed, too, that the ex-Communist forces could do business as they pleased. Each successor army was given a "Special Region."

At the same time, the border with China was opened. After the Tiananmen Square protest in 1989, China's government made a clear choice to combine political repression, a market economy, and globalization. Growth became white-hot. Burma became a backyard to the world's biggest ever industrial revolution. The result was a transformation of the Burmese economy and society.

"The seed capital of the Burmese economy is heroin," said Ronald Findlay, a Burma-born professor of economics at Columbia University. "If that's an exaggeration, it's not a huge one."[12] The cultivation of opium and the production of heroin in the Golden Triangle was nothing new. But with the collapse of the Communist insurgency and the newly agreed ceasefires, the illicit narcotics trade boomed liked never before, with tacit if not explicit official sanction. In addition to the former Communist forces, dozens of smaller militia, many of which had been set up by the army to fight the communists, settled into a new money-making existence. There's nothing to suggest that the top army brass set out to boost the drug economy and then profit from it; instead, it's likely they were motivated first and foremost by a desire for regime survival and their perceptions of national security. But the upshot was the same.

Logging became another big business. Burma in the early 1990s still had vast areas of virgin forest, with more than 90 percent of the world's teak and many other hardwood trees as well. Forests were cut down on an unprecedented (and unsustainable) scale.

In 1994, another insurgent group, the Kachin Independence Army, with up to 10,000 troops in the far north of the country, agreed to a cease-fire as well. They had stayed separate from the old Communist insurgency and enjoyed considerable support from their largely Christian communities. The Kachin region includes spectacularly rich jade mines, the stuff of legend—the only source anywhere of what the Chinese call imperial jade, more valuable to Chinese connoisseurs than diamonds. These mines now came under the control of the Burmese army, with the Kachin army taking a cut. Companies linked to either or both dominated sales to China. More forests were cut down. No one knows how much money was made from drugs, timber, and jade, but it was doubtless in the billions, possibly tens of billions of dollars a year over the 1990s and 2000s. This, in a country where the average income was then less than $1,000 a year.

Consumer goods flooded in from China. This was a good thing for many ordinary people, and in the years to come would provide affordable motorbikes, phones, electric fans, solar panels (the only source of electricity for most), and more or less everything else anyone wanted to buy. But the imports also decimated local industries.

Under the Burmese Way to Socialism, nearly everyone was poor together. Even top officials had little more than a modest house, a car, perhaps air-conditioning and a TV. Now there were at least two paths to getting rich, very rich. The first was in the northern and eastern uplands, where men with guns were kingpins and their associates ran the rackets. Alongside drugs, timber, and jade came a host of other illicit and illegal operations.

A man named Lin Mingxian headed one of the ex-Communist militias, the salubriously named National Democracy Alliance Army. Lin was Chinese and had been a Red Guard during the Chinese Cultural Revolution in the 1960s. In his revolutionary fervor he had joined the Burmese Communists and their fraternal fight for a dictatorship of the proletariat. In 1989, he was one of the mutineers. He set up a successor army, agreed to a ceasefire with Rangoon, and set up his own fiefdom, Special Region 4. Far from the jade mines and with few forests to chop down, Lin pioneered a new way to make money: gambling. Mongla, in the center of Special Region 4, became a booming casino town replete with brothels and eateries offering exotic animals, attracting gamblers by the thousands from across China.

Another way to make money was through a relationship with a Burmese army officer, if possible a very senior officer in an administrative position, ideally a minister or a regional commander. Some generals made money directly, through kickbacks (some were eventually sacked for corruption). Many more allowed their wives, children, and hangers-on to profit from their positions. Money could be made from a government contract (for example, to build a road, charging a few times more than the actual cost), getting land (say, a fifty-year lease on state-owned land which could then be subleased for a handsome profit), or gaining an import license. An import license for a single car might be worth $100,000 or more. A road contract could bring tens of millions of dollars from state coffers. And access to state projects could mean access to the official exchange rate of 6 kyats (the local currency) to the dollar, at a time when market rates were at least a hundred times more.

These two worlds interacted. Warlords who made "black money" (for instance, from heroin) could launder their profits through new banks by paying a tax (of around 30 percent). A warlord could then buy a fleet of expensive cars. The "national entrepreneur" who had the license to import the cars could make a killing. The warlord could also use money from his bank account to buy a nice house in Rangoon. Those already on the Rangoon real estate ladder would get rich too. By the late 1990s, the United Wa State Army, one of the successor armies to the Communists, owned both the Mayflower Bank in Rangoon and an airline company, Yangon Airways.

There were men in the insurgent armies who fought to protect their communities, and in the hope of a brighter future for their people. There were also men in the Burmese army who were good soldiers and who believed they were serving their country in the best way they could. But on all sides, there also were men with venal motives. For many, with markets opening and fortunes there for the making, temptations became too great.

As one sector of the economy after another was deregulated, new opportunities emerged. Some businessmen built up big portfolios. In addition to the warlords, kingpins, and cronies, there were also a few businessmen and women who played by the book and were largely free of army connections (though no one could be entirely free). Often, they tried to rely on new foreign investment and sectors like tourism. There were ups and downs. The 1997 Asian financial crisis and American sanctions wiped out many companies. Sanctions in particular made it almost impossible for the more independent businessmen to survive, leaving the field clear for those close to power.

By the early 2000s, billions of dollars' worth of new offshore natural gas finds were added to the mix. Global oil companies (specifically exempted from Washington sanctions) had discovered and developed the fields and built pipelines to export the gas to Thailand. Burma's share of the profits went straight to offshore accounts controlled by the junta for "special projects." A good relationship with the army meant access to a lucrative special project.

Rangoon mutated. As black money entered its veins, hundreds of charming colonial-era bungalows were torn down and in place of both the bungalows and their surrounding gardens sprang up gargantuan mansions of concrete and tinted glass.[13] Old hotels were given makeovers, a new cable TV service offered CNN and BBC News, and a gleaming new airport provided many daily nonstop flights to Bangkok, Singapore, and Hong Kong.

Land everywhere became more valuable as speculators speculated and those close to decision-makers grabbed hundreds, sometimes thousands of acres of farmland or forest in the hope of future windfalls.

Some ordinary people benefited. There were new jobs, especially in construction. There was a sliver of a new middle class. And there was growth in the narrow sense of more economic activity. At the same time, millions were impoverished. As land became commercialized, rural families across the country lost rights to their ancestral farms (a bribe could turn someone's ancestral land into "vacant" land ready for leasing by the state). The same families were broken up as one or more members migrated to Rangoon, Thailand, or overseas in search of work. Rivers were contaminated by mining runoff and forests cut down on an epic scale. Even tigers were not spared, as their habitat was wrecked and they themselves hunted for the sale of their body parts to an insatiable Chinese market. By the 2000s, Burma's tigers were on the verge of extinction.

A kind of capitalism was being restored. Some like to put an adjective in front: "crony capitalism," "ceasefire capitalism," "army capitalism." It wasn't the socially responsible capitalism the World Economic Forum might want to promote, but it wasn't too different from the system in colonial days: an extractive economy that benefited office-holders most, then a handful of businessmen, with infrastructure built to serve exports, and with little or no concept of the state as something meant to serve popular welfare.

By the turn of the millennium, no one thought anymore of Communism or socialism, the ideologies that had dominated politics for most of the 20th century. Democracy was the new buzzword. People wanted change and an end to military rule. But the iron fist of the junta meant that, in Rangoon at least, opposition became less a mass movement and more the symbolic resistance of one person, Aung San Suu Kyi. The combination of ceasefires, the opening to China, and Western sanctions threw up a rapacious new market dynamic. Power and money reconnected. And there was, as well, a rising ethno-nationalist impulse, grounded in older ideas about race and identity. Over the coming years, all these elements would congeal.

The future seemed bleak. But there were still opportunities to turn things around.

THREE

DRIFTING TO DYSTOPIA

MOE MOE MYINT AUNG was born in Rangoon in 1979, during the tranquil, stagnant days of Burmese socialism, and grew up in a leafy neighborhood of little wooden houses, close to the river and not far from the sea. Her father was a Karen Christian. Her mother was Shan, another minority people, from the hills east of Mandalay. Small and slender, with sharp features and neatly combed hair, she was wearing simple Burmese clothes, a cotton sarong and blouse, when we met in 2018.[1]

She told me that the first convulsion in her life took place in the late 1980s, when she was in the fourth grade. The army had just crushed anti-government demonstrations, and, to prevent the possibility of further unrest, hundreds of thousands of people were forced from downtown areas to makeshift townships miles away. Bulldozers flattened Moe Moe's home and her family was ordered to the newly created Shwepyitha or "Golden Pleasant City," a collection of hovels with little electricity and no running water.

There was, though, a school, and at school Moe Moe dreamed of being a doctor. "Not just any doctor. I wanted to be an army doctor. I watched movies on video and saw doctors who were looking after soldiers on the front lines. I wanted to do that too." But when she was in the seventh grade her father disappeared. He was, she said, a "simple man" who "fell into a bad crowd." As she was the eldest of three children, she felt she had a responsibility to help her mother as much as she could and look after her siblings. "I couldn't think of university any more. We were so poor. We sold what we could. Some days we had nothing to eat."

In 1996, when Moe Moe was seventeen, she got a job at a factory making T-shirts for export to America. She made 20,000 kyats a month (about $150) and gave all of it to her family. "It was a tough life, but I was okay and was able to provide for my mother and sisters." In 1997, though, as campaigns against doing business in Burma gained steam and the Clinton administration imposed sanctions on new investment, the garment factory shut down.

After a few months of occasional work, earning small amounts here and there, Moe Moe took a friend's advice and went to Victoria Point in the far south of Burma, then crossed a narrow estuary to the Thai port of Ranong. She thought she was going to waitress in a restaurant, but when she arrived, she discovered it was a nightclub where men paid to spend time drinking with women. Extras couldn't be refused. She was told she would receive 5,000 kyats a month (about $5). She was also told that if she wanted to leave before doing a year's work she would have to pay 300,000 kyats "compensation" to the owner. "It was a terrible life, spending hours every day with drunken men, both Burmese and Thai."

As soon as the year was up, she left. Determined to find decent employment, she worked for a while on a rubber planation, in a little eatery, and as a babysitter for a Thai family, before finally being arrested as an illegal immigrant.

It was her first time in jail. She shared a big room with many other women, mainly Burmese held on drug charges. She spoke little Thai and so could barely communicate with her jailers. "It was a really hard time, initially," she told me. But the prison staff were not unkind. They helped

her learn Thai and soon she was able to read the alphabet and then cartoons. In August 2005, as part of a prisoner amnesty marking the queen's
birthday, she was released.

"I was taken to one detention center after another and then left in the
middle of the water, in the estuary between Thailand and Burma," she
said. The reason that detainees like Moe Moe were often left in the middle
of the water was so that "brokers," in collusion with immigration officials, could fetch the recently "returned" illegals and bring them back
to Thailand for more illegal work. It was a racket. Moe Moe considered
herself now savvy in the ways of the illegal migrant world of southern
Thailand and thought she could do better the second time around. So she
hooked up with a broker and went back to Thailand.

She was right. After some trial and error she found her way to Phuket,
the resort island, and found work in a garment factory where she laun-
dered clothes. Her boss was nice, and the salary was good. After a couple
of years, she sent a message to her family in Rangoon through a woman
who was traveling back from Phuket. Months later, she got a message
back that her mother had died and that her brother had enlisted in the
army. Only her sister was left. With the savings she had accumulated,
she went home.

Being back in Rangoon was both good and bad: good, because she met
the man who became her husband, a government telephone department
worker, and bad, because a job at the government telephone department
meant only 20,000 kyats a month (less than $20). "We had a lot of difficulty
making ends meet. My savings were gone after not very long and we were
borrowing at 20 percent interest a month. I couldn't see how we could get
out of debt," she told me.

Burma's banking system was a mess. Almost no one had a bank
account or access to formal loans. Poor people turned to informal moneylenders, who were sometimes poor people themselves with some extra
cash to lend. Interest rates were astronomical. Some paid day rates of 20

percent—borrowing the equivalent of five dollars in the morning, spending one or two dollars in bus fares to and from whatever work they had, and paying back six dollars in the evening. Some had to borrow hundreds of dollars if they or a relative fell ill and needed medicine. Once in debt, it was nearly impossible to recover.

Soon, a childhood friend appeared and offered Moe Moe a job in Lashio, a town on the old Burma Road connecting Mandalay with Yunnan province in China. "She said I could get 200,000 kyats a month to help an old lady," she said. "My dream was to buy a sewing machine for 100,000 kyats and set up a small business. I wanted this so much. I thought this would be the way."

On the way to Lashio, her friend told her to drink from a small vial, telling her it was medicine for carsickness. Almost immediately, Moe Moe fell asleep. When she awoke, she was no longer in Burma.

"All around me was Chinese writing. All the people in the car were Chinese too. I had been taken to a small village and once there was told, 'Make yourself look nice or else we will beat you.' I still wasn't sure what was happening. Then I was put out for sale to visiting men like morning glory at the market." She tried to flee through a back door but was caught. She was kept in the village for a month and then sold for 40,000 yuan to a man who took her to his home near Shanghai, more than a thousand miles away.

"He wasn't bad to me," she said. "He was trying to make me like him. I didn't speak any Chinese so when he and I communicated it was just through gestures. His relatives were nearby and in the village were other Burmese girls. We were not allowed to speak to each other. I was there about three months.

"One day we went for a drive. He said he would show me the big city. He pointed to one place and said, 'That's where Jet Li lives.' At a tollgate, I gestured to my stomach and said I had a pain and needed to use the toilet. We stopped and as soon as I saw him going into the men's room, I ran as fast as I could. Several minutes later, I snuck inside a bookstore. The owner saw me and asked what was happening. He didn't understand me and I didn't understand him. I said 'Burma' in English. An older lady was in the bookstore and realized what I was trying to say, that I was from Burma, and told me to hide and call the police. I didn't understand what they were saying so she spoke for me. They gave me an egg and some maize and some water." At 6:30 that evening, the police came.

Moe Moe was held in a detention cell before being flown from Shanghai to Yunnan, and then driven to the border at Muse. Two Chinese police officers accompanied her the whole way, saying it was for her own safety in case her "husband" came looking for her, but also because some Burmese girls tried to flee. Back in Rangoon, she was reunited with her family. She also discovered that she had contracted HIV/AIDS.

MOE MOE MYINT AUNG's life was not dissimilar to the lives being lived by millions of young men and women throughout the country. In the early 2000s, Burma's estimated per capita GDP was little more than half that of Cambodia or Bangladesh, and less than half that of Laos or Vietnam. It was the poorest country in Asia. There was almost no electricity outside the main cities, and even in the cities power was available at best for only a few hours a day. Inflation was the highest in the region, running at nearly 40 percent a year. Shockingly, 73 percent of spending in the *average* Burmese household was on food (compared with, for example, 52 percent in Bangladesh). For some it was closer to 100 percent.

Skyrocketing poverty meant fast-rising malnutrition. More than 30 percent of children under five were malnourished. Burma was the only country in the world where the main cause of infant death was beriberi, a vitamin B deficiency. Extreme poverty also exacerbated the crisis in education; 40 percent of children were taken out of school by parents who couldn't pay the cost of a uniform or books, or who couldn't afford the time to walk a young child hours every day to the nearest school.[2]

HIV/AIDS was rampant. By 2003, Burma had the third highest rate of infection in all of Asia, after Thailand and Cambodia. Some of the worst-affected areas were along the China border, in the mining towns and smuggling hubs where migrant workers from around the country shot up heroin nightly and where sex workers knew little about protection from sexually transmitted diseases. Only an estimated 3 percent of those needing retroviral treatment were receiving drugs. About 20,000 people a year were dying.

In the early 1990s, Rolf Carriere, then UNICEF's country director for Burma, warned of a "silent emergency" facing the country's children. He was appalled at the level of need and at the minuscule levels of international assistance the country was receiving. Carriere argued passionately for a different approach, saying that without urgent help the lives of Burmese children would only worsen and that providing humanitarian assistance shouldn't wait for the "right government" to be in place. Few listened.

Would anyone listen now?

The generals wanted a modern future. But their vision was one of growth and the development of "the nation." This they would do through big infrastructure projects that would spur a Burmese industrial revolution. Individual people mattered little. There were corrupt motives, too. In any case, their underlings, drawing from a hodgepodge of statistics that were dubious at best, were telling them that the economy was growing at 10 percent plus per annum.

The opposition—the National League for Democracy and their supporters abroad—prioritized politics. Only a regime change, they felt, could lead to other improvements. There was, of course, something to this. Systemic change, even revolution, might be a good thing. It was not impossible, but it was improbable. And as the political stalemate wore on, year after year, and a merciless capitalist system took root, a generation of young people was fast losing whatever future they had.

The opposition offered no theory of how things might actually improve. By the early 2000s, the generals were more firmly ensconced than ever before. Isolation (except for the back door to China) was, if anything, cementing the environment in which the generals and their cronies were doing very well. Was tightening that isolation from the rest of the world likely to spur a different momentum?

There was also little thought given to what landscape could best prepare the country for democratic change and make change sustainable if and when it ever came. Legions of dirt-poor, uneducated, ill-fed, and sickly people were unlikely to undergird a robust democracy. And there was no thinking about whether democracy itself was really the best initial exit from military dictatorship. Could there, instead, be a combination of other steps: New ceasefires that actually benefited local communities? Economic reforms that lessened inequalities coupled with fresh international assistance, aimed especially at public health and education? Efforts to combat discrimination and address deep-seated issues around race and identity? Could there be a different conversation about Burma's future that placed front and center the lives of the poorest and most vulnerable? No one knew. But trying would mean engaging the generals. And that was anathema to many in the opposition, who believed engagement would only weaken the hand of the National League for Democracy.

THE NATIONAL LEAGUE FOR DEMOCRACY was in dire straits. Hundreds were locked up in the early 1990s and still serving long prison terms. There was no longer any countrywide organization, only a little office in Rangoon, and even less space to mobilize. And the incessant repression—the omnipresent spy networks, years of hiding, fear of the midnight knock on the door—meant that for many the rational thing to do was to quit, emigrate if possible, seek asylum in the West, or quietly move on to other things, perhaps business. Some stayed the course. They were the stalwarts, willing to make any sacrifice for what they believed was the highest public good. They also developed absolute faith in Aung San Suu Kyi.

At tea at home with David Rockefeller in early 2003, Aung San Suu Kyi joked about those who advised her to be "patient" with the generals and to "go slow," saying, "Slow is one thing, a snail's pace is another." The longer it takes, she warned, the more difficult it will be to "restart" the country under a new government. She worried about the state of the education system and expressed concern that Burma would soon become a country of "uneducated people," with terrible consequences for the nation's political and economic future.[3]

She was right. But it was not apparent what the NLD could do. Aung San Suu Kyi's core strategy was to demonstrate popular support, ask for dialogue, and hope the generals would respond. By 2003, it was clear that the generals were thinking no such thing.

On May 30, near the small town of Tabayin, not far from Mandalay, a swarm of men, many possibly drugged or drunk, and armed with makeshift weapons, ambushed a convoy carrying Aung San Suu Kyi and her supporters. She had been released in 2002 from her latest bout of house arrest and was traveling around the country giving open-air speeches calling for an end to military rule, and receiving a rapturous welcome from people wherever she went. Dozens were killed in the ambush. Aung San Suu Kyi escaped unharmed but was subsequently jailed.

The regime was testing its limits. The movement for democracy was effectively crushed. Could the outside world still help?

The Bush administration was keen to make a difference in Burma, in large part because of the personal interest of First Lady Laura Bush. A Bush cousin, Elsie Walker Kilbourne, who had for many years been drawn to Buddhism, introduced Laura Bush to a Tibet activist, Michele Bohana, who was also active in the Burma cause. Laura Bush began reading Aung

San Suu Kyi's writings, including her collection of essays *Freedom from Fear*. They made a deep impression. At a time when her husband and his national security aides were firmly focused on the Middle East, she tried in her own way to help Burma. For her, Burma meant Aung San Suu Kyi and, using a "back channel," she sent private notes of encouragement and items she thought might be hard to get in Rangoon, including books, fabrics, seaweed tablets to "share with friends in prison" who were in need of iodine, and aloe to "heal wounds." For now, all this was kept secret from the media, in order "to protect those who helped along the way."[4]

Support for Burma's democracy movement was bipartisan. It was also transatlantic. Tony Blair's government in the UK was a staunch ally of Aung San Suu Kyi, leading every effort within the European Union to impose ever tighter sanctions. Campaign groups targeted companies doing business in Burma with vigor. The Norwegian government not only awarded Aung San Suu Kyi the Nobel Peace Prize in 1991 but funded both a Burmese government in exile, headed by her exiled cousin Sein Win, and an exiled radio station, the Democratic Voice of Burma. In 2002, Bono won the Grammy Award for Record of the Year for "Walk On," a song he composed in Aung San Suu Kyi's honor.

America had just invaded Afghanistan and Iraq, and the idea that Western coalitions might successfully impose democracies around the world was still riding high. A decade before, the scholar Francis Fukuyama had written about the "universalization of Western liberal democracy as the final form of human government."[5] Neocons like Paul Wolfowitz were now in the uppermost echelons of the administration, motivated by a desire to aggressively promote liberal democratic ideals throughout the world.

The US was still the world's sole superpower. The Soviets had been vanquished, Russia seemed eager to embrace the West, and China was still little more than a giant new market for multinational companies. In 1999, NATO intervened in Kosovo to protect human rights, without a mandate from the UN Security Council. In 2003, Saddam Hussein was captured and later hanged. It seemed possible that the days of tyranny everywhere were numbered.

But then, over the following years, the interventionist tide waned. The disbanding of the Iraqi Army and the cavalier attitude taken toward other Iraqi institutions were based on an assumption by American planners that the country was a *tabula rasa*, needing only new constitutions and fresh elections. The assumption was wrong, and over the next few years the perils of state-building became clear. Afghanistan proved no easier. Neither did Somalia or Libya. Understanding grew that these places that needed fixing had their own histories, their own unseen and complex dynamics, and that any intervention might well do more harm than good.

Except in Burma.

ON JULY 28, 2003, a little less than a month after declaring the war in Iraq "mission accomplished," President George Bush imposed on Burma the toughest economic sanctions in the world.

The Burma Freedom and Democracy Act banned all Burmese imports to the United States, froze assets, and banned remittances to Burma, effectively preventing any financial exchanges involving the US banking system. The law also required the American government to block any loans from the World Bank and other international development banks. Coming on top of existing Clinton-era sanctions, the new act virtually cut Burma off from the global economy.

The new American law charged the ruling junta with failing to transfer power to Aung San Suu Kyi's National League for Democracy and for "egregious human rights violations" against its own people. The law also stated that the regime had been guilty of ethnic cleansing, which constituted a "crime against humanity."

This was a reference to army offensives over the 1990s and early

2000s against Karen rebels. The Karen are a partially Christian minority people spread across the south of Burma. Whereas ex-Communist and other armies in the north had signed ceasefires, the Karen National Union, an insurgent group with more than 8,000 men under arms and considerable local support, refused to do the same and bore the brunt of brutal counterinsurgency operations. Thousands of civilians were press-ganged into carrying army supplies. An estimated 700,000 people were forced to flee their homes, including 100,000 who sought refuge across the border in Thailand.

The bill passed overwhelmingly in both houses of Congress. Senator Mitch McConnell, the primary sponsor of the bill, said, "We must never tire in the pursuit of justice in long-suffering Burma until Suu Kyi is free and the struggle for freedom is won."[6] Senator McConnell, later Senate Majority Leader, was a diehard fan of Aung San Suu Kyi; on his office wall hung a framed letter she had sent the year before, thanking him for his support.[7]

On signing the law, President Bush issued a statement declaring that the "United States will not waver from its commitment to the cause of democracy and human rights in Burma." The aim was not simply to punish a rogue regime. The aim was to make a democracy in the heart of Asia.

Burma seemed to be a place where there was no downside to "doing the right thing." There were few business interests and no calculation (yet) that Burma was strategically important. In the UK, there was the added dimension of colonial ties, remembered in a rosy way, and the personal link to Aung San Suu Kyi, a fearless Oxford-educated heroine standing up to the most thuggish group of men imaginable in a faraway land. There was no attempt to analyze the roots of authoritarianism or Burma's complex interethnic relations. Nor was there an effort to understand the country's traumatic past or reflect on the legacies of colonialism. To the extent that people thought about Burma's myriad "ethnic groups," they were seen as victims too of military repression and on the side of "democracy." The ceasefires along the China border remained out of sight and mind. The seductively powerful Manichean narrative trumped all other considerations.

In May and September 2001, Buddhist–Muslim riots broke out in Pegu, Toungoo, and Prome, following news of the destruction by the Taliban of the Buddha statues at Bamiyan in Afghanistan. That same year, in Akyab (the main city in Arakan, also known as Sittwe), the army intervened to quell days of violence between Buddhists and Muslims that left at least a dozen dead. Human Rights Watch reported that "resentments are deeply rooted and result from both communities feeling that they are under siege from the other."[8] Few took notice.

In January 2005, at her Senate confirmation hearing, incoming secretary of state Condoleezza Rice listed Burma as an "outpost of tyranny," together with Cuba, Iran, North Korea, Belarus, and Zimbabwe, augmenting the original "Axis of Evil." In London, activists organized an "I'm Not Going" campaign, an effort to stifle any possible development of the country's embryonic tourism industry. In a special show of crossbench unity, prime minister Tony Blair, Conservative leader Michael Howard, and Liberal Democrat leader Charles Kennedy all pledged to boycott holidays in Burma, together with a raft of celebrities including Ian McKellen, Honor Blackman, Robbie Coltrane, and Joanna Lumley.

Voices in the West for democracy in Burma were growing louder.

MEANWHILE IN BURMA ITSELF, Senior General Than Shwe was quietly preparing his retirement. In the 1990s, he had been head of a collective; the other generals in the junta were only slightly junior in age and rank. Most were at the same time ministers and "regional commanders" in charge of large parts of the country. General Tun Kyi, for example, was both Minister of Commerce and the army chief in Mandalay. General Kyaw Ba was minister of hotels and tourism as well the head of the army's

Northern Command. They were viceroys with unlimited power. Some amassed fortunes.

Slowly and methodically, Than Shwe removed the other generals in power. He started with those closest to him in seniority, and the most corrupt. One general after another was purged. In 2002, as the old dictator Ne Win lay on his deathbed, Than Shwe arrested Ne Win's family. Until then, observers suspected that Ne Win was still wielding power and his family was still influential. Than Shwe demonstrated plainly who was now on top.

Next to go was the intelligence chief Khin Nyunt. The trim, bespectacled Khin Nyunt was for many foreigners the man in the regime they knew best. He was the one who met John McCain and Madeleine Albright. He liked watching himself on TV. He ran a vast network of well-trained spies and informants who were feared even within the army. Under him was an Office of Strategic Studies, with five departments, which monitored the opposition and plotted strategy. Some were urbane men who spoke English and presented themselves as reformers. Others ran the torture centers. This intelligence service, formally the Directorate of Defense Services Intelligence but colloquially known as MI from its earlier, British-bred incarnation, was the weapon used to grind down the democratic opposition.

On October 18, 2004, Khin Nyunt was detained by army officers at the airport in Mandalay, flown to Rangoon, and placed under house arrest. The next day, the state-controlled newspapers reported that the sixty-five-year-old had been "permitted to retire for health reasons." Within weeks, hundreds of military intelligence officers were arrested, interrogated, charged with economic crimes and other sometimes minor offenses (for example, illegal possession of a handgun), and sentenced to up to thirty years in jail. The entire secret police system, the bedrock of repression since the first days of army rule in the 1960s, was disbanded. More than 30,000 junior officers and soldiers in the intelligence service were summarily dismissed. Khin Nyunt's once ubiquitous image was everywhere taken down, and the cabinet and civil service purged of his supporters.[9]

Some might have worried that knocking off such a potent institution would lead to a backlash, but Than Shwe was by now confident in his dominance. He even left the country for India a few days later, posing for a photograph with his wife in front of the Taj Mahal and worshipping at the Mahabodhi temple in Bodh Gaya, where the Buddha attained enlightenment.

What had been a gang of generals was reduced to Than Shwe and his deputy, General Maung Aye. Before his ouster, spy chief Khin Nyunt had announced a Seven-Step Road Map to Democracy. This was kept intact. The government promised there would be a new constitution, fresh elections, and then (at some future, unspecified date) a transition to civilian government. A slew of political prisoners were released, though not Aung San Suu Kyi. In 2004, Than Shwe ordered army officers to buy their own personal computers and start surfing the Internet.

He did something else too: he built a new capital city, Naypyitaw. Various Burmese rulers had built new capitals in the past: Amarapura in the 18th century and Mandalay in the 19th were both the projects of kings who wanted to leave behind a special legacy. The word Naypyitaw simply means "the capital" and is normally only part of the appellation (e.g., "Mandalay Naypyitaw"). Perhaps Than Shwe was unable to come up with a good name. For the location, he chose an area smack in the middle of the country, halfway between Rangoon and Mandalay, bounded by a teak-clad ridge to the west and a limestone escarpment to the east, an area that at the height of the civil war in the late 1940s had been a stronghold of Communist insurgents.

Naypyitaw was far from the reach of George Bush's warships. The idea that the Americans might invade may have seemed risible in New York or London, but in the mid-2000s, it wasn't an entirely outlandish idea to a country which was the target of increasingly harsh rhetoric by an administration that had already invaded two countries, and was certainly not something that a risk-averse army would easily shrug off. A Wesley Snipes film that featured a cruise missile attack on a city that looked like Rangoon seemed to underline the danger, as did *Rambo IV*, which was set in the Burmese jungle.

Naypyitaw also created a revolution-proof geography. Far from the centers of population, the new capital stretched over an area almost as large as New York City but with a tiny fraction of the population, nearly all of whom were soldiers and bureaucrats. There were ten- and twenty-lane asphalt boulevards, government offices set apart by hundreds of yards of shrubbery, a vast expanse of concrete buildings (in a sort of cost-cutting tropical brutalist style) and little else. Street protests in 1988 had come within striking distance of overthrowing the government; a mob had disarmed soldiers guarding the Trade Ministry and nearly stormed the War Office itself. There was now no chance of a repeat.

At the astrologically auspicious time of 6:37 a.m. on November 6, 2005, on the Senior General's orders and with no forewarning to the general public, ministries began their move, with over a thousand army trucks carrying files, typewriters, and furniture up to what was still a colossal construction site.

Than Shwe was now in complete control. The new constitution would soon be finalized. It would be a hybrid system, with the army and elected institutions sharing authority. The plans were set. Events, though, would soon get in the way.

FAR FROM THE general's gaze, the country was careering toward a full-blown humanitarian crisis. Aid restrictions imposed by Western governments had reduced international assistance to approximately $3 per person per year, compared with $9 per capita in Bangladesh, $38 in Cambodia, $49 in Laos, and $22 in Vietnam.[10] The junta did little to help. The government's coffers were improving from their bankrupt state in the early 1990s, but next to nothing was spent on education and health care. In 2000, the World Health Organization had ranked Burma's health care at the very bottom, below Angola, the Central African Republic, and even the war-ravaged Democratic Republic of Congo.[11]

The Bush sanctions decimated Burma's nascent manufacturing industry, the garment sector in particular. At least 200,000 young women, most from impoverished rural backgrounds, were thrown out of work. Said Richard Horsey, the representative of the International Labour Organization in Rangoon, "When they lost their jobs, they had no safety net, because nearly all savings were sent home. They were mostly too ashamed to return to their villages and admit they had lost their jobs, and see the impact of that on their families." Many made their way to Thailand.

In 2004, Charles Petrie, a veteran of UN operations in Africa who had been in Rwanda during the genocide, was appointed the UN's first humanitarian coordinator for Burma. UN assistance in dozens of townships around the country was quietly expanded. The regime, though, was suspicious. Whereas before they had pleaded for international aid, now they drew back, as critics in the West started to use the idea of a humanitarian crisis in Burma to demand intervention. Charles Petrie and others in the Rangoon foreign aid community had to walk a fine line, attacked on one side by the government as a fifth column for a Western regime-change agenda, and on the other by the opposition and sympathetic Western politicians for being too willing to work with the generals in power.

The Global Fund, set up by Bill Gates and several European governments to combat HIV/AIDS, tuberculosis, and malaria, began providing help, but in 2005 withdrew its $98 million in grants to Burma under heavy pressure from pro-democracy activists in the West.

Some within the democracy movement tried to do what they could in extremely precarious circumstances. In 2002, Phyu Phyu Thin, then thirty years old, founded Rangoon's first hospice for HIV/AIDS patients, and over the following five years cared for more than 1,500 patients unable to get help from either government hospitals or international organizations. Even though she had been detained for over a month by the authorities (for organizing a prayer in support of Aung San Suu Kyi), she still believed that some collaboration with government to tackle urgent humanitarian needs was possible. "Let's set aside who you are and on which [political] side you stand," she said. "We are ready to cooperate not only with the government but also with any organizations to combat HIV/AIDS."[12]

Millions were now on the move. One was Maung Than. His parents were poor farmers who split up in 1982, when he seven years old. After dropping out of school in the sixth grade, he did what he could to survive, herding cattle, sweeping floors in Rangoon tea shops, then working for a while in construction, before traveling down south to clear forests for a logging company. In 2005, with little prospect of employment in Rangoon, he signed up for a job on a Thai fishing boat. He wound up a slave.[13]

Thailand is the world's fourth largest exporter of seafood, providing fish to supermarkets around the world. In the 2000s, this industry depended on thousands of Burmese men who were tricked, drugged, and kidnapped and forced to work for years at a time in brutal conditions.

The fishing boats sailed as far as Indonesia, fleeing at the first sign of a police boat. Maung Than and the other Burmese, when not working, were kept behind two sets of locked doors. The captain, his deputy, and the engineer were Thai; the workers, about a dozen, were Burmese. For two years they were paid nothing. They were fed irregularly. There were constant beatings. There were different captains over time; some "treated us humanely, but some were brutal," he told me. "We worked at times twenty-four hours straight, sometimes longer, with no rest. Some lost consciousness while working. If a net was broken, it might be days, literally days, of work. Sometimes we could take turns to sleep a few hours. We were given coffee and stimulants." Maung Than once saw four of his fellow Burmese workers shot dead. He was finally rescued by Issara, a charity devoted to helping Burmese migrant workers and the Thai military. By then he had spent ten years as a slave.

THE UN LIKES TO SAY that its mission everywhere is conflict prevention and peace-building. At UN conferences, nations agreed that the goals of peace, development, and respect for human rights were intertwined and must be addressed together in "holistic" ways. These lofty ideas were born of decades of experience in war-torn societies. They were, however, thrown out the window in the case of Burma, where the goal was democracy and little else.

Every year, the UN General Assembly passed a resolution drafted by the European Union that essentially called on the junta to give up power to the National League for Democracy. There was rarely any mention of the armed conflicts, or even of the country's dire poverty. There was certainly no discussion of how sanctions and aid restrictions might be tipping the country into a humanitarian disaster.

The UN had a string of special envoys and special advisors on Burma. In the early 2000s, the UN special envoy was the Malaysian diplomat Rizali Ismail. He remembers his first meeting with Aung San Suu Kyi:

"After a period of waiting she emerged, cool and composed, in a traditional blue blouse and sarong, with bunga melor [jasmine flower] in her hair. Call it a grand entrance, if you like. There was no question about it. She looked very attractive, what with the scent of the melor in the air at close quarters. At an early part of my conversation with her, I said, 'You are not only courageous but also attractive.' It was obviously an unthinkable faux pas."[14] He saw his role almost exclusively as one of facilitating dialogue between Aung San Suu Kyi and the generals. He didn't get far.

In April 2005, Kofi Annan became the first UN Secretary-General to meet Than Shwe himself. This was in Bandung, Indonesia, during a fiftieth-anniversary commemoration of the Bandung Conference, which launched the Non-Aligned Movement. Annan was meeting dozens of heads of government, and had been advised to speak first in his meeting with Than Shwe and to only mention Aung San Suu Kyi toward the end of what was meant to be a twenty-minute meeting. Tired from jet lag and hours of meetings, he asked Than Shwe to speak first. Than Shwe held forth, for nearly an hour, on the history of Burma (from the army's perspective) since the Second World War. Finally, Annan got a word in edgewise and asked about Aung San Suu Kyi. Than Shwe closed his big notebook and indicated that the meeting was over.

The next envoy was Ibrahim Gambari, a good-humored Nigerian scholar and former foreign minister. His first trip in 2005 had been a success. He met Than Shwe and was able to meet as well with Aung San Suu Kyi, then under house arrest and incommunicado. The regime thought they were making a concession, but when Ibrahim Gambari briefed the Security Council a few weeks later, the generals were livid. For them, any Security Council discussion on Burma was the first step on a ladder that could lead to international intervention. Kofi Annan tried to telephone Than Shwe. Than Shwe didn't take the call.

There was pressure on the UN from the pro-democracy camp, too. In May 2006, a little over a year into her tenure as secretary of state, Condoleezza Rice sent Aung San Suu Kyi's party, the National League for Democracy, a videotaped message of support. During this period of her house arrest, the party was being led by a group of septuagenarian "uncles," mainly ex-military men who had thrown in their lot with the Nobel Prize laureate. They were "delighted" with the message, they told the *Washington Post*. "Her words boosted our morale at a time when we were feeling ill at ease." They also told the *Post* that they were unhappy with Charles Petrie (the UN humanitarian coordinator), as he was more interested in humanitarian assistance than the political issues that were all-important, and were "not satisfied" with Kofi Annan. "Just get us in a meeting room [with the junta]," they said, "and we will do the rest."

In July 2007, the Chinese entered the fray and arranged direct talks in Beijing between the Burmese and American governments. The talks didn't achieve much but both sides agreed to meet again, with China hosting if necessary. Around the same time, the Elders, a new grouping that included Bishop Desmond Tutu, Jimmy Carter, and Kofi Annan (who had just retired from the UN), probed for ways to become involved in Burma.

Then, ordinary people tried to make their voices heard.

By early 2007, the Rangoon poor, mainly migrants from the countryside who had lost their land to army and crony capitalist confiscations, were desperate. Inflation was at an all-time high, shooting up nearly 50 percent over the course of twelve months. "Why is there severe malnutrition in this Garden of Eden? Because people are poor," said Frank Smithuis, a Dutch physician who had worked in Burma since 1994 and headed the medical charity Doctors Without Borders. "People are going from three meals to two meals to one meal. One meal a day just isn't enough."[15]

In February, there was a small demonstration, and in April, another. Twenty-two people were detained for calling for lower prices and improved health, education, and electricity. Protesters carried placards with slogans such as "Down with consumer prices." On August 15, without warning, the government hiked fuel prices by 500 percent, leading to an immediate spike in bus fares. Buses were the only transportation available to most workers to get to work.

A couple of days later, the '88 Students Generation led a march down Rangoon's main avenue. These were the youngsters who had led the nearly victorious 1988 uprising. Now in their forties, and released from prison only a couple of years before, they saw the political impasse between the junta and Aung San Suu Kyi and tried unsuccessfully to find a fresh way forward. They saw as well the extreme hardship facing poor people and suggested a mechanism involving both the generals and the opposition to "attract and coordinate" international aid. They had avoided confrontation but now decided they might as well roll the dice.

They were soon arrested. Ko Ko Gyi, one of the '88 leaders, knew what was coming. When the police arrived at his apartment, he had a bag packed with two sets of clothes, a toothbrush, and a copy of the *Oxford English Learner's Dictionary*.[16]

Sporadic demonstrations continued, but the authorities were responding harshly, rounding up dissidents and using thugs to break up gatherings. It looked as if things were dying down. Then came an unexpected turn.

On September 5, far to the north in the dusty riverside town of Pakkoku, not far from Mandalay and home to dozens of Buddhist monasteries, hundreds of saffron- and crimson-clad monks organized a protest of their own, to show their support for the detained demonstrators in Rangoon. Monks were close to ordinary people. Across the country, monasteries provided the social services the state did not, including education for orphans and children whose parents were too destitute to look after them. They provided adjudication at a time when courts were corrupt. And they depended on alms, which were now drying up. They knew well how desperate many people were.

Police beat three of the monks who took part in the protest. Word spread among Burma's approximately 400,000 monks, and Buddhist leaders demanded an official apology from the government by September 17. When the day passed without an apology, monks took to the streets in Rangoon, Mandalay, and towns across the country. They also refused to perform rituals for government officials, army officers, and their families, an exceptionally serious step in a fervently religious society.

By September 22, thousands of shaven-headed monks, a sea of reddish hues, walked along Rangoon's glistening, rain-swept avenues, chanting the *Metta Sutta*, an ancient discourse on compassion, which includes the lines:

> *sabbe satta bhavantu skitatta* [May all beings enjoy happiness
> and comfort]
> *sukino va khemino hontu* [May they feel safe and secure]

A line of monks passed in front of the house of Aung San Suu Kyi. Under house arrest, she had not appeared in public in years, but now, under a monsoon downpour, she opened her gate and stood by the roadside to accept their blessing.

Within a week, the crackdown began, with the army opening fire on protesters, raiding monasteries, defrocking and arresting monks. Dozens of people are believed to have died, but as with almost every event like this in Burma's recent history, there are no confirmed figures.

Burma became the focus of global media attention just as world leaders were congregating in New York for the annual UN General Assembly. The Dalai Lama issued a statement expressing his solidarity with his Burmese brethren. The actor Jim Carrey taped an appeal to Secretary-General Ban Ki-moon on YouTube. George Bush made Burma the centerpiece of his UN speech, announcing yet more sanctions and saying that "the people's desire for change is unmistakable."

On UN Day (October 24), Charles Petrie and the heads of UN agencies in Rangoon issued a statement drawing attention to the plight of the country's poorest, saying this had been the purpose of the Buddhist monks' protest. The statement included a figure for poverty that was far worse than the government's official statistics. Within days, Charles Petrie was told to leave the country. What really riled the junta was not criticism of their repression, but criticism of their economic performance.

The protests were rooted in the economic desperation of the poor, but the West chose to see these events as a pro-democracy uprising that was crushed. The protests were retroactively termed the Saffron Revolution, to draw parallels with the Orange Revolution in Ukraine and the other "color revolutions" in the former Soviet bloc. The economic dimensions of what was happening in Burma were almost entirely lost.

I REENTERED THE Burma scene around this time. From 1988–91, I had campaigned in Washington and London for the harshest possible stance against the junta. By 1992, though, I was feeling increasingly uneasy about aid restrictions and sanctions, in part because of their unintended humanitarian consequences but also because I felt anything that pulled the country out of its shell was a good thing, including the right kind of trade, investment, and even tourism. I wrote an article saying this, upsetting colleagues who still advocated an embargo, and then said nothing publicly about Burma for fourteen years. Instead, I wrote a PhD dissertation and then a book, *The Making of Modern Burma*, about 19th-century Burmese society and the transition to colonial rule. I studied the legacy of British control. In 1996, I was allowed by the government to visit for the first time in eight years. In writing a second book on Burmese history, *The River of Lost Footsteps*, I began to understand more clearly that the roots of Burma's problems lay not just in its military dictatorship but in the peculiar nationalism that had led to war, isolation, and impoverishment. What Burma needed was not simple regime change but a more radical process of transformation.

Over these same years I worked on and off for the United Nations. I served five years on peacekeeping operations, in Cambodia and the former Yugoslavia, and seven years at the UN's headquarters in New York. I had worked in different departments and finished as head of policy planning in the Department of Political Affairs. I saw close up how international diplomacy worked and the limitations of our global institutions.

I was in Sarajevo during the Bosnian War. At the time, I wanted nothing so much as NATO-led armed intervention on the side of the Bosnian government, to stop the atrocities and bring about a just settlement. But by 2007, I was extremely skeptical that any outside intervention could work, anywhere, unless it was part of a peace accord already agreed upon by all parties. I advised that the Iraq invasion would be a disaster, not because the US didn't have the might to overthrow Saddam Hussein, but because the "international community" would have next to no ability to deal with the day after. One of my last projects was to try and improve the UN's understanding of the countries it was working in. The project was a failure. Deeper understanding added layers of complexity for which few international institutions were ready.

By then I had visited Burma several times as a private citizen, reuniting with family and friends and traveling around as much as possible. Seeing the country's extreme poverty, at a time when neighboring Asian economies were doing so well, was difficult to stomach. Many of my own relatives were in dire straits. I left the UN because I wanted a break from the bureaucratic politics and a chance to try something different; I expected to go back after a year or two. I was troubled by Burma's descent and even more by what I saw as a completely counterproductive approach from the West, of further isolating a self-isolated nation. I didn't think revolution was possible. That meant some kind of engagement with the powers that be. I thought I'd see if I could help.

Few in Burma then knew who I was. But they all knew of my grandfather, the former UN Secretary-General. Because his burial had led to protests, anything to do with him (including me) was seen as potentially anti-regime. So when I began reaching out to Burmese diplomats abroad, they were guarded. But as I began writing op-eds opposed to sanctions, the regime grew curious.

A month after the monks' protests were crushed, I was invited to Naypyitaw. The new capital was still far from finished. It was immense.

The hotel zone was the size of the Upper East Side, with dozens of hotels. Some were rows of bungalows; some, with outlandish domes and turrets, looked like something out of a drug-induced nightmare; one was in the shape of a plane. I stayed at the Royal Kumudra, comfortable enough and empty except for a group of Russians from a Kazakh oil and gas company. I met a serving general and a government minister as well as other high officials. They were all polite, wary of me, and not sure where to take our relationship. The general told me he was meeting me on the express authority of Than Shwe himself.

Nearly all were incredibly distant from the outside world and had little understanding of Western politics or policy-making. They tended to deliver long monologues on Burmese history. Very few understood English. They also thought that they were fundamentally misunderstood. One general said, "If I were a Western policy-maker and only knew what was written about us in their media, I would do the same as them. I would be even tougher against us! But the media reports are wrong. We're not who they think we are."

After the protests, the UN Security Council had issued its first ever statement on Burma. The officers I met were incensed, saying that they had tried to work with envoy Ibrahim Gambari, and had even appointed an interlocutor with Aung San Suu Kyi a few months before, as he had requested. I told them that given what had happened and the depth of international feeling, they should be pleased with the statement; it was the very least that could have been expected. That was news to them.

I could tell even from these early meetings that their instinct was never to show any weakness. Change was possible, even desirable, but it could never seem to have come under pressure. "We've spent our lives on the battlefield," said one senior officer. "Stand and fight to the death is what we've always been told to do."

Over the same months, I traveled to Washington, Ottawa, London, and capitals around Europe, meeting with foreign ministers and development ministers and anyone else interested in Burma. I had a think tank fellowship at the time but did this on my own, reaching out through old friends and contacts I had from my time at the UN. I argued that sanctions and aid restrictions were simply not working and were only hurting the poorest. Addressing long-standing interethnic violence, as well as ending poverty, should be front and center of any international policy. A big hurdle was the bizarre psychology that had evolved during Burma's isolation. We should be looking for ways to break down that isolation, I said, including the right kind of economic engagement. No one really disagreed. But no one wanted to rock the boat. Burma was just not important enough. Showing solidarity with the democracy movement was politically expedient. Results didn't matter.

In the Asian capitals I visited, the view was different if no less cynical. There was no interest in "promoting democracy," but also not much interest in trying anything particularly innovative. Most felt the generals would muddle through and that was that. The exception was China, which had its own schemes in the making.

A referendum on the new Burmese constitution was set for May 2008. Opposition groups and supporters in the West denounced the charter as nothing more than a fig leaf for continued army rule. Jennifer Aniston and Woody Harrelson uploaded a video to YouTube entitled "Burma: It Can't Wait." On May 1, George Bush announced fresh sanctions. The next day, in New York, the UN Security Council adopted a US- and UK-backed statement again calling on the Burmese government "to establish the conditions and create an atmosphere conducive to an inclusive and credible process." It was a mild statement, watered down to gain Chinese and Russian approval. Nevertheless, it alarmed the Burmese generals, who were always fearful that the world was ganging up on them.

It was then Friday night in Rangoon. Cyclone Nargis had just made landfall.

FOUR

TEMPEST

THURA AUNG GREW UP in a little village named Amakan, near the town of Bogalay, deep in the delta, where the Irrawaddy River, from its snow-fed Himalayan sources a thousand miles to the north, after dividing and subdividing innumerable times, empties into the warm waters of the Bay of Bengal.

The Irrawaddy delta—about the size of West Virginia or southern England—was a swampy backwater until colonial times, when a combination of Anglo-Indian financing and migrant Burmese labor turned it into the most profitable rice producing area in the world. Ever since the Great Depression, the area had become increasingly destitute, though at the same time more crowded. As land became scarce, poorer people moved near the coast, cutting down the mangrove forests that separated the land from the water.

Thura Aung's family had taken part in clearing the area around Amakan when he was a teenager, in the early 1990s. After trying and failing to grow sesame, they turned to rice. This was a success, and the family came to own several dozen acres of paddy land. Thura Aung, a man of middling height and a ready smile, had a pleasant childhood, with four siblings, and attended school nearby and then Dagon University in Rangoon, where he studied history. He chose history, he said, because it was the easiest course. Rangoon was a new experience. He had never before been to a big city and during his first months there, he rode the buses for fun. As soon as he finished his course, he went back to Amakan to help on the family farm.

Amakan in the mid-2000s was a village of around four hundred people. Most families owned ten to fifteen acres. By this time, Thura Aung's parents owned ten times that. Each season they hired around twenty people, some from outside the village, to plant and harvest the rice crop. With the money they made, in a village of wooden and bamboo houses, they built the first brick house. There wasn't much to do at the end of the day except watch movies on a video player or by using a small satellite dish they had installed. They also had a karaoke machine. "This was the big new thing then," he remembered when I met him in Rangoon years later. After all expenses, the family was still able to save around 100,000 kyats a month, then equivalent to a few hundred dollars. By the standards of Burmese villagers, they were prospering.

On May 1, 2008, Thura Aung was visiting his grandfather's village, a few hours away by boat. Boats were the only way to get around the more remote parts of the delta, as roads and bridges only connected the main towns. Thura Aung's grandfather wanted to introduce him to a young woman, Wa Wa Khaing, whose family had a shop in the village. Both families thought the young people might be a good match. There were pleasantries over a Burmese meal of curries, salads, and light soups. Then it started raining heavily. Everyone advised Thura Aung to stay the night, so he did.

The next day, though the rain was tapering off, Thura Aung noticed that the water levels in the creek next to the village were still rising when they should have been falling with the tide. This was unusual, and reminded him of the tsunami six years before. He wondered whether another tsunami might be taking place. Though the tsunami of December 26, 2004, had been devastating in Indonesia, Thailand, and Sri Lanka, it hadn't done much damage in Burma. Thura Aung wasn't especially worried.

By 5 p.m., however, the wind was blowing extraordinarily hard. He again put off returning to Amakan. The creek overflowed onto the road. He tried to listen to the radio but couldn't hear anything. Then the phones lines went dead. At 7 p.m., a gust of wind tore off the roof of his grandfather's house. He and his grandfather, aunt, and younger sister huddled together, sitting on little plastic chairs under a tarpaulin, as a wall of seawater pushed past the house. "Outside was pitch black and the sound and strength of the wind like nothing we had ever experienced," he told me.

Three days before, on April 28, the Indian Meteorological Department in New Delhi had noticed a potentially threatening storm emerging in the Bay of Bengal. They named the storm Nargis, from the Persian word for daffodil, which was the name of a Bollywood movie star. They tracked the evolving system closely, worried at first that it might make landfall along India's Coromandel coast, then watched it veer north, gathering immense strength and causing panic in Bangladesh.[1]

On April 30, Bangladesh's military government met in emergency session, schools were closed, and hundreds of thousands of people in low-lying areas took shelter. Then, on May 1, Nargis, now upgraded to a "severe cyclone," suddenly made a very unusual ninety-degree turn and moved directly east, feeding off the steamy waters and building up a vicious intensity. At about six the next morning, Nargis slammed into Burma's southwestern coast, with winds of up to 215 miles an hour. An enormous storm surge followed, and a wall of water twelve feet high pushed as far as twenty-five miles inland. On the evening of May 2, the cyclone passed over Rangoon, weaker but still able to lash the city of five million with torrential wind and rain, felling thousands of trees and damaging hundreds of buildings, before disappearing over the eastern hills. For the delta—a level landscape of five million people nearly all living in rickety wooden houses—Nargis was a disaster of epic proportions.

At 8 p.m. that evening, cousins of Thura Aung arrived at his grandfather's house in a little boat. In their village, a few miles away, every single house had been destroyed. They had no idea what had happened to their neighbors. Thura Aung began to worry for his own parents. "Until then, I still wasn't really understanding what was going on, and in my mind kept thinking only our small area was affected." He and one of his cousins tied small LED flashlights to their heads and went outside to search for survivors. The water was over five feet deep and the currents powerful. Only with great effort were they able to inch through the water, moving from one coconut tree to another. It took them two hours to reach a relative's house just three hundred yards away. When they arrived, they found the house obliterated but four of their cousins, including two children, hunched inside the silo beside it. They all made their way back to the grandfather's house, carrying the children on their shoulders.

The grandfather's house was now the safest place, because a silo full of rice just behind it offered some protection from the wind. One of Thura Aung's cousins, weeping and very distraught, begged him to go out again to search for her father, his uncle. So he went out again, this time alone. He didn't find his uncle, but found seven other people huddled under a tree, and brought them back.

The water level was now going down fast, Thura Aung recalled, "but by now I was really scared. We had no idea what was happening. Everything seems so unreal." At 4 a.m., he and the others managed to sleep for a couple of hours. It was cold even under the tarpaulin but they found a few *longyis* (cotton sarongs) to wrap around their soaked clothes. The wind howled in the darkness.

Thura Aung remembers the next morning as no longer cloudy but very hazy, with an unusual greyish light. His relatives boiled up some rice from the silo but he found it difficult to eat, as they had to use salt water for cooking. There was no fresh water, but there was water from coconuts to drink. Everyone was in shock. Many were weeping quietly. All they could see outside were trees lying on top of destroyed houses.

He wondered if his parents were still alive. That evening, four people arrived, saying they were the only survivors from their village nearby. They also said that Amakan was gone. Thura Aung wanted to see for himself. Luckily his little boat was still intact. On the river, he first came across a local government official, who told him there was nothing left to see. Further along, on the shore, he saw people he thought looked like savages, naked or wearing only a tiny strip of cloth, their hair wild and covered in mud. He felt like he was in a dream. At the next village, he saw a sheet of aluminum that he recognized as being from his parents' house, even though he was still three miles away. He saw someone trying to cook over a fire. He kept going. There were bodies everywhere in the water and along the shore, including the bodies of little children. There were the carcasses, too, of dead dogs, water buffaloes, and oxen. Nearly every tree was down, and Thura Aung could see far into the distance.

"At one spot I saw a group of people running around almost naked trying to capture a pig. I wondered: why are they doing this? Are they really going to eat this pig? They seemed crazed. They called to me. I told them I was going to Amakan but I didn't want to take them on board. They might have lost their minds." At the next village, he saw no living people, only bodies and a single mango tree. He stopped the boat and wept for the first time. Another little boat appeared, carrying people who said they had been swept away for miles. It wasn't impossible, he thought, that some people from Amakan had survived.

When Thura Aung finally reached his parents' house, he saw it was smashed. Only one side was left. But his mother, brother, and brother's family were all there, crouched against the wall. At the same moment, his father appeared. He had been in the town of Bogalay when the storm struck, and had only just returned. They cooked some rice with salt water and ate it together.

Over the next few days, twenty-one people sheltered in what was left of the house. They gave away some of what little rice they had to people who came by. They worried about looters and people who might have turned violent. About half the villagers of Amakan had died or simply vanished without a trace. On May 7, Thura Aung was finally able to get to the nearest town, where he bought clothes and food for everyone. The next day, soldiers arrived with rice and beans.

AT LEAST 138,000 PEOPLE died between May 2 and 3. In Thura Aung's village tract alone, 8,000 of the 43,000 residents died. Some were killed by the impact of the ferocious winds and collapsing houses, many more by the inundation that followed. Across the southern belt of the Irrawaddy delta and toward Rangoon, 450,000 homes were destroyed and another 350,000 damaged. Seawater flooded 600,000 hectares of farmland, and 60,000 water buffaloes, essential for plowing, were drowned.[2] Three-quarters of all hospitals and medical clinics in the area lay in ruins, together with more than half of the schools. Scores of villages were entirely wiped away. Towns like Bogalay and Laputta, along the coast, lay devastated. In Rangoon, the streets were clogged with mud and littered with debris. Everywhere, power and telephone lines were down, bridges collapsed, and roads made impassable. In many communities, the dead far outnumbered the living.

It was, by far, the worst natural disaster in Burma's history. As news began to filter out, the world geared up to help. But this was to be no ordinary natural disaster: Nargis had not struck an otherwise trouble-free land. Over the next three weeks, the natural disaster would give rise to a political crisis of global proportions, a Burma crisis dominating interna-

tional television screens for the second time in less than a year and drawing in politicians and diplomats from around the world.

It's not clear what the Burmese government knew about the impending catastrophe, or when. They certainly received warning from the
Indian Meteorological Department of the cyclone's imminent approach,
but until a day or so before it struck, Nargis was expected to make land
in Bangladesh or perhaps on the Bangladesh–Burma border, not the
delta. On May 1, the state-run newspapers carried stories about the US
presidential election ("Obama's lead over Clinton shrinks to zero") and
the British royal family ("Britain's Prince William on secret Afghan
trip") and pictures from Australia's fashion week. There was warning of
a severe cyclonic storm, but only in the weather section, and only pre-
dicting widespread "rain or thundershowers." On the morning of May
2, commercial aircraft were diverted from Rangoon, but few other measures were taken.

By the morning of May 3, the magnitude of the devastation was becoming clear. Communications were down, and any information received in
Naypyitaw was sketchy and mainly from Rangoon. Nevertheless, a state
of emergency was declared in all the affected areas, and troops and vehicles were ordered south to Rangoon and on toward the delta. The prime
minister, General Thein Sein, was placed in overall charge of the response
and on the same day set up a committee of relevant ministers and bureaucrats.[3] The minister of health established a crisis center at Rangoon's General Hospital and ordered teams of doctors and nurses from around the
country to report immediately. But the enormity of the disaster was so
overwhelming that Burma's poor official infrastructure could barely begin
to move. The army was by far the best-equipped institution in the country, but it was essentially a counterinsurgency force, with no experience or
training in disaster relief.

The first instinct of the military leadership, as soldiers facing chaos,
was to ensure control. This sense of control would soon be challenged by

the scale of the task at hand, and by the demands and expectations of a 21st-century relief operation.

Over the next four days, from May 3 to May 7, as Thura Aung and his family huddled in what was left of their village house, the UN, international nongovernmental organizations, Burmese authorities, and the Red Cross hurried to assess the damage and provide what emergency aid they could. Rangoon was a mess, and frantic efforts were soon underway to clear the damage and repair basic infrastructure. Scores of local charities quickly went to work and private citizens mobilized by the hundreds of thousands. It was a heroic effort and a testament to the resilience of Burmese civil society—private businesses, professional groups, informal neighborhood associations, schools, Buddhist monasteries, Christian churches, and networks of friends organized spontaneously, raising money and rushing supplies to the delta any way they could.

By May 5, the extent of the death toll along the coast was becoming frighteningly apparent. Satellite photographs from NASA showed thousands of square miles of what had been villages and farmland covered in a pale blue blanket of salt water. What should have happened next was a major international relief operation, like the one that followed the 2004 tsunami. But several factors came together to prevent this, delaying assistance and leading to weeks of frenzied diplomacy.

First was the speed of the government's response, and foreign perceptions of this response. No one could have blamed the junta for not having the resources at hand to cope straightaway. No government could have done this, not even a major industrial power. But the typical opaqueness of the army's decision-making and information system meant that its own efforts were obscured. No one outside Naypyidaw really knew whether the government was doing anything at all. And given that the last big news story from Burma was the junta's violent suppression of the monk-led protests in 2007, few wanted to give them the benefit of the doubt. The government was instantly cast as the bad guy once again.

Existing (and cumbersome) procedures requiring visas for foreign aid workers to enter the country and permits to travel beyond Rangoon remained in place. Within twenty-four hours, hundreds of disaster relief experts were queuing up at Burmese embassies around the world, eager to help, and within forty-eight hours hundreds were shocked and frustrated at not being able to get in. In Rangoon, international UN staff waited impatiently for permission to travel to the worst-hit towns and villages. News crews from dozens of international networks arrived in Bangkok. But they too had no luck.[4]

The Burmese government had appealed for international aid, and had specifically asked UNICEF and NGOs such as World Vision, long present in the country, for special assistance. Planeloads of food and water and other emergency supplies landed at Rangoon airport from China, India, Thailand, and other nearby countries. Some charities, such as CARE Australia, stated that they were happy with the cooperation they had received from the government. But with UN and Western aid experts and journalists cooling their heels in New York and Geneva and Bangkok and elsewhere, the story quickly became one of the Burmese authorities barring the kind of global response necessary and again responding callously to the needs of its people.

On Monday, May 5, Laura Bush, the First Lady of the United States, went on television to criticize the Burmese response to Nargis, saying that it was "only the most recent example of the junta's failure to meet its people's basic needs." The next day, as the official toll rose dramatically to 22,000 dead and 41,000 missing, President Bush himself hosted a ceremony at the White House to award the Congressional Gold Medal—which, along with the Presidential Medal of Freedom, is America's highest civilian award—to Aung San Suu Kyi. This had been planned well in advance, but the combination of President and Laura Bush's appearances underlined to the Burmese leadership that aid from the US was aid from their enemy. The US routinely sends disaster specialists to assess damage in the wake of a natural disaster, but the junta refused to let them in, fearing that they were spies preparing to team up with underground dissidents and use the Nargis emergency to drive forward their goal of regime change.

What made the Burmese even more suspicious was the presence of US warships off the coast. The same day as the White House ceremony for Aung San Suu Kyi, a Pentagon spokesman reported that the Essex Strike Group, with four ships led by the amphibious assault ship the USS *Essex*, as well as the 31st Marine Expeditionary Unit, with twenty-three helicopters and 1,800 marines, were nearby and "ready to help."[5] The spokesman also said that the US Seventh Fleet's flagship, the USS *Blue Ridge*, the USS *Kitty Hawk*, and the aircraft carrier USS *Nimitz* were "all in the region." On board was an impressive capacity to deliver desperately needed assistance with superpower efficiency. But what was a good-faith offer of emergency help seemed to the Burmese authorities like their worst nightmares come true. Nargis had pulverized the Burmese navy's own base along the coast, and now an American naval force was steaming toward Rangoon.

To almost everyone's astonishment, on May 10 the government went ahead with the planned referendum on the new constitution. For the government's detractors, and there were many, there could be no better evidence of the regime's lack of concern for the plight of ordinary people or their willingness to use precious resources to further their own political goals rather than tending to the humanitarian emergency at hand.

On the ground, efforts continued—by the aid agencies already present, by Burmese groups, and by local authorities. It was far from enough. Rangoon was approaching a degree of normality, but in the delta the situation was very different. Casualty figures were soaring. It was now clear that over 100,000 people were dead or missing, and that over two million were in urgent need of help. The lower delta was now one big field of mud, without roads or bridges, crisscrossed by hundreds of streams and miniature waterways, the sea having created dozens of islets practically inaccessible by land. The skies blackened and new storms lashed the coast. Government roadblocks went up to make sure that no one without authorization, which essentially meant all foreigners, could leave Rangoon. No one knew how hundreds of thousands of survivors were coping. A week after the storm, experts warned that starvation could be setting in and that a wave of water-borne diseases threatened the lives of hundreds of thousands more.

Enter Bernard Kouchner, the founder of the Nobel Peace Prize-winning international humanitarian organization Médecins Sans Frontières, famous for its work in war zones and its principle of speaking out for the rights of victims. Kouchner was now foreign minister in the new government of French president Nicolas Sarkozy. He had railed against General Than Shwe's junta during the 2007 protests, and now cautioned that delivering aid through the Burmese government might not be wise.[6] A French as well as a British navy vessel joined the USS *Essex* and others in the Andaman Sea, waiting for permission to land.

On May 7, as international frustration turned to disbelief and then rage, the melodramatic Kouchner called for forceful action from the UN Security Council under the new doctrine of a "responsibility to protect." Others agreed, and just four days after the cyclone, pundits and opinion writers around the world began to wonder out loud whether or not Burma should be invaded.

Was it time to use force to help the victims of Nargis? The Burmese government clearly wasn't responding quickly enough, and was restricting outside aid. But could it be right to use military force to speed up the delivery of aid? Did it matter that thousands of lives were at stake? Or a million lives? Using force against the Burmese military—say, to secure parts of the delta, as some were suggesting—would effectively mean war.

It was an ethical dilemma. It was, in the end, an academic one as well. The reality was that neither the Americans nor the French nor the British nor anyone else was going to risk a firefight in Burma. With commitments in Iraq and Afghanistan, the West was not seriously thinking of starting a major conflict in Southeast Asia. Taking responsibility for a poor country of fifty million, with hundreds of ethnicities, dozens of armed groups, and little state infrastructure other than the Burmese army itself, was never in the cards. Moreover, China might have felt obliged to support the Burmese regime in any conflict.

And so diplomacy was instead revved up and the pieces began to fall into place. On May 9, the Americans and the Burmese agreed that a single US cargo plane with aid supplies would fly to Rangoon. The early insistence on a US assessment team going in first was quietly dropped. On May 12, the first American plane arrived, carrying not only supplies but also the highest-level US delegation to the country in decades. On board were Admiral Timothy Keating, commander of all US forces in the Asia Pacific region, the head of the US Agency for International Development, the State Department's senior official for Southeast Asia, and an assortment of other military officers and diplomats.[7]

The arrival of Admiral Keating was a surprise to the junta. The Americans had tried to keep it under wraps, but Thai diplomats had inadvertently tipped off the Burmese during a discussion with Kyaw Thu, a deputy foreign minister.[8] Kyaw Thu, alarmed, consulted his superiors in Naypyitaw, who also knew nothing of the visit. Ordered to stop it, he went to see Shari Villarosa, the US chargé d'affaires in Rangoon (there was no ambassador). Villarosa admitted that Keating was coming, saying that the US hoped merely for an informal chat at the airport. The junta, fearing more international censure, relented.

Admiral Soe Thane, the commander of the Burmese navy, was sent to meet the Americans together with Kyaw Thu. Soe Thane was well aware of the extent of the disaster. All his ships except one frigate had been lost, and a major base on the west coast of the delta wiped out. He had traveled to the affected areas by car and helicopter with prime minister Thein Sein (whose own family was from the delta and had their homes severely damaged).

When the call came to return urgently to Rangoon, he worried that he was going to be arrested. But it was to meet Keating.[9]

Niceties were exchanged, and the American side tried to impress upon the Burmese their goodwill and desire simply to help the survivors of Nargis. Soe Thane and his junta colleagues were worried that the Americans would come and never leave. They were happy to accept aid, Soe Thane said, but only via Rangoon. They also had Chinese sensitivities to consider.

The next day, May 13, I saw Admiral Keating in Bangkok. I had recently moved to Bangkok and was traveling often to Burma. I was researching and writing my book *Where China Meets India*, traveling often to the India–Burma–China borderlands, but also seeing senior government and army officers at least every few months, trying to build relationships and get a better sense of what was going on. At a time when most embassies in Rangoon had very little contact with anyone in the regime, I was regularly asked to meet VIPs passing through to give them my sense of the political landscape.

The admiral told me that while Soe Thane had seemed interested in striking up a rapport, other officers were much more inhibited. Another US Navy officer told me that "all options were on the table." I spoke as well to Marine General John Goodman, who had stayed behind in Rangoon to see if the US could reestablish communications with the Burmese military. There was a feeling that, in addition to coping with the present tragedy, a door could be opened to a different and better chapter in US–Burma relations—not the invasion the Burmese generals feared, but something else. No one was very sure. The week before, I had been in Washington where staff at the Senate Foreign Relations Committee told me of their hope that aid for Nargis victims could lead to a bigger assistance program, effectively easing sanctions policy.

Over the coming week, a string of high-level visitors tried their hand at Burmese diplomacy. Thai prime minister Samak Sundaravej, EU commissioner for development and humanitarian aid Louis Michel, the UK minister for Asia Mark Malloch Brown, and John Holmes, the UN undersecretary-general for humanitarian affairs, all came and went. I met them all in Bangkok or Rangoon to give them my best analysis of what future assistance relationship might be possible. Each tried to convince the Burmese of the urgent need to allow a proper international aid effort and allow foreign disaster specialists directly into the delta. There was no breakthrough, but a steady diplomatic pressure was building. The story was still at the top of the international news, with analysts warning daily of an impending catastrophe.

In a state-run newspaper, a cartoon showed smiling Burmese people being led by the military across the referendum toward a shining city of skyscrapers ("peace and development" in the distance), with threatening black demons coming from the coast labeled "Nargis and Internal and External Destructive Elements."

At the same time, more and more countries, including the US, did what the Burmese regime wanted, and flew in supplies to Rangoon. The UN's World Food Programme established an air bridge from Bangkok and requested permission to bring in heavy-lift helicopters to transport aid from Rangoon to the main towns in the delta. On May 18, General Than Shwe himself traveled to the affected areas for the first time, and was shown on national television meeting with survivors and inspecting relief efforts. But hundreds of thousands were still believed to be without any help. Nearly two weeks into the disaster, no one knew how many more were dying, or if an outbreak of disease was imminent. And the Western fleet was still hovering offshore, ready for action.

May 19 was the turning point. At a meeting of the foreign ministers of the Association of Southeast Asian Nations (ASEAN) in Singapore, the Burmese were presented with a clear choice: allow a UN-led humanitarian operation, allow an ASEAN-led operation supported by the UN and other international agencies, or have ASEAN simply stand back and see where Western pressure would lead. The Burmese chose option two. ASEAN's charismatic secretary-general, Surin Pitsuwan, was appointed head of a task force to oversee the effort, and jetted off to Rangoon to discuss next steps with Burmese ministers.[10]

Then came Ban Ki-moon, the first UN Secretary-General to visit the country since my grandfather was last there in 1970. With an entourage of aides and New York-based journalists, he was flown by helicopter over the delta and shown a neatly organized government-run camp. He then went to Naypyitaw and met with Than Shwe in the general's private residence. In all the frantic diplomacy of recent days, Than Shwe had remained elusive, but everyone knew that for real access to be granted, his personal stamp of approval was essential. After a cordial and frank hour-long discussion, the world's top diplomat emerged to tell the press, "I had a very good meeting with the Senior General. He has agreed to allow all aid workers regardless of nationality."[11]

Two days later, Ban Ki-moon presided over a hastily scheduled international donor pledging conference organized by the Burmese government in Rangoon.[12] It was an unprecedented spectacle. Sitting with Ban in the ballroom of the swish Sedona Hotel was the Burmese prime minister Thein Sein, together with the chair of ASEAN, the dynamic and forthright Singaporean foreign minister George Yeo, and high representatives of friendly Asian governments. Also in the room were an array of Western development ministers and senior aid officials, including some from countries such as the UK, Norway, and Sweden that had long been among the regime's most vocal critics. All the visitors wanted to demonstrate that politics had been placed to one side, and were anxious not to endanger the fragile opening that a week of mediation had apparently created. Money was pledged and handshakes extended.

At a national security meeting that week, the junta appointed Kyaw Thu, the deputy foreign minister, as chair of a body through which the UN, ASEAN, and the Burmese government would coordinate all international aid. Kyaw Thu told several of the top generals that he had no experience in disaster response and requested guidance on what to do. They looked at one another and smiled. Shwe Mann, the number three in the army hierarchy, said, "Neither do we. So just go down to Rangoon, try to understand the situation, and do the best you can."

Trips to the delta were organized for visiting VIPs. Within days, nearly all visa requests from UN agencies were granted and helicopters from the World Food Programme began flying directly into the delta.

It seemed like a breakthrough, and in a way it was. Diplomatic tensions were reduced dramatically and Burma returned to the back pages of the newspapers. In the end, though, nothing had been achieved that couldn't have been achieved without all the brouhaha. All aid was coming in via Rangoon, which had been the junta's main demand all along. The reason this didn't lead to a further crisis was because there was, so far, no "second wave" of deaths following the initial disaster.

The situation was still urgent. Hundreds of thousands of farmers had lost all their seeds. If they weren't replaced within weeks, they would miss their seasonal planting deadline and have no chance for a new crop. At a time when many aid officials were looking at longer-term planning, Debbie Aung Din pushed for an immediate focus on seeds. Debbie Aung Din was a Burmese-American who, with her husband, Jim Taylor, ran Proximity, one of the very few NGOs working on agriculture in Burma at the time. At one aid coordination meeting, she said, "Look, if there are no seeds in two weeks you guys can just forget it, the assessments, everything, it's as simple as that." The US Agency for International Development (USAID) stepped in to help, but in a low-key way, without any US flags; working through Proximity, they quickly got seeds to 55,000 homes in 1,200 villages. It was an important success. A month later, Debbie Aung Din was invited to meet George Bush.

The president and Laura Bush were in Thailand on an official visit, staying at the Four Seasons Hotel in Bangkok. Debbie Aung Din first met

Laura Bush, who was very inquisitive. The next morning, the First Lady flew to the Burmese border to meet with Karen refugees and others. Aung Din was given fifteen minutes to speak to the president, as part of a meeting that also included an American army colonel and a senior USAID official. It was all carefully scripted, but in the end she took up the entire forty-five minutes. She remembers George Bush as "super friendly and really curious," welcoming her by saying, "Hey, you're the first person from Burma I've ever met!"

The president seemed amazed that a person like Debbie Aung Din, a smart, articulate American, actually had her home in Rangoon. "How do you live in Burma?" he asked. He had only heard horror stories. "Just normally," she replied. "I have a house, we send our kids to school, go to the office." He was astonished and peppered her with questions.

"I'm really glad for your help with all these *facts*," President Bush told her. "Why then are these generals all dragging their feet?" He knew that aid access was still slow.

"Only good news gets to the guy at the top."

"I get that! Hey, if you were me, what would you do?"

"Lift sanctions."

"But we have just targeted sanctions."

"No, not really. There are trade and investment sanctions, sanctions on development assistance."

The president then turned to Chris Hill, his assistant secretary of state for Asia. "Hey, do we have trade sanctions on Burma?"

"Yes, Mr. President."

President Bush began pondering his next steps. "I'm going on VOA [Voice of America] soon, what should I say?" he asked Aung Din.

"That the US cares about you and wants to help," she replied. Later that day, he said exactly that. He also said, "Our aid is getting to people." This was an important thing to mention. Around that time, there were many stories saying that all aid was being stolen or siphoned off by the military.

At a lunch afterward with Debbie Aung Din and several exiled Burmese dissidents, the president reflected, "The further you get away from Burma, the more you really don't get all the facts."

A MODICUM OF AID was finally getting through. A new disaster was averted. But in the years to come, the victims of Nargis would receive nothing like the assistance they might have had if not for the political situation. And because of sanctions, there were limits to the type of relief that could be given. Housing, for instance, was a no-go area for Western governments, as it seemed to go beyond emergency aid and drift toward development assistance, which was forbidden. Aceh in Indonesia had received billions of dollars to rebuild after the 2004 tsunami. Burma's total foreign aid went up slightly in the months after Nargis, but slid back down again by late 2009 to around $5 per capita, a tiny fraction of what was being given to people in Vietnam and Laos next door (both countries under Communist regimes). Politicians in the West had contemplated using force to deliver aid, but when the door opened, few cared to follow up.[13] Two years after the cyclone, more than 100,000 families still didn't have a roof over their heads.[14]

If the monks' protests had wrecked the regime's legitimacy, the response to Nargis laid bare the state's weak institutional capacities. When outsiders imagine a military dictatorship, they imagine an all-powerful police state. The truth in Burma was very different. The army and the bureaucracy simply didn't have the wherewithal to do anything approaching what was needed, and so turned in panic to their cronies and other businessmen, who were each assigned a township to rebuild.

The generals also began to give both local and international charities far more room to operate. This was incredibly important. Burmese NGOs were now able to receive outside funding and shore up their institutional strength.

One local organization was Paungku, meaning "bridge" or "connection." Its founder, Kyaw Thu, tall, ponytailed, and with a trim beard, black T-shirt and jeans, looked the exact opposite of an army officer (and was no relation to his namesake the deputy foreign minister). He had for years been working with the poorest both in ethnic minority communities and around Rangoon, assisting them with small amounts of money he had raised to strengthen their own self-help networks. Those he assisted included sex workers, who were already looking after one another, for example with informal arrangements to take care of one another's kids. A small grant could make a big difference. Now he organized a major effort to aid villages in the delta, for the first time with international funding, and under the wary eye of the authorities.[15]

Four months after Nargis, I met the social welfare minister, a serving general, who told me that the junta had first been afraid of NGOs: "We didn't know what they were, what they would do." But now, a few months later, he felt much more relaxed about opening the door wider. Another minister was still distrustful, but said the government had to live with the new reality. It was, he said, "like feeding a tiger."

Into this picture stepped Noeleen Heyzer.[16] An energetic, Cambridge-educated Singaporean, she was the head of the UN's regional economic commission. She had been to Burma several times over two decades, and knew only too well the depth of the country's poverty. She was also a supporter of democratic change. She had previously been head of UNIFEM (the UN organization working on women's rights), and after the landmark Beijing Women's Conference of 1996 organized a big exhibition in New York, with a "Wall of Shame" showing ways in which women around the world were suffering discrimination and repression, and a "Wall of Hope" which featured Aung San Suu Kyi. The Burmese ambassador in New York told her to take it down. She agreed to do so but said that "UN bureaucracy takes a long time." It stayed up. Now, Noeleen Heyzer thought that the key was to see things from the Burmese junta's perspective, to talk in a language they understood, and thereby break the impasse. The goal was democracy, but the goal was also a better life for the poorest in Burma as soon as possible. She thought this post-disaster situation was a good opportunity.

In October 2008, Heyzer organized a big conference in Bangkok on post-Nargis recovery. Her UN colleagues were unhappy, believing she was wading into dangerous political waters. Almost anything to do with Burma involved huge risks—one was clobbered either by the regime or by the regime's detractors. A key interlocutor was Deputy Foreign Minster Kyaw Thu, now coordinating international assistance. They got to know each other well. Kyaw Thu was an urbane, even liberal figure, but was tired from bearing the brunt of criticism from all sides.

The evening before the conference, Heyzer and Kyaw Thu had a lively discussion. Kyaw Thu complained that the international community only wanted to see the bad things his government did, and not the good. Heyzer replied that people understood the challenges the government were facing but couldn't compromise on matters of principle. The conversation became heated.[17]

The next morning, Kyaw Thu failed to show up for the opening session, for which he was the main speaker. Even the Burmese embassy staff present became worried. At the coffee break, Heyzer saw him pacing up and down the corridor. He came in, put aside his prepared speech, and, to a packed audience of diplomats and aid officials, he spoke from the heart, saying that everyone was letting down the Burmese people. He pointed to the plastic water bottles in front of the delegates in the big air-conditioned hall and said, "You probably don't even notice them. They have no value to you. But in the delta, hundreds of thousands of people still have no clean water." People in the hall were almost in tears.

I worked closely with Heyzer in those months. I also met Kyaw Thu on several occasions. For two years I had been trying to explain Burma to policy-makers at the UN and in foreign governments, and at the same time explain the UN and foreign governments to policy-makers in Burma. I had no clear idea what would turn Burma around. But with every interaction I was increasingly certain that the current approaches, economic sanctions and international ostracism, weren't working and could not work in the future. The lives of millions of poor people were being impacted every day as a result of restrictions on aid. And Nargis had revealed clearly the weakness of state institutions. The country was far more mentally isolated, and more fragile, than most on the outside could imagine.

FOR THURA AUNG and his family in Amakan, late 2008 and 2009 were all about restarting their lives as best they could. Local charities and some foreign aid workers came, bringing food and other assistance. He married Wa Wa Khaing, the young woman he met at his grandfather's house the night of Nargis. Finding enough workers to work the land was a major challenge. "Even those who survived, like the ones who lost all their kids, their parents, they really couldn't think of working anymore.

"Our mentalities changed after Nargis," he told me. "We now save everything we can, and spend very little. We always feel there might be another disaster around the corner. Many over the years in our village became alcoholics. Some went mad."

By 2009, Burma was an impoverished country, with a sinister economic system and a mosaic of generals, warlords, and ethnic rebels, with millions more now traumatized by a natural disaster of unimaginable proportions. At the same time, Burma's isolation was being chipped away, ever so slightly, and civil society groups, which had started out as aid charities, were feeling their way into a new political environment.

January 22, 2009, was the centenary of my grandfather U Thant's birthday. Since the 1974 protest surrounding his burial, no one had dared to publicly commemorate his life in any way. My family and I suggested a simple reception for a few dozen diplomats, UN officials, and an assortment of Burmese: writers, heads of charities, businessmen, and political figures. The junta agreed and even sent representatives to take part. Erik Solheim, Norway's development minister, was in Rangoon that week— the first Western minister to visit Burma in decades. He came too. There had been no gathering like it in a very long time.

Burma was sliding in a new direction. There was the potential for something new. The risks, though, were greater than ever.

FIVE

FIGHTING CHANCE

A LL THIS TIME, Aung San Suu Kyi was under house arrest, at her stately colonial-era villa on the south shore of Rangoon's Inya Lake. She lived with a staff of two women, a mother and daughter. She was also visited regularly by her physician, Dr. Tin Myo Win, who brought her news from the outside and packages, mainly books, sent by friends overseas. She kept a strict regimen and listened at set times to the BBC and the Voice of America over her short-wave radio.

She played the piano as well, an assortment of classical pieces on an old upright Yamaha that had belonged to her late mother. Her favorite, she later told an interviewer, was the "Canon" by Baroque German composer Johann Pachelbel. She read voraciously. And she enjoyed an eclectic collection of more contemporary music, from Tom Jones to Bob Marley and the Grateful Dead. From her window she would have seen the little amusement park by the side of the expansive lake, children and their parents on the rickety Ferris wheel, hawkers selling fresh coconut juice, couples holding hands on the benches along the embankment.

She was scheduled for release from house arrest on May 27, 2009. The regime was just then trying to get its ducks in a row for the planned elections. Releasing Aung San Suu Kyi would be extremely risky. But, under the law, they would need a good reason to extend her confinement.

In 2008, John Yettaw, a fifty-two-year-old army veteran from Missouri suffering from post-traumatic stress disorder, developed an obsession with Aung San Suu Kyi while traveling around Thailand by motorcycle with his teenage son. Believing he had to help her, in October that year he flew to Rangoon and managed to get inside her house by swimming through a culvert and scaling a low fence. The house staff prevented him from seeing Aung San Suu Kyi. He left her the Book of Mormon. The authorities were informed but did nothing.

Back in Missouri, he saw visions that told him to try again. He was nervous but determined. He borrowed money for a plane ticket, downloaded Michael Bublé and Mormon sermons using the free WiFi at his neighborhood Hardee's, and set off.

On May 4, 2009, John Yettaw swam for a second time to Aung San Suu Kyi's house. The staff threatened to call the police (there were armed guards less than a hundred yards away), but when he complained of exhaustion, leg cramps, and low blood sugar due to diabetes, Aung San Suu Kyi saw him and agreed he could stay overnight. The next day, he was arrested as he tried to swim to an American diplomatic residence nearby. He was charged with several offenses including "illegal swimming."

Nine days later, Aung San Suu Kyi was arrested and charged with breaking the terms of her house arrest. She was transferred to the notorious Insein jail north of the city. Her trial, which lasted several weeks, became an international sensation. Gordon Brown, then UK prime minister, wrote in a public letter to her that "the clamour for your release is growing across Europe, Asia, and the entire world." With her sixty-fourth birthday approaching, he promised to "do all we can to make this birthday the last you spend without your freedom." David Beckham, Daniel Craig, Kevin Spacey, and George Clooney all sent words of encouragement.

On August 11, in a damp colonial-era courtroom packed with diplomats and media, the ceiling fans whirring overhead, the presiding judge sentenced Aung San Suu Kyi to three years of hard labor. Then, minutes later, the home minister himself made a dramatic entrance and announced that Than Shwe was personally halving her sentence and allowing her to serve the remaining time in her Rangoon home. She would be released in November 2010, just after the elections.

The National League for Democracy was in a grim state. Hundreds of their members were among over 2,000 men and women behind bars for their political beliefs. They included many of Aung San Suu Kyi's lieutenants, who were now in far-flung prisons with little or no contact with one another.

Yettaw was sentenced to seven years' hard labor, pardoned after two months, and sent home in the company of visiting US senator Jim Webb. He later told *Newsweek* that his conversations with Aung San Suu Kyi were "personal" and that he would never tell a soul, including his three ex-wives. "I will never be at peace, emotionally or psychologically, until that woman is free, until that nation is free." He also said, "I am not crazy. I am not insane."

SENIOR GENERAL THAN SHWE's retirement preparations were now complete. The junta would soon be dissolved and replaced by a new constitutional set-up. At the core of the constitution was a power-sharing arrangement between the army and a semi-elected parliament. The army would remain autonomous under its own commander-in-chief. Elections would fill 75 percent of the seats in a two-chamber parliament. The army would appoint the other 25 percent from within its own ranks. Parliament would elect the president, who in turn would appoint ministers. But the ministers of defense, "border affairs," and "home affairs" (in charge of the police and local administration) would be military men nominated by the commander-in-chief. The president would also appoint the chief ministers in charge of the country's fourteen states and regions.

The constitution was virtually identical to the one first proposed by the army in 1993. The National League for Democracy had rejected this, and years of attempted mediation by the UN on a constitutional process acceptable to both sides had led to nothing. Now Than Shwe pushed through what he and the other generals had always had in mind.

The constitution enshrined basic rights, including the rights to free speech, association, and peaceful assembly. The constitution also prohibited discrimination on the basis of "race, birth, religion, and sex." It did, however, add the qualifier that nothing should "prevent the appointment of men to positions that are suitable for men only."

The constitution was also concerned with identity, sanctifying a concept of the Burmese nation that had been fermenting for decades. The first sections included a summary of Burmese history up to independence in 1948, which began with the lines:

> Myanmar is a Nation with magnificent historical traditions. We
> the National people have been living in unity and oneness, setting
> up an independent sovereign State and standing tall with pride.
> Due to colonial intrusion, the Nation lost her sovereign power in
> 1885. The National people launched anti-colonialist struggles and
> National liberation struggles, with unity in strength, sacrificing
> lives and hence the Nation became an independent sovereign State
> again on 4th January 1948.

The "Basic Principles" went on to declare: "The State is where multi-National races collectively reside." The "multi-National races," or *taing-yintha*, were now at the very center of the state narrative. In this worldview, Burma was less a community of equal citizens than an amalgamation of the "multi-National races" that had lived side by side since time immemorial, except for the period of "colonial intrusion." Resurrecting and protecting this unity was paramount. "National race affairs" was listed in the constitution as a primary issue, alongside foreign affairs and the economy.

During the 1990s, the junta began to speak of "135 National Races." There was never an exact list, and the lists that were produced were nonsensical mixes of apples and oranges: dozens of language dialects alongside overlapping ethnic designations. What was important was the concept that the country was comprised not just of the Burmese and a few other major peoples (who might then deserve equal billing) but of a jumble of tiny races that needed to be welded together.

What was unspoken was a racial feeling. The "Europeans" were long gone, and the sizeable Anglo-Indian and Anglo-Burmese population had either emigrated, over the 1940s and 1950s (mainly to Australia and the UK), or had blended into Burmese society, taking on Burmese names and intermarrying. There remained only those accepted as part of the 135 and those who were left out, people deemed Indian or Chinese. A negative identity grouped all the "National Races": they were neither *kala* nor *tayok*, centuries-old terms for those from across the Bay of Bengal or from over the Shan and Yunnan hills. The *kala* and the *tayok* looked different and acted differently. This was a distinction that superseded language or religion or culture. It wasn't based on anything like the race science of the early 20th century, but it was about identity and physical appearance and its relationship to biology and ancestry. The root of the Burmese word for "national," *myo*, originally meant "seed" and is a cognate of an older word for semen.[1]

The constitution also included an arcane formula tied to race. Any *taing-yintha* "whose population constitutes at least 0.1% of the national populace" (around 50,000 people in 2010) was entitled to representation in local legislative assemblies and ministerial portfolios in local administrations. If a *taing-yintha* constituted more than half of two contiguous townships, it was entitled to an "autonomous zone." So, in addition to ethnically-based states for the Shan, Kachin, and five others, there would now be "self-administered zones" for the Nagas, Danus, and a few smaller ethnic groups.

I've heard many Burmese warn that giving Muslims in northern Arakan *taing-yintha* status, as "Rohingya," would lead automatically to their being entitled to a zone of their own. "A part of Burma would fall under sharia law," a university lecturer whispered. To consider the Muslims of northern Arakan as one of the "National Races" fused anxieties around both race and religion. The ethnonym "Rohingya" was particularly toxic for this reason, as it means literally "of Arakan" and therefore implied that those to whom it referred were indigenous. On the other hand, if they were called "Bengalis," they could be seen—like the other *kala* and *tayok*, who were believed biologically as well as culturally distinct—as immigrants and not natives deserving special protection and special rights.

THAN SHWE ALSO retired dozens of generals and promoted in their place a new generation of officers, men in their late forties and early fifties (Than Shwe was then seventy-eight). This was critical for the retirement scheme: for the foreseeable future, until he was in his afterlife, the men in charge of state violence would be men who were unreservedly loyal, protégés whom he had himself pulled up through the ranks. They would be the steel frame. They were told they were the "guardians" of the new constitution. And for the coming elections a new party was created: the Union Solidarity and Development Party, or USDP. "Solidarity" meant the solidarity of the *taing-yintha*. It was well funded (from the junta's coffers) and sought to coopt as meaty a slice of Burmese civil society as possible, by reaching out to local worthies—businessmen, doctors, schoolteachers, retired civil servants—and encouraging them to run under the USDP banner.

By late 2010, Naypyitaw was looking finished. The few visitors were welcomed at a new airport (my favorite in the world—where one can arrive twenty minutes before a flight, check in, speed through security, shod and with little hassle, enjoy a good espresso, and board). There was a zoo and "night safari," several golf courses, a big fountain, and even bigger statues of the warrior-kings who had crafted past empires. There was a sprawling Legoland parliament complex with thirty-one buildings, representing the thirty-one planes of existence in Buddhist cosmology. About a mile away was a hundred-room presidential palace with a state-of-the-art fitness center and, in the main hall, a golden replica of the throne of the last king of Burma.

Than Shwe didn't want to be president. He would watch the stage he had set from behind the scenes. And so he built a house for himself nearby, overlooking a 400-foot-high gilded pagoda, an almost exact replica of the centuries-old Shwedagon in Rangoon.

At a time when strongmen like Robert Mugabe in Zimbabwe were hanging onto office well into their eighties, and others like Muammar Gaddafi were being hunted down and killed in the street, Than Shwe concocted his own exit. His predecessor, General Ne Win, had died eight years before, powerless to stop Than Shwe from arresting his kin. Than Shwe didn't want another military dictator to come after him and do the same to his family. He preferred to engineer a very specific transition, to a more diffuse and popularly acceptable structure of power.

He thought for a while of creating a "Defense Commission" that he would chair and that would oversee the army—an insurance policy in case the rest of the retirement scheme didn't go according to plan. But in the end he decided against it. Things seemed to be falling into place.

Almost everything. A few days after Aung San Suu Kyi and John Yettaw were arrested, junta leaders and their wives led a special ceremony at the 14th-century Danok Pagoda on the outskirts of Rangoon. The pagoda had been renovated, and dignitaries including Than Shwe's wife were there to install a new diamond-encrusted spire. On June 6, during Aung San Suu Kyi's trial, the pagoda mysteriously collapsed, killing twenty people and injuring dozens more. There were rumors of a supernatural cause. In a very superstitious country, it wasn't a good omen.

There remained, as well, two outstanding questions, neither one minor: how to deal with China and, relatedly, the country's unfinished civil war.

In the early 1950s, when Than Shwe first became a soldier, the entire country was a sea of rebellion. Half a century of pitiless counterinsurgency campaigns followed. By the beginning of the 21st century, the authority of the Burmese army alone ran over the entire Irrawaddy valley. The delta and nearly all the coastline were also in the hands of the generals. In the west, toward India and Bangladesh, there were a few small militant outfits. Most, like the United Liberation Front of Assam, were fighting the Indian state, using bases inside Burma to attack Indian positions across the border. In the southeast, in the hills bordering Thailand, were the Burmese army's oldest foes, the Karen National Union. They had been formidable adversaries, but their headquarters had been overrun in the 1990s and much of their territory seized.

In the north and northeast, big ethnic-based forces remained. All, however, had agreed to ceasefires in the late 1980s and early 1990s. There had since been little or no fighting. The focus of elites on all sides had been making money. Villages on the Chinese border became boomtowns.

The biggest of these rebel forces, by far, was the United Wa State Army. It was the largest of the successor armies to emerge from the old Communist insurgency, fielding over 25,000 well-armed men. The Wa are a mountain people of the China–Burma borderlands who speak a language more similar to Khmer and Vietnamese than either Burmese or Chinese. Some had become Lutheran in the early 20th century. Drugs— heroin, and more recently methamphetamines—were now a major part of Wa business, making their rulers rich. The Wa had their own television station, schools, and hospitals. More importantly, they enjoyed a good relationship with their patrons in Beijing. The "Wa state" was on the Chinese telephone and electricity grid, and they came and went from China as they pleased. From a Wa perspective, the past twenty years had been good. The last thing they wanted was to surrender power to Naypyitaw. A Burmese army officer I met in 2009 told me, "We don't lose much sleep thinking about the West or Aung San Suu Kyi. But we really don't know how to deal with the Wa and the Chinese."

In the mid-2000s, the junta were hopeful that the Wa and other insurgent armies would accept the new constitution, disarm, form their own political parties, and contest the elections. By 2008, it was clear that wasn't going to happen. The junta then suggested they become "Border Guard Forces": they would only partially demobilize, but their remaining troops, though still commanded by their own officers, would come under the ultimate authority of the Burmese army. Four rebel groups accepted. More than a dozen others refused.

In June 2009, Sri Lankan president Mahinda Rajapaksa made an official visit to Naypyitaw to meet Than Shwe and cement the already close ties between the two countries. He also came to give advice. Just weeks before, Rajapaksa's army had wiped out the Tamil Tiger rebels, ending a bloody, quarter-century-long war. As many as 40,000 civilians, as well as Tamil Tiger fighters, died in the onslaught. Rajapaksa told Than Shwe to forget about negotiation and do the same.

One of the groups that refused the Border Guard Force proposal was the fetchingly named Myanmar National Democratic Alliance Army. It was the army of the Kokang warlord and heroin producer Peng Jiasheng. At a meeting in June 2009, Peng met with a Burmese general and told him that his militia had no desire to change current arrangements. Some members of his Executive Committee differed, so Peng expelled them. The split provided an opportunity for the Burmese, who began making allegations about drug trafficking and illegal arms production. On August

22, police issued a summons ordering Peng and his two sons to appear in a Burmese court. They refused. A warrant was issued for their arrest.

Heavy fighting soon erupted between the Burmese army and Peng's militia. The faction that wanted to accept the Border Guard Force proposal fought alongside the Burmese army. Nearly 40,000 civilians fled to China. Than Shwe personally directed the attacks, even telephoning the battalion commanders on the ground. The fighting ended when 700 Kokang fighters—the bulk of Peng's troops—crossed the border and were disarmed by the Chinese People's Liberation Army.

The Chinese government was extremely unhappy. They had maintained close relations with all the armed groups along the border and wanted the Burmese to find a negotiated way forward. The images of ethnic Chinese refugees fleeing Kokang, shared widely over Chinese social media, were particularly galling and had inflamed Chinese nationalist sentiment against Burma.

The Burmese were unhappy, too, feeling that it was exactly these close relations with China that were keeping the rebel militias going. A couple of weeks after the clashes ended, the junta organized a special tour of Kokang for ambassadors in Rangoon. The Chinese sent their most junior diplomat, saying their ambassador was busy with a visiting Inner Mongolia Cultural Troupe. The same week, state-controlled media in Rangoon ran a story about the Dalai Lama visiting Taiwan, the first mention of the Dalai Lama for over twenty years in any Burmese newspaper.[2]

THE CIVIL WAR in Burma had started in the late 1940s primarily as a Communist insurrection. But soon there were other armed factions that rallied people around rival identities. Burmese nationalism called for the assimilation of all who were deemed to belong to a timeless Myanma nation. But there were other nationalisms, too, such as the growing nationalism of the Kachin. "Kachin" is a Burmese word for the peoples living in the northern hills. They speak different languages, all related to Burmese, some distantly, some quite closely. But their culture, tied to their upland ways of living, is sharply different from Burmese. Previously animist, they are today predominantly Christian, of various denominations. Little wooden churches take pride of place in nearly every Kachin village.

The Kachin experienced colonial rule very differently from the Burmese. The Kachin Hills had never been ruled by an outside power, either Burmese or Chinese. And the British administered the hills with a light hand: an occasional 'tour' and not much else. There was little development, which meant little capitalist intrusion. American missionaries in the early 20th century converted the majority. And during the Second World War, Kachins fought with distinction against the Japanese alongside British and American special forces (unlike the nascent Burmese army, which fought on the side of the Axis powers until the final months of the war). At independence, Kachin chiefs agreed to be part of the new Union of Burma on condition of equality and a state of their own. They received a separate state, but over the 1950s saw any dream of real equality fading into the distance. In the 1960 election, the leading political party campaigned in part on a platform of making Buddhism the state religion. Kachin Christians were appalled. Some drew inspiration from the Karen ethnic rebellion far to the south. By the early 1960s, a Kachin Independence Organization was organized and in full revolt against the dictatorship of General Ne Win.

Thirty years of bloody fighting followed, with thousands killed or wounded and thousands more displaced or used as forced labor, to build roads or carry army supplies. Finally, in 1994, five years after the ceasefires between the government and the ex-Communist forces along the Chinese border, the Reverend Suboi Jum, a former general secretary of the Kachin Baptist Convention, mediated a separate ceasefire between the Kachin Independence Organization and the junta. Over the decade or so that followed, his daughter, Lahtaw Ja Nan, noticed an ever stronger spirit of Kachin nationalist sentiment.[3]

In the late 1990s and 2000s, Ja Nan was a teacher at the Kachin Theological College in Myitkyina, the capital of Kachin state, only a few miles from the ceasefire line. Though it was in name a theological college, many different subjects were offered, from English to mathematics, and the college attracted students from over the Kachin Hills. The junta saw it as a training ground for rebels but, as the ceasefire was intact, tolerated it nonetheless.

"We read the Bible according to the local context," explained Ja Nan, moon-faced and soft-spoken. "There was the idea of contextual theology. We used sticky rice and rice wine at communion instead of bread and wine. We connected what was happening around us to what we read in the Bible. A rights language developed linked to Christian beliefs. The idea of 'walk another mile,' from the book of Matthew, for example, was placed in the context of local forced labor.

"We were part of the North American Baptist Convention, not the more conservative Southern Baptist Convention," she continued, "so we had ties to the ideas of Martin Luther King, his ideas on nonviolent resistance. 'Social rights' and 'civil rights' became part of our vocabulary. Some teachers gave after-school classes at their homes, for discussions about injustice. Kids connected this to their own experiences growing up. Kachin nationalism became stronger over these years."

Ja Nan believed that the Kachin had not been prepared for the economic changes that came with the 1994 ceasefire. The thinking had been political and military; there wasn't a clear economic agenda. The jade industry boomed, and though the Kachin Independence Army continued to profit from it, the lion's share now went to outsiders. Big machines were brought in from China, and the mainly Kachin people who had been working the mines were thrown out of work. Commercial logging also grew exponentially. Land was confiscated for watermelon and banana plantations. A new capitalist class—Kachins, Burmese, and Chinese, with ties to armies on either side of the ceasefire—became rich, while everyone else stayed poor.

Ja Nan said that up to 2009, the Kachin Independence Organization had the idea of "change from within." Unlike the NLD, they participated in the junta's Constitutional Convention to the very end. They even participated in the referendum held in the days after Cyclone Nargis, the chairman of the Kachin Independence Organization casting the first ballot (in favor of the constitution) at the polling station in Laiza, their headquarters. A Kachin State Progressive Party was formed. But by 2010, there was no agreement on the Border Guard Force proposal, which would turn insurgent armies into smaller militias under the army's command. As a result, the junta refused to allow the Kachin State Progressive Party to register. Ja Nan felt that, despite the political differences, relations between the Burmese army and the Kachin Independence Organization were still amicable. "They had been doing a lot of business together," she told me. But by late 2010 tensions were mounting fast.

FOR CHINA, the possibility of fresh fighting along the border was a growing irritant. Beijing had bigger things in mind. Over the past twenty years, the Chinese economy had grown by leaps and bounds, and was now the engine powering much of global growth. The 2008 financial crisis in the West seemed to presage a more general Western decline. In 1990, Deng Xiaoping had ordered the Chinese to "hide your strength, bide your time," but now China was moving into a higher gear and making its ambitions better known. Remaking Burma was one of its ambitions.

On a map, Burma and China are neighbors, and it's easy to assume that this has always been the case. But the borders of both are new, and until modern times China was a faraway place, with many other kingdoms belonging to other peoples, neither Burmese nor Chinese, like the Yi, Dai, and Naxi, in the high mountain valleys in between. Whereas India was a few weeks' sail away, across warm and pacific waters, reaching China meant months of arduous travel by foot and mule. It was this geography that was now being altered. Yunnan, the Chinese province closest to Burma, had only a minority Han Chinese population until the 20th century. Now it was fully integrated into the People's Republic. It was also industrializing rapidly, tying its markets closely to Burma's.

By the 2000s, the Chinese were hoping that Burma would provide a route to the Indian Ocean. This was a very old ambition, going back to the first Chinese explorers two thousand years ago who searched for a way from today's Yunnan, via Burma, to the sea. Burma served as a back door to China during the Second World War, when the Americans trucked supplies over the Burma Road to Chiang Kai-shek's besieged forces at Chungking. In the 1990s, Chinese scholars began discussing what they termed "the Malacca Dilemma," the fact that nearly all China's shipping and energy supplies depended on the narrow Straits of Malacca, a potential chokepoint that could be blockaded by the American or other navies. Beijing wanted a new Burma Road, a permanent one, and much else.

In November 2009, Burma and China finalized plans for a $2.5-billion oil and gas pipeline that would connect a port in Arakan to refineries in Yunnan and beyond. A tenth of China's imported energy would flow across central Burma. Gas from Burma's newly discovered offshore natural gas fields would do the same. New highways and railway lines would run parallel to the pipeline. In addition, China began work on a massive $3.5-billion hydropower project in Kachin state, four times the size of the Hoover Dam and projected to be the fifteenth biggest in the world. A slew of other dams were also planned, along the Irrawaddy and Salween rivers, as well as a giant nickel mine worth $1 billion.

In Burma itself, China's push was controversial, to say the least. Given Western sanctions, the junta felt it had little alternative. The junta had few qualms about the environmental destruction some of these projects would cause, or the land confiscations they would entail, but many ordinary people did have qualms. An image of a rapacious China, taking advantage of Burma's international weakness, took root.

In Beijing, I met with both government officials and analysts. They understood far better than their counterparts in the West that change was on the horizon. At a seminar I attended, a scholar working on Burma said, "After the elections there will be an end to sanctions and a normalization of Burma's international position. The West will not only accept the process but will welcome it and respond positively. After all, Burma will have elections with different parties, and though it's a scripted process, there will be different possible outcomes. This is much more than the Chinese or Vietnamese (or the North Koreans!) will do for decades." There was much laughter in the room.

Earlier that year, Barack Obama became president of the United States. His secretary of state, Hillary Clinton, quickly ordered a review of American policy on Burma, saying that the "path we have taken in imposing sanctions hasn't influenced the Burmese junta."[4] Just as Than Shwe was embarking on his transition, the US was also looking for a way to change tack. What Than Shwe had in mind was still far from anything that could easily justify fresh US engagement with Naypyitaw. But an opportunity was emerging.

Over the spring and summer of 2009, I traveled over a dozen times to Rangoon and Naypyitaw, meeting with generals and other high officials, trying to get a better sense of what they had in mind. In formal meetings, they spoke admiringly of their new constitution, the economic achievements of the regime, and the prospects for rapid development. In informal meetings, they said that what was intended was "new system, old people." There would be a genuinely new set-up but, for the first five years, perhaps ten, ex-military men would dominate institutions, to break them in. They wanted to make sure reform didn't lead to revolt, to protect their families and safeguard their wealth. Not all generals were corrupt, but many had family members who had profited from their positions. Perhaps more than anything, they seemed to want their legacy respected. But beyond that, they were open to ideas.

In all my meetings in Burma, I tried to repeat my primary message as many times as I could: any steps away from military dictatorship were good, but they had to be accompanied by economic reforms that would genuinely benefit ordinary people and bring a just end to decades of internal conflict. I had no idea if anyone was listening.

Over those same months, in both Western and Asian capitals, I met with more than a dozen government ministers. The international media at the time were almost unanimous in saying that the new system would be nothing more than a fig leaf for Than Shwe's continued dictatorial rule. I suggested that what was taking shape was the best chance in a very long time to influence Burma. Speaking at the European Union parliament in Brussels in June 2009, I argued that the new constitutional set-up would not lead to democracy, but would be the biggest shake-up in the Burmese political order in a generation. I advocated trying to take advantage of this shake-up, thinking not just about politics but also about the economy and the armed conflicts. I also said that China should loom large in anyone's analysis of Burma's future.

I also met Jim Webb, US senator from Virginia. Webb was a Marine Corps veteran of the Vietnam War and a former secretary of the navy. In 2009, he was leading efforts to rethink policy on Burma. Webb called sanctions "overwhelmingly counterproductive." He pointed as well to China's growing economic footprint and argued that America should speak to the Chinese rather than simply isolating Burma from the West.[5] And he said that the United States needed to develop clearly articulated standards for its relations with the nondemocratic world. In an op-ed in the *New York Times,* headlined "We Can't Afford to Ignore Myanmar," he wrote, "Our distinct policies toward different countries amount to a form of situational ethics that does not translate well into clear-headed diplomacy."[6]

In mid-August, Jim Webb flew to Burma and met with both Than Shwe and Aung San Suu Kyi, becoming the first senior American political figure to do so. This was at the height of the Kokang fighting, something perhaps not lost on the Chinese. On his return, he held hearings on Burma policy. I was invited, and in my testimony said that Burma was at a watershed and that any effective policy would need to address seven decades of ethnic-based armed conflict as well as half a century of isolation.[7]

The Norwegians were also very active. Development minister Erik Solheim visited in early 2009, together with his Danish counterpart, Ulla Tørnæs, and toured villages devastated by the cyclone. As the first European ministers to visit Burma in well over a decade, they attracted criticism for doing so. Erik Solheim returned a year later. He was convinced that an end to Burma's isolation was a prerequisite for any progress. Norway, which had previously taken the hardest line on Burma, not only pivoted toward a new approach, but tried to persuade counterparts in Washington to do the same.

Most governments, however, followed the old approach. It was easy to see why. There was no reason to trust anything the junta said. They were inarticulate in English and anything in translation was at best garbled. Few could see the granular changes already taking place in Naypyitaw. The visits of people like Jim Webb and Erik Solheim did have an important effect, however: they demonstrated to the regime that taking the first steps out of dictatorship would be recognized. These early moves would prove a crucial ingredient for the transformation to come.

NEW STRATEGIES were emerging within Burma as well. A central character was the erstwhile businessman, magazine publisher, and think tank founder Nay Win Maung. A small, wiry man with a cigarette always in hand and a chain-smoker's cough, he was gregarious and good-humored, and by the late 2000s single-minded in his desire to find a way out of his country's political and economic morass. His life story made him a good fit for the role he would come to play.

Nay Win Maung grew up in the 1960s and 1970s in the old colonial hill station of Maymyo, a rambling collection of mock-Tudor homes and once well-manicured lawns. A century ago, it was where the British went when Rangoon was too hot. His parents were lecturers at the Defense Services Academy, Burma's equivalent to West Point or Sandhurst, known to generations of army officers. He was a reasonably good student, but he was also rebellious, always questioning both his teachers and his parents, something not often done in conservative Burmese society. He read Harold Robbins and Arthur Hailey in translation and later tried his hand at writing fiction. After graduating with a medical degree, he decided not to practice as a doctor and turned to business instead. There were ups and downs. He became fascinated by the world of business—or, more precisely, the dysfunctional world of Burmese business and the policies behind its dysfunctionality.

In 1997 he founded *Living Colour* magazine, which focused mainly on stories about the economy. Starting a private publication wasn't an easy thing to do under the dictatorship. But the magazine did well, and it allowed Nay Win Maung to meet often with an ever wider circle of people. Whereas others saw the economic mess and threw up their hands, Nay Win Maung began scheming quietly. For him, the faceless generals were not faceless. Some he knew through his parents. What he lacked was any real background in public policy, so in 2004 he accepted an offer to be Maurice R. Greenberg World Fellow at Yale, spending four months intensively studying and discussing comparative politics. It was a turning point.

When he got back, he teamed up with Tin Maung Thann, an old school friend and an ichthyologist. Like Nay Win Maung, he was, he said, part of the "hopeless generation" that grew up under the Burmese Way to Socialism.[8] After university in Rangoon, he continued his studies in aquaculture in Thailand. He worked in Vietnam, Bangladesh, Laos, and Cambodia before returning home to promote tilapia farming. Soon he was caught up in Nay Win Maung's plans to change the country. In November 2006, Nay Win Maung set up a think tank called Egress. Tin Maung Thann was a founding member, together with Hla Maung Shwe, a successful shrimp exporter and former political prisoner. Both would play pivotal roles in the politics to come.

I first visited Egress in 2007. It was located in a warren of rooms and corridors at the back of the Thamada, a dilapidated 1970s hotel with a movie theatre at one end and the 365 Café on the other. Across the street was the red-brick Presbyterian church. Egress was partly a school offering short courses in "capacity-building," an innocuous term used to hide its teaching of comparative politics. Hundreds of young people attended.

One of the lecturers was Kyaw Yin Hlaing, a jovial and loquacious PhD from Cornell University who had just returned from a teaching position abroad. He believed that Burma was "in a social and political deadlock" and in desperate need of "a critical mass of young people who could think critically and differently and become agents of change." He focused on issues of identity: "Young people didn't have access to new ways of thinking. They hated the military. But they still had the same idea as the military of a Burma that was unchanged from millions of years ago. They didn't know what had been the product of the British and what was not. We talked about all these things. About how the country's borders themselves were new. This opened their eyes. Some were very upset. 'No, Myanmar was always there!' some said. But then they changed. With that they came to accept a more pragmatic approach. It wasn't going to be about bringing back a glorious past."

Egress was also a think tank aimed at influencing regime policy. "The regime's information systems were down," one former Egress member told me in 2018. "They had no intelligence service, no one to explain their options. If we can manipulate that, we push them toward reform. If we make one mistake, though, we'll wind up in jail." Nay Win Maung was by that time writing hundreds of short papers with ideas on every aspect of government policy, and sending them to top generals. He also had a weekly newspaper, *Voice*, in which he tried, carefully, to challenge official thinking. He even wrote to Than Shwe. He got away with much of what he was doing only because so many of the generals had been students of his parents. In Burma, the teacher–student (*saya-tabè*) relationship is considered second only to the one between parent and child.

For many in the democracy movement, Egress represented nothing less than a sellout. By implicitly accepting the new constitution, it was turning its back on the National League for Democracy and its goal of revolution, at a time when the NLD and Aung San Suu Kyi were especially vulnerable. The other side was also suspicious. Nay Win Maung and other Egress officials were interrogated several times by the police Special Branch (responsible for monitoring dissent) and briefly detained in the summer of 2010.

By then, a growing circle of people were working together informally. It included Egress, along with Burmese exiles, political figures outside the NLD, Western diplomats and aid workers in Rangoon, and an array of people in various capitals, from desk officers to ministers. They shared the beliefs that sanctions were counterproductive, that revolution was not around the corner, and that the opportunities around Than Shwe's impending retirement could be used to push Burma in a reformist direction.

Egress was also active in Bangkok, running a series of quiet meetings ("the Bangkok process") with Burmese exiles gearing up to return. Nay Win Maung was almost manic in those days, working incessantly. He started wearing short shorts all the time. He fell asleep once while smoking and typing, setting fire to his laptop. He changed his email address, without explanation, to brattpytt@gmail.com. He emailed me and dozens of others every day, maneuvering between diplomats, generals, aid officials, businessmen, and exiles, trying to get the next steps just right. His hope wasn't radical change in 2011, but a gradual evolution that would lead to democracy by 2016.

My personal desire was to see discussions broaden away from politics and toward the economy and the armed conflicts. Then, as now, I felt that the plight of the poorest needed to be placed front and center, together with new ways of thinking about race and identity. In May 2009, in Bangkok, I organized the first ever conference on economic reform in Burma, bringing together the UN, the World Bank, the Asian Development Bank, and Burmese economists from both inside and outside the country. I also became a part-time advisor to the Livelihoods and Food Security Trust Fund, or LIFT, commuting weekly from Bangkok to Rangoon. LIFT was a several-hundred-million-dollar fund set up by the European Union, the UK and Australia in the aftermath of Nargis to address extreme poverty in rural Burma. I acted as a bridge, working to convince the government that this was a good thing, at a time when most generals were still extremely suspicious of the West. Conversely, Western governments needed reassurance that aid under the military regime was not further entrenching the status quo. LIFT was a test. As part of the LIFT team, I traveled to some of the most destitute villages in the country. I hoped and believed that, at the very least, in the years to come, the situation of the poorest would improve.

OVERSEAS, A SMALL but growing number of Burmese also realized that a once-in-a-lifetime opportunity might be around the corner. One was Min Zaw Oo, then working with aid agencies in Afghanistan. At the time of the abortive uprising in 1988, he was fifteen years old. He soon joined an underground movement and later the All Burma Students' Democratic Front, or ABSDF, an insurgent group on the Thai–Burmese border. For years, he and a ragtag group of mainly boys from the area lived on a hilltop. There were many close calls. Once, during a firefight with government soldiers, six bullets missed his head by inches, lodging in a jackfruit tree just behind him. He nearly died several times from malaria and typhoid. He began to wonder: what I am doing on this hill? Many Western embassies, including the American, were in regular touch with the ABSDF as well as other rebel groups along the border, via their liaison offices in Thailand. One day, he received word from the ABSDF liaison office of a scholarship opportunity to go to America. "For everyone in the camp there were two habits: one was not to talk about family back home, to prevent breakdown in morale. The second was not to think about the future." But now he did. He went to Bangkok, got an application, and filled out the forms in his hut on the muddy hillside.

Before long, he was at the University of Maryland, where the political scientist Ted Gurr was working on state failure. "Somalia was then big in the news and the US government was setting up a Somalia-linked 'state failure task force,'" he told me. Ted Gurr was involved in it, so Min Zaw Oo became involved too. He eventually completed a PhD at George Mason University in conflict analysis and resolution.

By this time, Min Zaw Oo knew that sanctions and isolation weren't the way forward for Burma. The 2003 attacks by the junta on Aung San Suu Kyi's convoy had angered him deeply. But the weakness of the democracy movement also suggested the need for a strategic review. "The army's plan for a new constitutional set-up needs to be used in some way," he thought. Then he met Nay Win Maung at a conference outside London. I was there too. They kept in touch. In 2008, he met his future wife, a Burmese woman living in the US. He told her he might not be a good boyfriend, let alone husband, as he was determined to go back to Burma one day and become involved again in political work.

Min Zaw Oo's idea was that any change would be an elite-driven transition. He felt there were two requirements: "a more open political space and the emergence of new agents for reform." By 2010, he was seeing both taking shape.

———

In March 2010, after months of internal debate, the National League for Democracy's leaders who were not in prison met and called for a boycott of the coming elections. This was Aung San Suu Kyi's wish, which her physician was able to convey to the others. A minority disagreed, left the NLD, and formed a new party, the National Democratic Front. This was good news for the junta. According to new election laws, all parties had to take part or face automatic dissolution. The NLD was officially dissolved.

Win Tin was a journalist who had spent nineteen years locked up for his beliefs, often beaten, denied medical care, and kept in terrible conditions. He was now out of prison and eighty years old, with a shock of white hair and clad always in a sky blue prison shirt that he wore as a show of solidarity with those still behind bars. He told the *New York Times* that taking part in the elections would mean "giving up all of our political convictions." Instead, he urged the international community to "please put more pressure on the government." "For me it's as if I were still in prison," he said. "I feel like the whole country is imprisoned."

In September 2010, the official campaign period began. In addition to the regime's own Union Solidarity and Development Party and the NLD's breakaway National Democratic Front, a total of forty parties were registered for the polls. One was the National Unity Party, a resurrection of General Ne Win's old ruling Burma Socialist Programme Party. Many were ethnic minority parties, some genuinely independent, others created by the junta to give them a local front.

Than Shwe's intent was that his Union Solidarity and Development Party win the election. But he wanted the party to win cleanly, if possible. The odds were already stacked in its favor. It had lots of money to spend. And with the NLD out of the picture, there were few nationwide rivals.

There was real campaigning. Recently retired generals were now parliamentary candidates. After a lifetime in uniform, some were not entirely comfortable wearing civilian *longyis* in public; they chose safari suits instead. They toured constituencies, shaking hands and kissing babies, promising better roads and better schools.

On November 7, 2010, the elections went ahead. The result was a landslide win for Than Shwe's Union Solidarity and Development Party. There were probably some who voted for the USDP because they genuinely supported the regime, or wanted to be on the winning side, and the NLD's call to boycott the election took away many potential votes from the other opposition parties. Added to this was outright fraud and vote rigging, which was engineered almost entirely via "advance votes" (absentee ballots). When preliminary returns suggested significant wins for the National Democratic Front (the NLD breakaway), including in key Rangoon constituencies, the top generals suggested a helping hand. By morning, a wave of additional ballot papers had swung the results in the other direction. A few weeks later, when Myanmar lost a soccer game to Vietnam, the joke in Rangoon was that Myanmar first lost 2–0 but then won 3–2 on advance votes.

The election was also something of a watershed for the Muslim communities of northern Arakan. The junta not only granted them the right to vote but sought to win their votes as well, promising better times ahead. To mobilize the Rohingya, they used Rohingya real estate tycoons from Rangoon. The USDP won all three majority-Rohingya constituencies. Rohingya politicians would soon join the new parliament.

Some, though, had an intimation that things were not quite right. Tin Hlaing was a Muslim businessman in Sittwe, the capital of Arakan. He was part Rohingya and part Kaman. The Kamans were a separate Muslim community living mainly in the south of the state. He had grown up in Sittwe and remembers only "a happy time" in school, which was about two-thirds Muslim. "There was no discrimination, either from teachers or the other kids. I had good friends from all communities and backgrounds. In town there might occasionally be a fight at a bar between people of different religions, but nothing too serious. Up to 1990, we could also travel freely, including to Rangoon. It was in the 1990s and 2000s that things gradually became difficult."[9]

Tin Hlaing went to university in Sittwe, studying mathematics. He taught himself Hindi on the side, from books and watching Indian films, becoming almost fluent. His English was also good. These language skills won him a job with an Indian company, ESSAR, helping them rent houses and hire workers.

During the approach to the 2010 election, things began to change. While dining at the Mayu restaurant, he overheard a discussion in an adjoining room organized by the main Arakanese party, the Rakhine Nationalities Development Party. There were Arakanese Buddhist leaders from Rangoon as well as from around the state. "They talked about the need for a *lu-myo seit* [a "racial" or "national" spirit—the words are interchangeable in Burmese]. They said, this is our land. It's a Buddhist land. Some said, 'We need to be careful about the *kala*.' Hearing this made me uneasy for the first time."

Several months earlier, in a letter to all heads of foreign missions in Hong Kong and the local media, the Burmese consul general Ye Myint Aung pushed back against reports alleging discrimination against Rohingya Muslims in Arakan. He said that the Rohingya were not one of "Myanmar's ethnic groups" and compared their "dark brown" complexion to that of the Burmese, which was "fair and soft, good-looking as well." For good measure, he noted that his own complexion was a "typical genuine one" for Burmese "gentlemen": "You will accept how handsome your colleague Mr. Ye is." The Rohingya, by contrast, were "as ugly as ogres."[10] Mr. Ye was never reprimanded. Instead, he was promoted.

ON NOVEMBER 13, 2010, a week after the election, Aung San Suu Kyi was released from house arrest. She spoke that evening to a weeping and cheering crowd outside her gate, saying, "People must work in unison. Only then can we achieve our goal."[11] Many in the crowd wore T-shirts with her image and the slogan "We stand with Aung San Suu Kyi."

Six weeks later, she was connected to the Internet. In an interview with the BBC, she said her hope was still for a "nonviolent revolution." She didn't know how long it would take, but she would take "any opportunity to speak to the generals." She added, "I don't want to see the military falling. I want to see the military rising to dignified heights of professionalism and true patriotism."[12]

The stage was set, but the script was unfinished. Than Shwe and his cohort could still have calibrated the transition in different ways. A new element weighing on their minds was the news they watched on their television sets every evening: the Arab Spring. In January 2011, Tunisian president Zine El Abidine Ben Ali was overthrown and chased into exile. A month later, Egypt's Hosni Mubarak was ousted and jailed. In March, a revolt began against Bashar al-Assad in Syria. By the summer, Libyan dictator Muammar Gaddafi would be dead, killed by a mob. All this focused minds in Naypyitaw. They were ready for help.

At this point, Noeleen Heyzer (the head of the UN's regional economic commission, who had played an important role after Nargis) stepped up her dialogue with the generals. After traveling around the country in 2009, she told them: "You really have a big problem. Kids are not in school. People don't have enough to eat. You say you're building dams, but there is not enough water in most villages. Do you really want to have an economy that's only about exporting cheap labor and raw materials? Or do you want something different? We can bring the best minds here to work with you."

Heyzer invited Joseph Stiglitz to visit Burma. Stiglitz, a Nobel Prize-winning economist and former chief economist at the World Bank, was (and is) a heavyweight. The generals hesitated to allow him to come, then relented. It was an incredibly big step. These were the same generals who had kicked out Charles Petrie just three years before for saying that poverty was worse than the junta were prepared to admit. And it wouldn't just be a flying visit. Stiglitz would speak at a grand conference with Burmese civil society organizations as well as with government officials. The generals were nervous, and only at the last minute did Than Shwe allow his prime minister, Thein Sein, to attend.

In the Chinese-built Myanmar Convention Centre in Naypyitaw, Stiglitz talked to the assembled participants about the need to increase spending on health and education, invest in agriculture and rural development, and use new revenues from oil and gas wisely. He stressed the need to help the poorest and drew attention to the appalling state of rural credit markets. There were many questions. Afterward, at a press conference in Singapore, he said, "There is the hope that this is the moment of change for the country."

In most countries, a lecture and discussion with a prominent economist, even a Nobel Prize winner like Joseph Stiglitz, would barely count as news. But in Burma, after decades of isolation, it was a tipping point. It wasn't what was said that was important; it was that an analysis implicitly critical of the regime's record was aired in public—and reported. What had been taboo was suddenly appearing in state-run media. The retired United Nations economist U Myint, who had helped organize the event, said at a press conference afterward: "I hope it is realized that Professor Stiglitz's visit here is not only to share his knowledge with us but to help create this space, for us as well as for others in the country who want change."[13]

As 2010 turned to 2011, Burma was in limbo. Aung San Suu Kyi was free. Than Shwe was about to give up the reins of power. New structures were taking shape. And those focused on profits were busy filling their pockets. There was a fire sale of state property, and businessmen close to the generals were able to buy prime real estate at bargain-basement prices. Forests were cut down at a ferocious pace. To me, this was the clearest sign that something would change. Like frogs picking up positive ions in the atmosphere weeks before an earthquake, it was the businessmen who sensed most clearly that the old way of doing things was about to end.

These businessmen had enjoyed a good run over the past couple of years. But, to be fair, so had many others. Moderate economic growth had led to noticeable changes in Rangoon. Hotels were spruced up and there were more restaurants to choose from, along with first-rate supermarkets and a sleek and efficient airport terminal, as good as any in the region. Much of the new money was tied to jade and a related inflation of the city's real estate prices. The building of the new capital, financed in part by rising natural gas prices, also enriched a select few. A house worth $200,000 ten years ago now fetched ten times that amount. There was a trickle down to an incipient middle class, though very little trickled down any further. Inequalities remained colossal.

Over the previous two decades, ever since the jettisoning of the Burmese Way to Socialism, money had reshaped the political landscape. Everyone—soldiers and civilians, government and rebel armies, Burmese Buddhists and ethnic minorities—was dependent on the market. A few made money honestly. Many with access to guns or high office did not. Collusion and racketeering knew no linguistic, racial, or religious divides.

But what of the future?

Would money continue to shape the next iteration in Burmese politics? Or would race thinking trump all?

Meanwhile, nearly four decades of repression and impoverishment had produced a psychological impact. I saw this in my own extended family as well as in others, where each generation had enjoyed fewer opportunities than the last and there was no one to hold to account. The anxieties of the free market were coupled with a sense of impotence. Many people turned to Buddhism or other faiths. Burma in 2010 was as religious a society as it had ever been. Millions also spent time each week in charity work, either at their local monastery or church or in one of the many *parahita* (literally "the welfare of others") associations that had sprung up. Millions more coped by keeping their heads down and minding their own business.

The generals themselves lived in a hermetically sealed world. They lived together, their wives socialized together, they attended the same religious ceremonies, and their children went to the same schools and married one another. They told themselves that they were the true patriots and their opponents were traitors.

Over that winter some of the generals, now ex-generals, crept onto the new stage. Two of them came quietly to listen to lectures at Egress. The more optimistic observers hoped for at least some economic reform, an easing of political restrictions, and an outreach to the West. What came next went far beyond anyone's wildest imagination.

SIX

ALIGNMENT

O VER THE FIRST FEW MONTHS of 2011, the doubters, those who had dismissed the new constitutional set-up as a sham, seemed to be proven right. Many of the generals were now ex-generals, but there was little sign that much beyond the change of clothes was likely to be different.

Rangoon gossip was focused on which of these ex-generals might wind up as the first, nominally civilian president under the new constitution. Than Shwe had made it clear in private meetings that he had no desire to take the top job. For years, his only rival had been his deputy, Maung Aye, just a few years his junior and a powerful figure with his own network, in business and in the army. Than Shwe's aim was to retire and to make sure Maung Aye retired as well. He also intended to fracture power between the army and the two new institutions he was creating: the presidency and the parliament. He wanted to live out his last years confident that no new strongman could emerge. He felt he had already outmaneuvered Aung San Suu Kyi.

The smart money had been on Shwe Mann, number three in the junta hierarchy, just below Than Shwe and Maung Aye. Born in 1947, he had spent most of his life in combat, fighting Communists in the teak-forested hills south of Mandalay and leading bloody campaigns against Karen insurgents in the steamy, malaria-infested jungles near Thailand. He was awarded the rare title *Thura*, meaning "brave," for distinction in battle. By the mid-2000s, he was in charge of all day-to-day military operations and was increasingly seen as Burma's next leader, trusted by both Than Shwe and Maung Aye. Square-jawed, with a soft-spoken charisma, Shwe Mann seemed to fit the part. A UN diplomat who met him together with other generals in 2006 remembered him as friendly and inquisitive, asking many questions and taking extensive notes. During his visit to Beijing in 2009, the Chinese rolled out the red carpet for the man they believed was the heir apparent.

Shwe Mann was also in close touch with Nay Win Maung and Egress. Nay Win Maung sent him notes at least every week on almost every conceivable policy issue, from liberalizing car imports to relations with the new Obama administration. Shwe Mann's son sat in on Egress classes and sent taped recordings of the lectures to his father. Like a slew of other generals, Shwe Mann formally retired in 2010 to contest the elections, won a seat, and waited for his moment.

So, at the end of January when parliament was convened and another ex-general, Thein Sein, was chosen as president, many were left scratching their heads. Shwe Mann was given what was seen as a consolation prize and made Speaker of the lower house of parliament. Nay Win Maung was discouraged. I remember many discussions with him over the preceding months on likely presidential picks. None had included Thein Sein as a possibility.

Thein Sein had been prime minister in the old system and number four in the junta hierarchy, below Shwe Mann. Sixty-five years old, mild-mannered and owlish, Thein Sein was slightly built and suffered from a heart condition. Whereas Shwe Mann was ambitious, Thein Sein had long sought a quiet retirement. He had a reputation for being extremely hard-working. He also had a reputation as "Mr. Clean," as one of the very few in the military top brass whose family had no business ties whatsoever.

The plan unfolded. In his aim of fracturing power, Than Shwe had placed the less ambitious man in the most powerful new position and the more ambitious in charge of the weakest institution. The new cabinet was packed with ex-generals (all chosen by Than Shwe), some in the very same posts they had held under the old regime, a mix of personality types that were meant to offset one another: conservative types were given deputies who were eager for change, and vice versa. "He's locked everyone in place, to make sure nothing can change very quickly," marveled a businessman over dinner one evening.

Than Shwe then abolished the junta, formally retired, and appointed General Min Aung Hlaing, twenty years younger, as the new head of the armed forces. Min Aung Hlaing was a protégé who had personally led the recent offensive against the Kokang militia.

Those who had predicted "old wine in new bottles" seemed exactly right.

But then words began to change. In February and March, the six hundred or so members of the new parliament met almost daily in their cavernous, air-conditioned complex. Almost all were middle-aged or elderly men, a good proportion former army officers or businessmen, clad in the white cotton jackets, silk headdresses, velvet slippers, and patterned *longyis* of Burmese officialdom. The majority were from the ruling Union Solidarity and Development Party. The rest were from ethnic minority parties (with appropriately different headgear) or the NLD breakaway National Democratic Front. These opposition MPs tabled discussions on a range of until now sensitive issues, from tax evasion to low Internet connectivity, the high cost of schooling, press censorship, and even a possible amnesty for political prisoners. The discussions were not only freely debated but reported almost verbatim the next day in the state-run media.

This was extraordinary. No one had heard anyone in an official capacity talk about the real problems people were facing in decades.

Shwe Mann, wounded by being denied the presidency, was keen to show that the institution he had been given, the parliament, would quickly come to life.

On March 30, the new president gave his inaugural speech. He highlighted the need for both "good governance" and "clean governance" and vowed that his administration would be "transparent" and "accountable." He also underlined the urgent need for economic reform, saying that "there are still many people whose life is a battle against poverty, whose life is a hand-to-mouth existence," and that one of his principal tasks would be "reducing the gap between rich and poor." He even called for robust protection of the environment.

In many countries, this would be run-of-the-mill political talk. But this was Burma, whose rulers had for half a century banned any suggestion that things were not exactly as they should be. Thein Sein also said that he wanted to cooperate not only with other political parties but also with other "political forces and well-meaning individuals"—meaning, implicitly, Aung San Suu Kyi. An American diplomat who had served in Moscow in the late 1980s told me it reminded him of the beginnings of glasnost.

Then came a bigger turn: the appointment of outside advisors. In the 1960s, the then-dictator General Ne Win had gutted the civil service. The top bureaucrats, graduates of Cambridge and London universities, were summarily dismissed. Many went into exile. Unlike other military-run governments in Asia—say, South Korea or Indonesia, with its "Berkeley Mafia" of economists—Burma's regime relied on no experts, sought no outside advice. The army knew best, always. An anti-intellectual instinct was strong.

So when U Myint, a Berkeley-educated former UN economist was appointed chief economic advisor (and one of several new outside advisors) there was a feeling that the ground was beginning to shift, a tremor before the bigger quake. For U Myint was not just any economist. He was a friend of Aung San Suu Kyi who pulled no punches in his criticism of the junta's policies. He talked openly of cronyism and high-level corruption. He had worked closely with Noeleen Heyzer in setting up the Joseph Stiglitz conference just months before. The president now tasked him with drawing up plans for economic change.

Building on the Stiglitz conference, a second conference, on rural development and poverty alleviation, was held in May. Tight timetables were set for new policy papers, workshops, consultations, presidential decisions, and if needed new laws, on everything from banking and currency reform to encouraging foreign investment and environmental protection. The mood was transformed. Civil servants dared for the first time in their careers to challenge the status quo and suggest alternatives. And people outside government started speaking openly, including to the media, about their ideas on what needed to change.

Doubters were still unconvinced. John McCain warned the authorities: "Governments that shun evolutionary reforms now will eventually face revolutionary change later. This choice may be deferred. It may be delayed. But it cannot be denied."[1] The authorities, keen to show they were different from the old regime, responded by reporting his remarks in full in the state media.

By early July, words were turning into actions. The president announced a massive boost to state pensions, significantly reduced tariffs on imported goods, liberalized the trade licensing system, and, most importantly, took the first steps toward currency reform. These last three seemingly technical measures were actually direct assaults on the existing system of regime privilege. Though Burma's currency enjoyed an official exchange rate of 6 kyats to the dollar, the market rate was about 750 to the dollar. Those with the right connections, who could buy dollars at 6 kyats, made a killing every time. Currency reform was also a crucial first step to properly accounting for the state's multi-billion-dollar annual natural gas revenues. The president officially asked for help from the International Monetary Fund. There was feverish opposition from within his own government and parliament, but the president pushed these reforms through nonetheless.

No one had seen anything like this in decades. Those hoping for bold steps on the economic front were encouraged. But would anything happen on the political front?

OVER THAT SPRING and early summer of 2011, Aung San Suu Kyi was not quite ready to accept that real change was taking place. She was working hard, catching up with her party members (those not still in prison) after years of separation, and spending long hours at the NLD headquarters, a small, unprepossessing concrete building next to a furniture shop, with exposed electrical wires, dusty tables stacked high with papers, and a flight of rickety stairs to her little office above. Her physician, Dr. Tin Myo Win, regularly monitored her blood pressure, occasionally giving her injections of a "cocktail drip"—a blend of vitamins, proteins, and glucose—to keep her from collapsing from exhaustion.[2]

She knew she had to carefully calibrate her next steps and judge whether recent developments amounted to something more than the cosmetic changes she'd expected. Some of her supporters wanted her to be more active in challenging the new government. She considered traveling outside Rangoon, something that in the past had provoked her arrest. Others wanted her to be more conciliatory and call for an end to Western sanctions. Was the new president someone she could work with? There was fear of a trap.

IN MID-JULY, I met ministers Aung Min and Soe Thane for the first time. Both had been senior military men. Aung Min was a retired major general and had been minister of railways for many years. Soe Thane had been minister of industry for a couple of years, since retiring as navy chief. Both were now plotting to take the country along an entirely new and uncertain path.

I had heard of Aung Min from Nay Win Maung. "You should really meet the railways minister," he told me repeatedly over many months. "He's not like the other generals. He listens very carefully and takes notes of everything. You will see." We met in a downstairs meeting room at his ministry. There was a painting on the wall of a big train. Sweet, milky tea and little fried vegetables were placed on the coffee table in front of us. As I had never met the two men before, throughout the meeting, I didn't know who was who.

They started by saying that they were my *parisad*, my audience. The person I later knew was Soe Thane said, "We have read your books and your articles. We have been isolated all our lives. We need new ideas, new knowledge. Please let us know what you think we should know." It was a disarming introduction. He continued, "We are at a really important moment in the country's history. Anything can happen. But we have to push for change. We don't know where we'll be in six months, we might be in prison, but we have to try." They explained that their focus was on persuading the president to move fast in a "reformist" direction.

The other man, Aung Min, was the quieter of the two, studying me. He had been an intelligence officer before becoming an infantry commander. He prided himself on being a simple soldier. "I'm not educated," he said. His interest now was in helping his friend, the president. They had known each other for decades, fighting together against the Communists, living together in remote villages.

Thein Sein had wanted Aung Min to be the ruling party's general secretary.[3] The other generals questioned whether Aung Min knew enough about the policy challenges ahead and pushed back. Aung Min now wanted to prove his doubters wrong. For months he had been secretly meeting with Nay Win Maung and others in the Egress team, listening to briefing after briefing on every imaginable topic, using a back room in his house. "It was like an intensive care unit," said one Egress member. "We sat him down and used a projector to show him one PowerPoint after another, for hours a day." Now Aung Min wanted to hear from me as well.

"Old mentalities need to be overcome!" said Soe Thane. They asked me for my wish list. I had met several generals over the past three years, but no one had ever asked me for anything like an agenda going forward. Not having prepared anything, I simply suggested it would be best if the new government could show initiative in many different areas at once: a release of political prisoners, an outreach to Aung San Suu Kyi, continued economic reform, the beginning of fresh peace talks, and visas for international journalists. "You need the outside world to understand what's happening," I argued. I had no expectation that any of my suggestions would go any further than the little Railway Ministry meeting room we were in.

"It's bad karma to be *bayins* in Burma," said Soe Thane. *Bayin* means "king." He meant that the country's problems were almost impossible to fix. He said the new constitutional government, like the army regime, felt it had to prioritize security over everything else. I suggested that the concept of security could be looked at more broadly, as human security, and include new challenges such as climate change. They liked that.

Two weeks later I met them again, this time at Aung Min's home in Rangoon. It was a suprisingly modest house, smaller than an average middle-class house in an American suburb, surrounded by a high wall. Soe Thane and a number of Egress members, including Nay Win Maung, were already there. There was much discussion of the various reform processes underway and possible next steps. Aung Min and Soe Thane showed me a loose-leaf binder with printouts of foreign news reports welcoming the new president's actions. They had shown the same loose-leaf binder to the president. It was a way of encouraging him to do more. Aung

Min also took out a little notebook, read the suggestions I had made two weeks before, and said they were now working on all of them.

Were these actually the ministers at the heart of the shifts taking place? What really was their relationship with the Egress people I had come to know? Was it all a confidence trick, or the beginning of historic political change? I wasn't sure. What was clear was that Aung Min and Soe Thane were now working hand in glove with Egress. And they wanted me to be involved and give them ideas on how best to engage with the West.

The mood was informal and candid. Indian dishes were available in the dining room for anyone who wanted to eat. Though everyone was respectful of the former general and admiral, everyone also spoke his mind. There was talk of "hardliners" and "corrupt interests" that were already trying to scuttle the president's agenda. Aung San Suu Kyi was seen as a possible ally.

On July 14, Aung San Suu Kyi was invited to the annual Martyrs Day ceremony in Rangoon. The ceremony marked the assassination of her father and his colleagues in 1947, but she had been barred from attending it during her years of house arrest. Permission was given, too, for NLD party members and supporters to march to the tomb where the ceremony was held. For the past twenty years, any NLD procession would have been met by police with batons or worse. A day later, Aung San Suu Kyi was allowed to travel to the nearby city of Pegu and give an open-air speech to over a thousand well-wishers. Her staff worked with the army to ensure security. Private newspapers and magazines were for the first time permitted to report her activities.

Changes unthinkable just a few months before were coming thick and fast. In mid-August, the president invited all "armed groups" to peace talks. He said he would soon appoint his negotiation team. He also welcomed back the previously banned UN Special Rapporteur on Human Rights, Tomás Quintana, who had not long ago called for a war crimes tribunal against the former regime. The Red Cross was given access to the country's prisons. That same week Thein Sein, in a speech to an unprecedented gathering of Burmese charities and activist groups, including ones closely affiliated with the opposition, encouraged exiles to return, stating that only those who had committed serious crimes such as murder risked prosecution.

Next came a watershed. U Myint, the former UN official and now chief economic advisor to the president, had organized a National Workshop on the Reforms for National Economic Development. Aung San Suu Kyi was invited to attend. On August 19, after days of quiet meditation, she traveled to Naypyitaw for the first time, arriving in an official motorcade accompanied by the chief of the Special Branch (the secret police). Hla Maung Shwe, the shrimp merchant, Egress leader, and one-time political prisoner, helped make arrangements.[4]

Once in Naypyitaw, she met Thein Sein in his office for over an hour, just the two of them. A photograph released to the press afterward shows them standing together, smiling, underneath a portrait of her father. Thein Sein then walked her over to his private apartments and introduced her to his family. His wife embraced her. Aung San Suu Kyi told journalists afterward that she was "happy and satisfied" with this first encounter.[5]

The workshop itself was a big success. Several hundred people attended, including leading government officials, businessmen, and scholars who had been in exile until just days before. There was open and often heated debate. Aung San Suu Kyi attended two of the sessions, escorted by a beaming U Myint. During the coffee break she met separately with Aung Min and Soe Thane. The ministers said they wanted to work with the Nobel laureate. "Let us know how we can assist," they said.

The next month, I met Aung San Suu Kyi myself for the first time in over twenty years. She had lived in New York from 1969–71, working at the UN, and some of my earliest memories were of seeing her at our home in Riverdale. In the 1980s I visited her a couple of times in Oxford. And in 1996, on my first trip back to Rangoon after the 1988 uprising, I tried to see her again. We spoke over the phone and she invited me to lunch the next day, but at the army checkpoint near her house I was told in no uncertain terms that I was not allowed to proceed. The regime made it a condition of any future trip back to Burma that I was not to communicate with her in any way.

I met her at her little office upstairs at the NLD's headquarters. She was relaxed and friendly, asking after my family, in particular my parents, who had been her contemporaries back in her New York days. She said, "Come over for a meal soon, so we have more time to properly catch up." I assured her I would be pleased to help in any way I could.

Nearly everyone in the country now felt a positive momentum. A door that no one thought would ever open was being unlocked. But the question remained: was Thein Sein, a career Burmese army officer and former junta member, genuine in his desire to move the country toward true democracy?

THEIN SEIN WAS BORN in a little village next to a creek at the western end of the Irrawaddy delta, not far from the sea. Just offshore was the island of Negrais, where in 1759 over one hundred English traders and their African servants were massacred by a Burmese king. For half the year, the village baked in the hot sun. During the other half, monsoon rains flooded the seemingly endless paddy fields and turned the roads to mud. In the 1950s, when Thein Sein was growing up, there was no electricity, only wood and bamboo huts. His parents were landless and poor, doing odd jobs when they could. Thein Sein was the youngest of three, with an older brother and sister.[6]

Thein Sein did well at the village monastery school and so the headmen sent him to Bassein, the nearby town. It was a precarious existence. After the fifth grade he had to drop out for a time and work back in the village because of lack of money. When he finally finished, rather than going to university, which he thought would be too expensive, he took the entrance exam for the Defense Services Academy. He was accepted, and became an officer.

From graduation in the late 1960s onward, the army was his life. He was posted all around the country. In the 1980s, he fought in pitched battles against Chinese-backed Communists. It was in those years that he first met Aung Min. In 1995, he received his first regional command, in the eastern highlands near Laos. By then he was a senior figure in the military hierarchy, having been promoted step by step by Than Shwe. Than Shwe asked him to chair the National Convention that drafted the constitution, and in 2007 appointed him prime minister. He ran day-to-day administration, traveling extensively to every corner of the country.[7] Around 2008, a businessman told me that Thein Sein sometimes phoned him after visiting a village to tell him how desperate the people were and that there was no budget to do anything, and asking if the businessman could make an urgent donation. The businessman said that no other general ever made that kind of request.

When Nargis struck, Thein Sein's village was devastated. And though he was already number four in the junta, his relatives were still there, ordinary village folk who suffered terribly. Thein Sein himself was placed in charge of relief, and chaired emergency meetings day and night. He says he was shocked both by the impact of the cyclone and by the government's inability to provide the necessary help. It was, say many people who know him, a psychological turning point.

He had never wanted to be president. He had a pacemaker and his wife hoped he would retire with the transition to a new system. "But I'm a soldier and have to take the task given to me and do the best I can," he said. Now he found himself president of a nascent quasi-democracy. "I had no experience in democracy," he told me. "I was too young in the 1950s [before the military regime took power] to remember anything. When I first came into office, I wasn't sure what to do. So I asked myself, what do people really want? I felt that for ordinary people, the most important things were to have enough food to eat, to send their kids to school, even if they had no money, and to have access to health care. Growing up poor in a village, what I wanted more than anything was to improve the lives of villagers. This was my deepest desire."

Thein Sein grew up in a wooden house. Now he lived in a twenty-one-room presidential mansion. An elevator took him up to his office and his private suite, where he lived with his wife, one of his daughters, and his grandchildren, and maintained the rigorous daily schedule of a staff officer: 5 a.m. wake up and walk, 7 a.m. breakfast, 8 a.m. at the office for paperwork, lunch at noon, then afternoons for meetings with ministers and others. He was an experienced manager and tried to cut down unnecessary meetings as much as possible. And he tried always to leave the office by 5 p.m. He knew his staff wouldn't leave as long as he was there, and he wanted them to be able to spend time with their families. People who worked for him said he never lost his cool. He was also a good listener.

Thein Sein was a loyal public servant who was trying to do the best job he could. At the urging of ministers like Aung Min and Soe Thane and outside advisors like U Myint, he was taking ever bolder steps toward reform. But he was not a revolutionary. For him, the military past was something to be proud of, not rejected. He was not seeking to overthrow an evil system. He wanted only to improve on what he saw as the decent legacy of the old regime. Than Shwe trusted him to take things in a reformist direction without going too far. It was a line that would be tested.

IN THE WEEKS after the president's meeting with Aung San Suu Kyi, the issue of the Myitsone dam reached boiling point. The dam was the biggest of the Chinese investment projects approved by the old junta. It had the potential to answer all of Burma's electricity needs for decades to come, and bring in billions of dollars in revenue by selling surplus power to China. Critics were appalled. The dam would flood an area the size of Singapore, including four villages. Nearly 12,000 people were being relocated. The location of the dam, where two Himalayan rivers joined to form the Irrawaddy, was of considerable cultural importance to the Kachin people. Activists also drew attention to the massive environmental damage that could be caused to the Irrawaddy River itself, the lifeblood of the country. No one knew exactly what was in the contract, but most believed the terms favored the Chinese and that bribes had been paid to army generals and their crony businessmen. In the past, ordinary people would have had no choice but to accept what was happening. The issue would now be used to probe the bona fides of the new administration.[8]

In September, a petition titled "From Those who Wish the Irrawaddy to Flow Forever" was signed by nearly 1,600 influential Burmese, including politicians, writers, movie stars, and artists, and sent to Thein Sein.[9] A "Save the Irrawaddy" campaign gathered steam. Rising figures in the NGO community, like Kyaw Thu, the ponytailed head of Paungku, were tireless in mobilizing grassroots support against the dam.

In Rangoon, where any political gathering would have been met with brute force just nine months before, demonstrators were allowed to mark the fourth anniversary of the monks' protests of 2007. Many wore "Stop Myitsone" T-shirts. An "anti-dam" art exhibition was organized and attracted Aung San Suu Kyi herself, who called on people to "unite if they are to achieve what they want."[10]

Thein Sein was in a bind. He had allowed the demonstrations and this snowballing of public sentiment. Mass protests led by Aung San Suu Kyi would be a nightmare and could, he thought, bring down his government. On the other hand, the dam had been agreed by his former boss Than Shwe and by China. He personally believed that the dam was a good idea. He didn't want to upset his former boss or do anything that might bring the old dictator back into the picture. He also knew the Chinese could make trouble. It would be the most difficult decision of his presidency. He stayed up all night. The next morning, September 30, he penned a statement to parliament stating that the construction of the dam would be suspended for the duration of his administration.

It was a bombshell, and the first clear sign that this was a government that would respond to popular concerns. Aung San Suu Kyi told the media, "It's very good of them to listen to the voice of the people."[11] The Chinese government was shocked and outraged. Thein Sein had not so much as informed them before announcing the suspension. But their howls of displeasure seemed to fall on deaf ears. So they retreated into the background, for now. There would be grave consequences in the years to come.

Thein Sein was buoyed by growing popular confidence in his government, and pressed on at a blistering pace. All restrictions on the Internet were lifted; until this point, hundreds of exile news sites and sites related to opposition supporters abroad had been banned. Weeks later, a new labor law was signed, allowing workers to form unions for the first time since 1962. Over a hundred unions would be formed over the coming year. In October, about two hundred political prisoners were released.

Soon after, Thein Sein approved a bill amending the party registration law. The bill had been negotiated with the National League for Democracy, to allow the party again to become a legal entity. Aung San Suu Kyi then met with other NLD leaders and agreed to register under the revised law, in effect accepting the new constitution—the same constitution they and their supporters had railed against for years. The door was now open to the NLD contesting by-elections planned for the spring and Aung San Suu Kyi herself becoming a member of parliament.

It's important to take a step back and recognize that this was a historic compromise. It both allowed Burma to move forward and sowed the seeds of future discord and uncertainty. In the mid-2000s, Thein Sein had chaired the Constitutional Convention, which the NLD had adamantly condemned as falling far short of democracy. Thein Sein and his ministers then embarked on a series of liberalizing measures, and Aung San Suu Kyi in return agreed to register her party and become part of the new system. But from the NLD's viewpoint, this was meant as an expedient, not an endgame. They decided to join the system in the belief that the government would not only continue reforms but also reform the constitution itself.

There was resistance on both sides. Some in the opposition feared being maneuvered down a dead end. On the side of the generals and ex-generals, there was unease at the extent to which Thein Sein and some of his ministers were veering away from the original script. Aung San Suu Kyi wasn't meant to be part of the picture at all.

At this point, the policies of several Western governments made a difference. Norway had carefully cultivated ties with Burmese both inside and outside government since the late 2000s, believing that change was coming and that this change, however tentative and imperfect, would be the country's best hope in a generation. Ministers Erik Solheim, Jonas Støre, and Espen Barth Eide all came in quick succession to support the reformist push. Australia did the same, with foreign minister (and past and future prime minister) Kevin Rudd making a personal visit to assess the situation firsthand and demonstrate Canberra's readiness to assist. For Thein Sein and his team, this early encouragement from two Western governments provided more than anything the psychological boost they needed to move ahead.

I spent these months working closely with the president's office to maximize this sudden rapprochement with the West. I sat in on most meetings with visiting ministers, sometimes translating for Aung Min or Soe Thane. More often than not, I met the visiting ministers first to give them my analysis of what was happening and why. In Burma, the personal always trumps any institutional loyalty, and I could see that for the Burmese these new relationships were personal. The ministers had little sense of Norway as a country different from any other European country, but they judged the individuals. Some Western interlocutors, they felt, came only to lecture; the Norwegians were sincere in a desire to help. Norway's ambassador at the time, Katja Nordgaard, who tried hard to understand Burmese perspectives, was seen as a friend.

The same was true of Derek Mitchell, the new US Special Representative to Burma and soon to be its first ambassador in Rangoon in twenty years. All high-level meetings with ambassadors took place in rooms designed for the occasion: two rows of highly ornamental teak chairs facing each other, with two slightly bigger chairs at the end, set at a diagonal. The Burmese minister and the visiting ambassador would then have to speak to each other at this awkward angle. For Mitchell's first meeting with Aung Min and Soe Thane, it was proposed (by the American side) to do away with normal protocol and meet over a beer.[12] The Burmese were nervous, as no minister had ever had a beer with an American ambassador, certainly not as part of the first courtesy call. But they decided to take the risk, and it broke the ice. Derek Mitchell would have many difficult conversations with Aung Min and Soe Thane in the years to come, but he, too, was always seen as a friend.

The Norwegians and Australians had helped pry open the door. Now the Americans threw the door wide open. In November 2011, Barack Obama traveled to Bali for the annual East Asia Summit to proclaim America's "strategic pivot" to Asia. His close advisor, Ben Rhodes, later wrote that the pivot, with the "Trans-Pacific Partnership [a proposed free trade agreement] representing our economic strategy; the deployment of Marines to Australia representing a deepening security commitment; and the opening to Burma representing a commitment to promote democracy and expand relations in Southeast Asia . . . was widely and rightly interpreted as a challenge to China."[13]

Three weeks later, Hillary Clinton became the first US secretary of state to visit Burma since John Foster Dulles in 1955. There was still ambivalence in Washington over whether the reforms in Burma were "real." So Obama first telephoned Aung San Suu Kyi from *Air Force One*, on the way home from Bali, to get her approval. She spoke well of Thein Sein and said that the Americans should be thinking about "rewards, not punishments." On the way to Burma, Clinton watched *The Lady*, Luc Besson's hagiography, in which Aung San Suu Kyi battles murderous generals and sacrifices all for democracy.

Her first stop was Naypyitaw, which she reached just before sundown (there were still no runway lights at the airport). Her meeting with Thein Sein was friendly and wide-ranging; both were policy wonks. The president said he hoped to "open a new chapter in relations."[14] For those, like Aung Min and Soe Thane, who wanted closer ties with the West, this was a big step. But there were legions on the Burmese side suspicious of the Americans. Aung Min later explained to me that in the Burmese army, whenever anything went wrong, the blame would often be ascribed to the CIA. The US was after all a country that had resolutely backed regime change in Burma for decades. Naypyitaw that day was festooned with billboards welcoming the visiting prime minister of Belarus.

Hillary Clinton also called on Shwe Mann. As Speaker of the Lower House, Shwe Mann had been busy getting parliament off the ground. He had brought in experts on parliamentary procedure from abroad, organized workshops, and encouraged open debate. He also encouraged cooperation across party lines. "Some thought parliament would just be a rubber stamp, meeting fifteen minutes in occasional sessions, but I wanted it to be a real force, part of a system of checks and balances." He, too, had a long discussion with Clinton. When I spoke to him in 2018, he remembered her congratulating him on his success. "I was really surprised. No American had ever said this to me." He told her he wanted to learn from the US Congress. She suggested otherwise.

If the encounters in Naypyitaw were friendly, the meeting with Aung San Suu Kyi was like a reunion with a long-lost friend. The two women had never seen each other before, but they immediately embraced and kissed each other on the cheek, held hands during part of their joint news conference, and burst into laughter before hugging each other goodbye. Clinton had brought a gift for Aung San Suu Kyi's pet dog. They talked about the changes taking place, the long road ahead.

What was important, though, was not what was said but the visuals beamed across the world: Hillary Clinton and Aung San Suu Kyi happy together. It was the third part of a three-step move: Thein Sein's liberalization, Aung San Suu Kyi's acceptance of the constitution, and now this vividly clear blessing from the West.[15] Sanctions would soon be rolled back, first by the Norwegians.[16] What had taken place in the course of 2011 was not a transition to democracy, but greater political freedom combined with a rapprochement with the West.

ON NEW YEAR'S DAY, Nay Win Maung died from a heart attack. He was forty-nine years old. He had been a crucial catalyst in the reform process so far. He was also a coordinator. He had become a trusted aide of Aung Min and Soe Thane—the ministers closest to the president. And he had supported Shwe Mann in his attempts to bring life to the new parliament. To these most senior leaders he sent boxed sets of DVDs of *The West Wing* so they could better familiarize themselves with the workings of a democratic government. I communicated with him daily and saw him frequently, as did dozens of others, including diplomats and UN officials.

Over the previous months, he had begun to see his work bear fruit. He pushed himself harder as a result. Even after his heart attack in the early hours, before he died that morning, he was still on his mobile phone, relaying thoughts for the president's meeting with George Soros the next day. Shwe Mann, Soe Thane, and Aung Min immediately sent their condolences. Aung San Suu Kyi visited the Egress office a few days later, to pay her respects and see a photo display about Nay Win Maung's life put together by his former students. With his death, one of the few people who might have brought Burma's disparate factions together was gone. It was an irreparable loss.

For a while, though, the positive news kept coming. On January 12, a government team led by Aung Min agreed to a ceasefire with the Karen National Union, the oldest rebel group in Burma and the longest-running insurgency in the world. A day later, as part of a separate process shepherded by Soe Thane, hundreds of political prisoners were released, among them the organizers of the 1988 uprising, the Buddhist monks who led protests in 2007, and activists from many different ethnic minority communities. Freed as well that January was Khin Nyunt, the old spy chief who had been jailed in 2004. Not long after, the government would remove nearly all the 2,000 names on the official blacklist, effectively allowing anyone, including those who had until recently been seen as a threat to national security, to obtain a visa and come and go as they pleased.

Many of the reforms of 2011–12 were the results of efforts by individuals who took advantage of a new dynamic to finally do something positive for their country. Aung Min and Soe Thane were vital in convincing Thein Sein to take risks in a reformist direction. But others also played key roles. Aung Kyi, for example, was then minister of labor. Also a former army general, he was now working hard to stamp out one of the old regime's worst legacies: the use of forced labor. The practice had died down considerably over the past years, but legislation permitting it was still on the books. Because of this, Burma was under International Labour Organization restrictions, which in turn were linked to European Union sanctions. He coordinated with both Thein Sein and Shwe Mann to undo the legislation and then traveled to Geneva to negotiate a lifting of the restrictions. It was all touch-and-go. He had learned the critical importance of amending the law only forty-eight hours before going to Geneva, accidentally, from a visiting UK diplomat. He rushed to the airport to catch Thein Sein, who was about to take off on a trip to China. The amendments were rushed through just in time.[17]

Ye Htut was another who played a key role. A former army officer, he was deputy minister of information. He would soon be minister, as well as the president's spokesman. With the help of a German foundation, he had since 2008 been quietly training ministry staff in how to work in a more open media environment. Now he reached out to exiled media organizations such as the Democratic Voice of Burma, a radio station based in Norway. In early 2012, he organized a conference with the exiled journalists in Rangoon—people who would have been imprisoned if caught inside Burma just a year before. Later in the year, all censorship was ended.[18]

Over the course of 2012, hardliners—men who opposed the liberalizing reforms—were sidelined. They included the vice president, Tin Aung Myint Oo, who chaired powerful economic committees. "Our enemies are still our enemies," he said to Thein Sein at a top-level meeting. Like several others in senior circles, he thought Thein Sein was wrong in relying on outside advisors, who couldn't be trusted; he was getting too cosy with the West, giving away too much. His dissent, like that of the other hardliners, was based not on a strategic analysis or a clear alternative agenda, but on gut instinct.

That spring, things came to a head. Aung Min said he would resign unless the reforms already underway were further strengthened. The president took his side. The vice president then felt cornered and even feared arrest. In May, he retired to a Buddhist monastery and became a monk.

Thein Sein now had a freer hand. The reformist agenda was ascendant. Aung Min and Soe Thane were moved from their ministries (railways and industry) and placed in charge of the president's office as "coordinating ministers." Aung Min was responsible for all aspects of the peace process. Soe Thane was the economic czar. "We formed a protective layer for the president," explained Soe Thane. The reorganization also allowed the president to focus on the most strategic issues: he went from being nearly overwhelmed with decisions to dealing with a maximum of ten files a day.[19] Around the same time, the Myanmar Development Research Institute was established, as a think tank on the economy. The president also expanded his advisory team to include me and others as part of a new National Economic and Social Advisory Council. It was my first official appointment. At our first meeting, I argued that the proper management of new international aid was important, and that aid should be connected to a clear government agenda to fight poverty. I also said that international interest in Burma might not last long and that we had a very narrow window of opportunity, perhaps a year, to get things right.

The president's office was soon beefed up with the addition of Waiyan Moethone Thann, all of twenty-two years old and a recent graduate of Singapore Management University. Waiyan acted as assistant to both Aung Min and Soe Thane, and kept in touch daily, sometimes hourly, with me and with other advisors in Rangoon. His little office was about ten yards away from the ministers, and behind the office was a tiny room with a mattress on the floor. Fluent in both Burmese and English, Waiyan literally worked around the clock, taking calls overnight from Western capitals.

Foreign governments began offering ideas and assistance. So, too, did individuals. George Soros met the president and asked what might be most useful. Soe Thane requested experts to help reform public finances. Tony Blair came with suggestions on a range of issues, from cabinet procedure to communications. There were proposals to place people in the president's office for short periods as experts in different fields, such as communications. I asked a colleague whether having foreigners in the president's office was wise, from a security perspective. The colleague replied, "Don't worry. It will take any foreigner at least five years to understand anything about what's really going on here."

On April 1, 2012, by-elections were held, and the National League for

Democracy won a landslide forty-three out of forty-five seats. Aung San Suu Kyi became member of parliament for Kawhmu, a small town south of Rangoon. It was, as much as anything, a referendum on half a century of army rule. People were thrilled to be able to vote freely and show their disdain for the generals. There was growing, begrudging, respect for the ex-general Thein Sein, but he enjoyed nothing like the adulation reserved exclusively for Aung San Suu Kyi. What was clear in those days leading up to the polls was that the fear so prevalent just a year ago had disappeared. I remember jubilant NLD supporters, confident of victory, cheering wildly as they drove around downtown Rangoon in open-air trucks. Expectations were also rising, among many ordinary people and foreign observers, that all Burma's problems would soon be solved. The Americans and the European Union almost immediately relaxed sanctions. Burma was rejoining the world.

Aung San Suu Kyi then took her victory lap, with Thailand her first stop. It was her first time outside the country since 1987. Departing from a Rangoon plagued by chronic electricity shortages, and allowed by the pilot of the Thai Airways flight to join him in the cockpit, she found herself "completely fascinated" by the bright lights of Bangkok. She attended the East Asia Summit of the World Economic Forum, and received a standing ovation as she entered the conference hall to give a keynote address.[20]

She soon flew to Oslo to finally accept in person her 1991 Nobel Peace Prize, more than twenty years after the award was made. Just outside Oslo, she attended a conference on peace mediation. I was there, too, as was Soe Thane. One of the other attendees was Bono, who seemed curious about Soe Thane—the former junta man turned reformist—and asked to see him in private. I joined them, at Soe Thane's request. And so, for about an hour in a little room, the windows revealing a brightly lit Norwegian forest just outside, Soe Thane, Bono, and I talked about Burma and its potential. Bono was excited and drew attention specifically to a UK-led effort called the Extractive Industries Transparency Initiative, which aimed to improve the management of natural resources worldwide. "We're already working on it, Mr. Bono!" said Soe Thane. "Please come to Burma, Mr. Bono, and help us. We are trying our best and need all the help we can get."

Bono then whisked Aung San Suu Kyi off in his private plane to Ireland, where she received a prize from Amnesty International in a packed Dublin theater. Three hours of special performances followed, including songs by Bono and the cast of *Riverdance*. Bono admitted he was star-struck. A couple of days later, on her sixty-sixth birthday, Aung San Suu Kyi received an honorary degree from Oxford. John Le Carré, who also received an honorary degree that day, said, "It was magic." Eliza Manningham-Buller, the former head of MI5, was also there, and said, "I don't think there was a dry eye in the house."[21]

In London, Aung San Suu Kyi was given the very rare privilege of addressing both houses of Parliament. John Bercow, the Speaker of the House of Commons, described her as "the conscience of a country and a heroine for humanity." When she met Prince Charles that day at Clarence House, nearly all the staff gathered outside to watch her plant a tree in the garden. The prince joked, "Is nobody doing anything in the office today?" before turning to Aung San Suu Kyi to say, "They are all very pleased to see you."

In September, she was in Washington. At the White House, President Obama expressed his admiration for "her courage, determination, and personal sacrifice." And at the Capitol rotunda, in front of a packed gathering of American political leaders, she was given the Congressional Gold Medal, the country's highest civilian award, which she had been awarded in absentia four years before; George Washington, the Dalai Lama, and Pope John Paul II were past recipients. "It's almost too delicious to believe, my friend," said Hillary Clinton.[22] John McCain called her his "hero." Mitch McConnell compared her to Gandhi and Martin Luther King. Laura Bush was there, too, and credited her for "breaking the legitimacy" of the military regime. Aung San Suu Kyi called the day "one of the most moving days of my life."[23] She thanked everyone for their steadfast support during the dark days of dictatorship, and graciously acknowledged "the reform measures instituted by President U Thein Sein." Aung Min was in town on a separate trip, and watched from the side.

THERE IS A MYTH in the West that Burma's reforms in 2011 were the result of a desire to tilt away from China. The truth was much more complex. But there was one person in the top leadership who, though not anti-China, was keen to bring the country as close to the West as possible. That person was Soe Thane.

Soe Thane was born a little more than a year after Burma's independence, at the height of the civil war, in Twante, a little town just west of Rangoon. From childhood he knew that he wanted to join the navy. After graduating top of his class at the Defense Services Academy, he took part in operations around the country, against Karen rebels in the Irrawaddy delta, bandits in Arakan, and around the islands off Mergui. This was in the 1960s and 1970s, when Burma had few international contacts.

In 1979, the up-and-coming naval officer was chosen to be part of the Burmese military delegation that attended the funeral of Earl Mountbatten of Burma, a much-loved figure in Burma. As Allied commander in Southeast Asia during the Second World War, he had decided to aid the Burmese partisans led by Aung San (Aung San Suu Kyi's father), at a time when many British Army chiefs wanted them strung up as erstwhile Japanese collaborators. Until he was assassinated by the Irish Republican Army near his summer home in Ireland, Mountbatten maintained a friendly relationship with Burmese leaders, including the autocrat Ne Win.

The trip was Soe Thane's first time overseas. Together with five other young officers, Soe Thane arrived four days before the actual funeral, staying at a little bed and breakfast in Bayswater, central London. The Burmese embassy had given them only three pounds a day to live on, so the men settled on daily meals of fermented fish paste (the Burmese condiment of choice) which they had brought in a little jar from home, spread over nan bread bought from an Indian restaurant next door. London in the late 1970s was an eye-opener for them. Soe Thane visited the British Museum, Madame Tussaud's, and Foyle's bookshop. "And the buses ran on time!" he told me. He was very impressed.

After the funeral, he stayed on as an official guest of the British government, which put him up at the Hyde Park Hotel ("full of sheiks"). He was now with his boss, Admiral Chit Hlaing, who told him it was English custom to slip ten pounds under the pillow every morning for the maids ("Don't forget!"). They traveled together to Portsmouth for a naval exhibition, and the British sold them a corvette warship on loan. These were the days when Western militaries had no compunction about helping the Burmese. He rode in a hovercraft for the first time.

A few years later, he went to Denmark to buy an Osprey gunboat with a loan from the Danish governmental aid agency (ostensibly to guard fisheries), and spent a month training in the North Sea. Soe Thane loved his time in Denmark. He remembers the cleanliness, the well-lit highways, and the "well-to-do people who rode public transportation."

Soe Thane didn't care much about politics. "I joined the navy to see the world," he said. He rose through the ranks, and by 2005 was navy chief and a member of the ruling junta. By then the West was off-limits, so he encouraged ties with India, visiting the country often and sending his men there for courses. By 2010, Soe Thane was the only Western-trained officer left in the Burmese military leadership. By 2011, he was the principal architect of the normalization of ties with the West.

Soe Thane was very unusual for a Burmese minister. Whereas others tended to shun foreigners, he sought them out. At diplomatic receptions, other ministers liked to stay in a penned area together with just their host ambassador. Soe Thane eagerly mixed in the crowd. He deliberately imitated what he considered the ways of a Western government or organization. He had visitors sit around a "working table." And he wanted to send a generation of Burmese youngsters to the best universities in Europe and America.

In 2012, Soe Thane was pushing hard on multiple fronts for an end to Western sanctions. He went to Davos for the annual economic forum and hobnobbed with top businessmen and political leaders. Short, with little round glasses and a ready smile, he became Burma's main cheerleader abroad, speaking frankly but optimistically about the country's prospects and the challenges facing his boss, whom he referred to as "Mr. President."

He negotiated the visits of a slew of Western leaders, and was keen to direct the aid that was now beginning to flow into the country. At a meeting with visiting Danish prime minister Helle Thorning-Schmidt, he responded to her comments on democracy, media freedom, and the remaining political prisoners by saying, "Don't worry, we will take care of all that. From Denmark what we need is help with dairy. Please help us set up a dairy industry." He would not take no for an answer.

He also arranged President Thein Sein's trips to London, New York, and Washington. I worked with him in writing speeches and talking points. In New York, Henry Kissinger dropped by to "see with my own eyes the generals who were giving up power."

BARACK OBAMA CAME to Burma in November 2012. Ulysses Grant had visited in 1879 as part of a post-retirement round-the-world tour. Herbert Hoover worked in Burma as a mining engineer at the turn of the century. And Richard Nixon made a trip as vice president, stepping out of his motorcade to confront left-wing student protesters on the side of the road. But Obama was the first sitting US president to visit Burma.

From the airport to Rangoon, tens of thousands lined up to cheer the leader of the free world. His arrival represented for many Burma's readmission to the international community, after a quarter century of self-imposed isolation and then twenty more years of Western sanctions. Along the way, he turned to his assistant secretary of state for Asia, Kurt Campbell, and said, "Tell me about Burma." In his memoir, Campbell wrote that he gave the president a ten-minute "abbreviated history of this most enchanting, vexed place." He told Obama of the country's "still pristine hardwood forests, raging rivers, and native tigers," the "many contending and distrustful ethnic groups," and "years of brutal, unrelenting military rule."

As they passed the towering Shwedagon Pagoda, Campbell declared, "No visit to Burma is complete really without a visit to the Shwedagon." Obama replied, "If it's so amazing, why aren't we going?" The Secret Service had earlier vetoed the idea, not least because it meant they and everyone else would have to enter the pagoda precincts barefoot. Obama insisted. And so they made an impromptu stop, performing a little ceremony at the shrine for people born on a Friday (as Obama had been) and ringing a giant bronze bell with a wooden stick.[24]

Obama then called on Thein Sein, remarking on "the incredible potential of this beautiful country." Thein Sein said his meetings with Obama "were the best of all his meetings with foreign visitors": friendly, businesslike, and productive. Obama then met Aung San Suu Kyi, who spoke at length about the minutiae of the current political scene. "The young people have very high expectations," she told him, "and of course we don't want to let them down."[25]

The highlight of the short (six-hour) visit was a speech at Rangoon University. The messaging was perfect: it was the site of first anti-colonial and then anti-military regime protests; its sorry state was symbolic of all that was wrong with Burma's past. Hundreds of leading figures from across Burma's political spectrum were in the spruced-up Convocation Hall, with Hillary Clinton sitting next to Aung San Suu Kyi.

I was there too. Obama gave a stirring speech. In a country used to generals and bureaucrats reading long-winded papers, it was without a doubt the best speech any Burmese in the room had ever heard. "Something is happening in this country that cannot be reversed," Obama said, "and the will of the people can lift up this nation and set a great example for the world.

"It was here that U Thant learned the ways of the world before guiding it at the United Nations. . . . This country, like my own country, is blessed with diversity. Not everybody looks the same. Not everybody comes from the same region. Not everybody worships in the same way. . . . I say this because my own country and my own life have taught me the power of diversity." He received a standing ovation.

An hour later, on *Air Force One*, Obama went over to his close aide Ben Rhodes and said, "That was worth doing."[26]

THE STORY HAD CHANGED, but the world saw only a fairytale. Few did their homework to really understand what was driving the positive momentum and how best to keep it going.

By 2013, there was a deepening split between the president and Soe Thane on the one side and Shwe Mann on the other, more a personal falling-out than a difference in worldview. As Aung San Suu Kyi drew closer to Shwe Mann, her relationship with Thein Sein steadily deteriorated. In September 2012, Aung San Suu Kyi was still very positive about the government and her partnership with it. A few months later, she was warning Obama, "We have to be very careful that we are not lured by a mirage of success."[27] Those wanting simply to support change found themselves divided between the two different camps. After our first meeting I tried several times, over many months, to see Aung San Suu Kyi again as she had suggested, but without success—likely because some around her felt that I had become too close to a presidential team she no longer trusted.

There were also other warning lights flashing. Over the summer of 2011, the seventeen-year-old ceasefire in the north between the army and the Kachin Independence Organization broke down, leading to all-out war. In Arakan, over the summer and autumn of 2012, savage clashes between Buddhist and Muslim communities left almost 200 people dead and around 140,000 displaced. And in Rangoon and Naypyitaw, with the easier economic reforms out of the way, the entire future of the economy seemed up for grabs.

There had been an alignment of the stars: at exactly the same moment when Washington was looking for ways to engage the Burmese generals, the generals did just enough to justify that engagement. This dynamic led to greater political freedom for the Burmese than any time in half a century, and a rapprochement with the West. But now, deeper issues around race and money were coming to the fore.

SEVEN

BLOOD AND BELONGING

To ACHIEVE SUCCESS, it was worth trying the unexpected. Aung Min told me he had watched *Lawrence of Arabia* and drew lessons from the Englishman's unorthodox ways. In 2011, he became the government's chief peace negotiator. Whereas Soe Thane was an extrovert with long-time experience of the West, a halting English speaker who enjoyed foreign company and thought in broad strategic terms, Aung Min was the opposite, an introverted former intelligence officer who spoke next to no English, had never been to the West, and who always looked for tactical advantage.

Aung Min was a much decorated soldier who had survived a Communist ambush that killed all twelve others in his column, then killed seventeen of the insurgents single-handedly before help arrived.[1] He was also an intensely practical man. In the late 2000s, as minister of railways, he was keen that his ministry win at least one medal in the annual inter-ministry sports tournament. To ensure this, he had an aide go to Chinatown in Rangoon and find the best ping-pong player he could, give him a contract as a Railways Ministry employee, and enter him in the tournament. He won a gold medal.

He was an accidental soldier. He had attended the prestigious St. Paul's School in Rangoon, and took the exams for the Defense Services Academy on a whim. He thought he would serve just the minimum four years. But within eleven months he received an award for bravery after his encounter in the jungle with the Communists, and was recruited to hunt down Communist leaders. A few years later, he joined the intelligence service, first serving in Mandalay, where he had to deal with dissidents, black marketeers, narcotics traffickers, and "underground" leftists. He drew the line at imprisoning a suspected dissident's wife who had just given birth— but not for sentimental reasons. "If you imprison her, this baby will be your enemy for life," he said. All his colleagues thought that was the end of Aung Min's career. Instead, he was promoted.

In Rangoon, he was part of the powerful Section 6 of the intelligence services: the administration department. This was the section that looked after the top brass and their families. The children of the generals often got into trouble, and any scandal had to be handled sensitively. There were also more mundane tasks. One day, Aung Min and his immediate superior were told to bring dinner for the then dictator Ne Win, who wanted Chinese takeout. They went to Chinatown, then to Ne Win's residence on Ady Road, where they presented him with what the other officer said was Mandalay kung pao chicken. Ne Win seemed annoyed and brusquely asked, "Why do you have to say *Mandalay* kung pao chicken, why not just kung pao chicken?" The dictator's anger froze the other officer. Aung Min stepped forward and said, "Mandalay kung pao chicken is the preferred type of kung pao chicken, eaten by rich Chinese. Rangoon kung pao chicken is an inferior dish, with mainly gristle."[2] From then on, Aung Min was in charge of all catering.

There were more promotions to come. In the late 1990s, he left intelligence and received a series of increasingly senior appointments in the army, including as a regional commander. In 2003, he became minister of railways. He bought new trains from Japan, China, and India, but didn't have the budget to do much more. In 2008, he met Nay Win Maung, whose parents had been his lecturers at the academy. Nay Win Maung and the rest of the team at Egress began to change his thinking. He met Debbie Aung Din (who had met George Bush after Nargis). He felt he had power but didn't know what to do with it, like "a monkey with a coconut."[3] He wanted Burma to have a better future, and that, he was increasingly certain, meant marrying knowledge with power. It also meant being fearless. "If I'm given responsibility, I won't look back."

On August 18, 2011, a little more than four months after taking office, President Thein Sein formally invited the leaders of the insurgent groups to new peace talks. He didn't have a clear strategy, but he knew that his core agenda of economic development would be constrained unless he could also find an end to Burma's seven decades of armed conflict. He appointed Aung Min negotiator—at first, one of several. His orders were clear: do not agree to anything that might lead to the breakup of the country or damage Burma's sovereignty. Otherwise, anything is acceptable.

Within weeks, Thein Sein received a positive response from the country's oldest insurgent group, the Karen National Union. The Karen lived across the south of Burma. They included both Buddhist and Christians, but in the eastern hills most villages, as well as the leadership of the KNU itself, were primarily Baptist. Colonial-era maps showed the Karen Hills as only "loosely" administered. In 1947, the KNU demanded independence. Their aim now was for autonomy within a federal union.

The KNU controlled a sliver of territory along the Thai border and had over 5,000 well-trained men (and some women) under arms. Over 400,000 Karen villagers had been driven from their homes over recent decades. Nearly 100,000 fled to Thailand as refugees, and some were resettled in America. Thein Sein sent Aung Min to the Thai town of Mae Sot, on the border, where the KNU leadership was based.

From the start, Aung Min acted completely differently than any past Burmese general or envoy. He eschewed the existing bureaucracy, preferring to depend on the Egress team to arrange the visit. He arrived in Bangkok with no fanfare and drove in a private car to Mae Sot. The journey took place during the epic floods of 2011, so what should have been a six-hour drive took fifteen hours. At first, the meetings were businesslike, even tense. The KNU were unsure what to make of the spectacle: a former general, with an NGO entourage, coming to their town without any security, inviting them to his hotel suite, and asking them to trust him. Aung Min brought with him an invitation from Thein Sein to come to Naypyitaw. Before leaving, Aung Min asked KNU deputy leader Zipporah Sein whether he could report back that there was at least a 50 percent chance they would accept. Zipporah Sein whispered, "You can make it 75 percent."

There were other early moves. Thein Sein wanted peace as well with the Shan State Army North, another major ethnic-based insurgency. At Aung Min's request, the president released their general, Hso Ten, who was serving a 106-year prison sentence. The very day of the release, Aung Min invited the rebel officer to his house for dinner, making sure it was an early dinner as he knew that in prison Hso Ten would have eaten his last meal each day at 4 p.m. Over the coming weeks, he would meet with the leaders of another prominent rebel group, the Restoration Council of Shan State, as well as with the KNU and several other armed organizations. He worked incessantly. After one meeting, he told me, "I may not know much, but I know how to deal with a man who has a gun in one hand and a bottle of whiskey in the other."

Over the coming year, Aung Min negotiated no fewer than a dozen ceasefires. He kept the president regularly updated but acted decisively on his own, going back to his boss after the fact and saying, "You can fire or jail me if you want, but this is what I've done." The momentum seemed incredible and, in 2012, it added to the overall feeling that Burma was finally breaking free of its past and heading in a peaceful and democratic direction. Until then, the very word "federalism" had been taboo in official circles. But Aung Min knew that the idea of a federal system of government was important to ethnic minority leaders, and saw no danger in accepting this in principle. He convinced a reluctant Thein Sein.

He told me that around this time he also "started giving the president a lot of strange ideas," things that went well beyond the repertoire of past army regimes.[4] One strange idea was the Myanmar Peace Center. By early 2012, it was clear that Aung Min couldn't just rely on the ad hoc support of Egress and various hangers-on. There needed to be a new institution to support continuing peace talks. After Nay Win Maung's death, two men—Tin Maung Thann (the fish expert) and Hla Maung Shwe (the shrimp exporter)—had taken over as the heads of Egress. They were now Aung Min's key lieutenants in the peace process.

Over several weeks, we discussed options. The president decided on a three-part structure: a Myanmar Peace Center as a quasi-government institution, a Myanmar Peace Fund to mobilize and direct international financing for development in places where the fighting had stopped, and a Peace Donor Support Group. This last was meant to be a bridge between Aung Min and the growing number of governments and organizations (like the World Bank) keen to be involved in what looked an imminent success.

I was made one of four special advisors, and would attend most of the formal negotiations in the years to come. My particular focus was anything to do with foreign governments and international organizations. I often sat in on Aung Min's meetings with visiting foreigners, interpreting for him as needed. Sometimes Aung Min gave very detailed and candid explanations of the dynamics at work. Other times, he would say a few words and then say to me in Burmese, "Just add whatever you think the foreigners want to hear." If I added anything, it was to underscore both the urgency as well as the complexity of the situation, the big hills left to climb. Aung Min's instincts were to show that he was different from past generals and to open the door as wide as possible to outside help. My instincts were to be very careful in not allowing the global peace-building industry to gain too big a foothold. I had seen from my perch at the UN in New York too many well-meaning efforts based on far too little local knowledge.

Over that year, the Myanmar Peace Center, or MPC, grew to over a hundred staff, mainly young Burmese, many from Egress, some newly returned from overseas. They worked around the clock from a compound of colonial-era houses in the middle of Rangoon. The MPC acted as well as an unofficial secretariat for the president's office, assisting in everything from the president's weekly radio addresses to the deluge of foreign visitors. Neither government body nor NGO, it was a many-tentacled organization tailored specifically for the political environment of 2012–13. Tony Blair dropped by one day. Bill Clinton came to give a speech. Western governments, the European Union, and Japan queued up to provide funding, eager to be part of one of the most successful peace processes in recent times.

Burma was not, however, on the verge of peace. The ceasefires signed were significant, but they didn't include any of the big rebel armies on the Chinese border. Many of the leaders of those armies—which had agreed to the earlier generation of ceasefires—had been doing business with the Burmese army since the 1980s. Aung Min was initially instructed only to focus on the Karen National Union and other rebel groups along the Thai border, and leave relations with Chinese border insurgencies to other ex-generals, the same men who had been in charge of them for years, and who were following old instincts and old motivations, trading in money and power. But the earlier ceasefires were unraveling. In 2008, the junta had attacked the Kokang militia. In 2011, tensions between the Burmese army and the Kachin Independence Organization boiled over into all-out war.

When the KIO refused to become a Border Guard Force, the army responded by blocking KIO trading routes. The KIO then shot and killed a Burmese battalion commander after he led troops into KIO territory without prior agreement. In June 2011, clashes broke out between the two sides at a Chinese-operated dam. Within days, the KIO placed all troops on a war footing and destroyed a number of bridges in the area to prevent government resupply of bases.[5] The Burmese army then attacked KIO positions, first along the Taiping River and then all across the ceasefire line.

What followed was the bloodiest fighting in Burma in decades. By the end of the year, Burmese forces were inching over frost-covered hills toward the KIO headquarters at Laiza, a town of about 50,000 people on the Chinese border, deploying Russian-built helicopters to transport troops and supplies. Hundreds of troops on both sides were killed or wounded, and thousands of civilians displaced. Before Christmas, Thein Sein ordered the army not to take Laiza itself.

In the spring of 2012, with a string of successful negotiations behind him, Aung Min was asked by the president to try his hand at ending the Kachin fighting too. From the start, he wanted to try something different, and went to Maijayang, in KIO-held territory, to meet directly with Kachin leaders. Venturing into enemy territory during an active conflict was something no Burmese envoy had done in decades. Just getting to Maijayang was no easy feat, as it meant crossing several front lines. Aung Min and his team passed dozens of burnt-out villages. They could smell the stench of death. A Burmese battalion commander constantly hovered over him. "Are you afraid I will try to escape?" Aung Min asked. "No, I am responsible for your life, minister," was the reply.

There were many more meetings. There were also quiet gestures. Aung Min sent a set of expensive golf clubs from the president to the Kachin commander, Sumlut Gun Maw. He assumed Gun Maw would want to keep the gift discreet. But a few weeks later, Aung Min received a photograph Gun Maw had taken of himself, with the clubs and in full golfing attire, at the Laiza Golf Club.

In October 2012, Chinese diplomats insisted on a role. Talks had been going reasonably well and the Chinese government convened a high-level negotiation at Ruili, across the border inside China. Ruili was a boomtown, with bustling shopping centers and high-rise hotels, which had become prosperous from Burmese jade and timber. Aung Min wanted to move discussions toward an actual deal to separate forces, to prevent future clashes, and worked frantically to secure senior Burmese army participation. But the KIO, in what was perceived on the Burmese side as a snub, didn't send any of their top leaders to Ruili. It's possible that the KIO were irked by continuing Burmese attacks, or that they had not yet reached an internal consensus on a new ceasefire. They were also unfamiliar with the new politics in Naypyitaw, and unaware of the political capital Aung Min had to expend to secure army participation. Regardless, the snub weakened Aung Min's hand with the Burmese military.

Fighting raged again, including around the fabulously lucrative jade mines at Hpakant, leading to thousands more men, women, and children fleeing their homes. In a fresh offensive near the KIO headquarters of Laiza, government forces reportedly lost over a hundred troops with four hundred more wounded, as the Kachin put up spirited resistance. The Burmese army used Russian-made Mi-35 helicopter gunships for the first time, the kind that had been used during the Soviet invasion of Afghanistan, as well as Karakorum-8 jet fighters bought from China years before.[6] This use of airpower marked a major escalation and worried the Chinese.

In January 2013, the Burmese army, now within a mile of Laiza, fired artillery directly into the town, killing civilians. Shells also landed on the Chinese side of the border. This was a wake-up call to senior echelons in Beijing. The vice foreign minister Fu Ying and deputy army chief Qi Jianguo both arrived in Naypyitaw to discuss "border stability." The Chinese then called both sides to a new round of talks in Ruili, and assertively attempted to direct them. Their negotiator suggested a very formal process, in which the Chinese would meet with each side first in different rooms before everyone met together in one room. Both the Burmese government and the Kachins piped up, "But we know each other already!" The Chinese pushed. Aung Min at one point told them, "This has nothing to do with you!" and shut the door. In a way, Chinese heavy-handedness helped to bring the two sides together.

At last, in May 2013, a final round of negotiations were held, not in China but in the Kachin state capital, Myitkyina. By then, thousands were dead and up to 100,000 civilians had been displaced by the fighting. A Chinese envoy, Wang Yifan, was there, as well as a senior UN diplomat, Vijay Nambiar. It was the first time the KIO had set foot in government-controlled territory since fighting had broken out nearly two years before.

Heading their delegation was their charismatic army vice chief, General Sumlut Gun Maw. A few years before, many Kachins had felt that the KIO's top leaders were too eagerly stuffing their own pockets, along with their Burmese counterparts. Gun Maw was of a younger generation. The recent conflict had aroused deep nationalist feelings among the Kachin. They knew the KIO had put up a tough fight against overwhelming odds.

When a seven-point agreement was signed, hundreds of Burmese reporters were there to cover the event. Gun Maw received a hero's welcome along the streets of Myitkyina. It was impossible not to feel the raw emotion of thousands of ordinary Kachin people as they cheered Gun Maw's convoy. The Burmese in Myitkyina seemed like an occupying power. I could only hope that a just and lasting peace would be possible before too long, so that another generation, Burmese and Kachin, wouldn't have to fight this senseless war. But any rational analysis suggested we were still far off. One of the senior Chinese diplomats said to me, "If we were serious, we would be looking at revenue substitution." He meant weaning the men with guns away from illicit money. No one had even begun to talk about the economy.

With the Kachin agreement, the peace process reached its high-water mark. The image of a Burma heading toward inevitable peace and democracy was stronger than ever. Foreign governments jostled for pole position. Many provided financing for ethnic armed group negotiators. They funded visiting experts and teams of consultants. Hardly a day went by without a Western nongovernmental organization proffering help and looking for a role.

The idea of a "Nationwide Ceasefire Agreement" was now introduced. The proposal was first made by several ethnic minority leaders, who wanted to avoid a situation in which the government could divide and rule. By the summer of 2013, Aung Min came to see this as a useful aim as well: it could lock all sides, including his side, into a political process, especially if there was maximum fanfare and international acclaim. The nationwide agreement was originally meant to be a simple document which would repeat key elements from the ceasefires already agreed, such as a commitment to end fighting, set up liaison offices, and seek a negotiated peace.

Many of the ethnic minority leaders began to sense that what the government wanted was not just a step toward peace but a political victory as well. Elections were two years away. A nationwide ceasefire agreement would provide a very attractive feather for Thein Sein's cap. So some began pushing for a new, more political agreement that would go well beyond the terms of the existing ceasefires. Time would not be on their side.

In November 2013, top representatives of seventeen "Ethnic Armed Organizations" (their preferred moniker) met in an unprecedented summit at Laiza, the Kachin headquarters. There they attempted to hash out how best to negotiate the proposed nationwide accord. There was much heated debate. Some saw the need to move quickly. They had waited their entire lives for this moment, and wanted to use the positive momentum. Others distrusted the government's sincerity. And there was inertia: after seventy years of fighting, some were settled into a way of life. Peace, after all, meant change.

A set of eleven principles was nevertheless agreed upon, which included the aims of a "federal union" and a "federal army." They also included the demand that "the fundamental rights of the *taing-yintha* (indigenous) people" be defended. The drafting of the points was done overnight by a Baptist theologian named Lian Hmung Sakhong. "People ask me how I drafted these eleven points overnight," he told me. "The answer is simple: these have been my feelings for my whole life."[7]

Lian Sakhong, a tall man with hooded eyes and a broad smile, was a Chin and the descendant of Chin chiefs. The Chins (known in India as Mizos) are a tribal people who were independent until about a hundred years ago, when the British divided their upland territory between Burma and Assam. Many later converted to Christianity. At Rangoon University in the 1980s, Lian Sakhong first thought of becoming a doctor, then a writer, before training to be a pastor in the North American Baptist Convention. He was from early on attracted to the ideals of freedom and democracy. On Friday nights he watched movies at the US embassy's American Center, which had been set up in the 1950s and was one of the very few outside institutions never dismantled. After the 1988 uprising, he felt strongly that there should be an ethnic minority element and perspective in the struggle against military dictatorship.

Lian Sakhong came to believe that federalism was essential for equality. By this, he meant that places like the Chin hills should govern themselves as part of a "Union of Burma." He also came to fear arrest. By 1990, he had fled to India, where relatives were able to secure him an Indian passport. He applied for asylum in the West. Once Aung San Suu Kyi won a Nobel Prize, it was easy; he merely went to the Delhi office of the UN High Commissioner for Refugees and showed them a photo of himself with Aung San Suu Kyi. He was offered asylum in Sweden. "Great! Abba!" he thought. That was all he knew about his new home.[8]

For the next twenty years, Lian Sakhong tried, from Sweden, to draw attention to the plight of ethnic minorities in Burma. No one was interested. It was too complicated and muddied the simple story around Aung San Suu Kyi and the generals. He completed a PhD at Uppsala University, all the while talking, debating, attending conferences, and keeping in touch with allies along Burma's borders, including in the different armed organizations.

In 2011, he was excited about Thein Sein's invitation to peace talks. He had met Ye Htut (the president's spokesman) the year before and had been impressed. Until then, he had no idea that there were "thoughtful people like that in the regime."

The Chin National Front, with which Lian Sakhong was affiliated, signed a ceasefire agreement in early 2012. In late 2013 Lian Sakhong, now with salt-and-pepper hair, became a core member of the negotiation team on the side of what were now officially called the Ethnic Armed Organizations. He was often at the Myanmar Peace Center, for both formal and informal talks. There were others who came back from overseas, men like Harn Yawnghwe, son of Burma's first president and an ethnic Shan, who had been in exile since his father's imprisonment at the hands of Ne Win in the 1960s. He too became a key player. At the Myanmar Peace Center, Aung Min recruited not just the old Egress team but an assortment of others, including former exiles and even former insurgents. They included Min Zaw Oo (the former rebel and PhD from George Mason University) and Kyaw Yin Hlaing (who had a PhD from Cornell University and had been teaching for Egress).

The two sides worked together well. They were amazingly compatible, at least on the surface. After formal talks there were invariably boisterous dinners, sometimes leading to karaoke singing. There was much use of the word "trust" and a free flow of whiskey. But was it all just a show of bonhomie? I couldn't tell. I remember a UN colleague, an experienced mediator, who told me that the peace talks that were the most successful were the ones in which the hatreds were visible and the sides trusted the process but not each other. Here, there was familiarity, but the process seemed to be lacking in a strategic direction.

I worked closely with a project set up by my wife, Sofia, called the Beyond Ceasefires Initiative. She had worked at the UN for many years as well, most recently with the peace process in Nepal. Our idea was a simple one: to bring people who had led successful peace processes in other countries to Burma, and have them share their experiences with their Burmese counterparts. These included the former UN mediators in Georgia, Libya, Guatemala, Burundi, Liberia, East Timor, and Colombia. It also included both the Nepal Royal Army's top negotiator and his principal counterpart from the Maoist rebels.

We wanted to make sure the issues our visitors came to discuss were the ones most relevant to what was happening at that time in the peace process. We worked carefully with both ethnic armed group leaders and Aung Min's team to identify the issues. We also wanted to make sure the foreigners, even though they would be speaking about their own experiences, understood the local context. We spent weeks preparing them.

Perhaps most importantly, we spent a lot of time on language and translation. I had been to many meetings where a good part of what was said was mistranslated and 100 percent of the nuance was lost. Burmese is a wonderful language for telling stories and expressing human feelings and experiences, but it is not very good for expressing policy ideas. Many words related to government are neologisms. "Human rights" is translated as *lu-akwint-ye*, where the word for "right" is the same as the word for "license" or "opportunity"; it's related to the word meaning an opportunist. The words for "economic" and "business" are the same: *si-bwa-ye*. So an economist is literally a business expert.

At one of our first events, over a hundred people involved in the peace process from all sides came to listen to Nepali general Shiv Ram Pradhan and Maoist commander Comrade Pasang talk about how they had loathed each other at first ("I wanted to kill him!") but learned to work together as friends. General Shiv Ram said that his army had been reluctant to engage in talks, and had seen UN involvement as an insult, even thinking at times of overthrowing the government in order to scuttle the negotiations. But in the end, with peace, everyone, including the army, was much better off. We made sure his remarks were properly translated.

We worked hard on the Beyond Ceasefires Initiative. Others worked harder. Aung Min himself was tireless, traveling around the country to the most remote rebel bases, then to Naypyitaw to see the army and report to the president, trying to keep everyone on track. But by 2014, the peace process was hitting one roadblock after another. Clashes continued, especially between the Burmese army and the Kachin despite the earlier agreement. Sometimes these were because of local misunderstandings, when small companies of soldiers inadvertently came into contact with one another. Other times, they were the result of one side trying to maximize its position before whatever came next. The negotiations for the nationwide ceasefire agreement also proved to be a nightmare. What was meant to be a catalyst for further quick advances became a drag. The formal discussions were like UN drafting sessions, with literally hours, if not days, spent on a single word or the positioning of a subordinate clause. And the swirl of foreign and press attention began to make progress increasingly tough to achieve, as everyone played to the galleries.

The Chinese watched the unfolding landscape in Burma with increasing alarm. They had long advised the Burmese to reform, make up with the West, get sanctions lifted, and stop being an embarrassment to them at the UN Security Council. But they were not prepared for a genuinely freer and more democratic Burma, which not only "suspended" big Chinese projects such as the Myitsone dam but seemed to be embracing the West with abandon. Their concern sharpened when the old ceasefires began to break down and fighting intensified along the common frontier. Refugees fleeing into the People's Republic were bad enough, but stray shells killing civilians inside China, as they would several times over these years, was an affront to their dignity.

As the Chinese watched the peace talks inch ahead, they saw the European Union and the Norwegians in leading roles. They also saw the Japanese becoming ever more influential. The Nippon Foundation positioned itself as a broker, funding all sides and then attempting to bring them together. Tokyo appointed Yohei Nishikawa, head of the Nippon Foundation, as its special envoy to the peace process. Nishikawa's father, Ryoichi Nishikawa, had been a prominent supporter of the Japanese military during the Second World War. Yohei Nishikawa was now a regular feature of the peace talks, often dressed in full Burmese costume. The Chinese, whose own popular history of the Second World War was of brutal mistreatment by the Japanese invaders, were not impressed.

The Chinese were even more perturbed when, in April 2014, General Gun Maw of the Kachin Independence Organization traveled to Washington. The very notion that the Americans were now influencing insurgent armies right on their border was a troubling one. Gun Maw met with an array of senior State and Defense Department officials, including UN ambassador Samantha Power. On his arrival, assistant secretary for human rights Tom Malinowski escorted Gun Maw to the Lincoln Memorial. Malinowski later affirmed the close ties of "the Kachin and American people" going back to the Second World War.

From the Chinese perspective, it got worse. By 2015, it wasn't just the border groups going to Washington; it was Washington coming to the border. In January that year, a visiting American delegation held a "human rights dialogue" in Naypyitaw, and this was followed by discussions in Myitkyina, the Kachin capital, about 60 miles from China. Those in the delegation included General Anthony Crutchfield, the deputy commander of the US Pacific fleet. The leadership in Beijing started to take notice: fighting was bad, but the wrong kind of peace could be worse.

Just four weeks after Crutchfield's visit, a heavily armed ethnic

Chinese militia crossed into Burma and seized the Kokang town of Laukkai, leading to weeks of heavy fighting. The militia was loyal to Peng Jiasheng, the warlord who had been ousted by the Burmese from his Kokang base following the first round of fighting in 2009. He was now trying to claw his way back into the picture, and perhaps win a seat at the peace talks.

The fighting sent 60,000 refugees, nearly all ethnic Chinese, into China. On Weibo, a Chinese social media site, Peng used images of these refugees and appeals to racial solidarity to crowd-fund financial support. The Chinese government allowed him to open a bank account to receive the money. It also allowed Peng's troops to quietly use Chinese territory to outflank Burmese positions.[9] The Burmese responded with air strikes. In March 2015, Burmese Air Force jets accidentally bombed inside China, killing four civilians. The Chinese military establishment reacted angrily, promising "resolute measures to protect the safety of Chinese people and their assets."[10]

Beijing now had to take a hard look at the situation. Continued fighting was not in Chinese interest. The border needed to be stable, not least to facilitate the growing trade and economic ties they wanted. But an accord reached through a Western- and Japanese-supported process was not ideal, especially if it led to anything resembling international peacekeepers, or even foreign ceasefire monitors, on China's southwestern flank.

By this time, Burma was looking less and less like a country on the verge of what negotiators called *htawara-nyeinchan-yay,* "permanent" or "everlasting" peace. Over 100,000 people had been displaced in fresh fighting since the peace process began, and another 100,000 temporarily displaced by the battle for Kokang. UN aid agencies estimated a million people in need of humanitarian assistance.[11]

But there was a deeper problem. The peace process began as a quest for ceasefires between the new government and the Burmese army's long-time battlefield opponents. But who should be involved? Was this simply an armed conflict between government and rebels, or an inter-ethnic struggle between the majority Burmese and ethnic minorities? Whose voice was important, and whose voice was legitimate?

Many of the people actually negotiating on the ethnic armed group side were political figures, motivated by long-held political beliefs and divorced from the war economies of the border. The biggest rebel group of all, the United Wa State Army, chose to stay on the sidelines and didn't attend any of the talks. Also not present at the table were the Border Guard Forces or any of the literally hundreds of militias, most allied to government and often neck-deep in illicit industries. These smaller militias seemed a breed apart, but it seemed unlikely that any peace deal could be sustained without their consent. And the National League for Democracy and Aung San Suu Kyi were not involved at all.

It wasn't clear who really spoke for whom. Were the armed groups the principal voices of the minorities they claimed to represent? Nor was it clear whether the aim was simply an end to fighting (in which case, an old-style ceasefire with lucrative business deals might have done the trick), or the start of an effort to completely remake state–society relations. If the latter, who had the legitimacy to decide? For the army and the insurgents, legitimacy came from fighting. The more the peace process became the flagship of Burma's reform drive, the more it was the men with guns who held the cards.

There was also an even deeper problem. The peace process did nothing to address questions of identity, and how Burma should see itself as a multiracial and multicultural country. The concepts and language of indigenousness were assumed. The peace process was about the "indigenous peoples of Burma" finding a new formula to live together. But there were other ethnicities, other identities, and the shadow of colonial-era race-based conflicts in play. They would now retake center stage.

ON THE EVENING OF May 28, 2012, three men killed a woman named Thida Htwe, near her village in southern Arakan. The story quickly spread that the three men were "Bengali Muslims" and that the woman had been raped as well as murdered. Five days later, a mob attacked a bus in a nearby town, believing the culprits were on board. Ten people, all Muslims, died in the assault. In the weeks that followed, both Rohingya Muslim and Arakanese Buddhist gangs destroyed shops and houses belonging to the other's community. Over 75,000 people were forced to flee their homes.[12]

In Maungdaw, in the far north of Arakan on the border with Bangladesh, clashes began on June 8 with the torching of several Muslim houses. Muslims comprised four-fifths of the population of Maungdaw, and within hours there were retaliatory attacks. Riots spread to other areas of the state, including the state capital, Sittwe, a seaside town of about 150,000.

Aye Aye Soe, a twenty-eight-year-old staff member of Save the Children, was in Sittwe on the first day of the riots, visiting from her hometown farther south. She remembers crowds of young Muslim men armed with knives and holding Molotov cocktails, as Arakanese Buddhists, both men and women, ran and shouted, "The *kala* are coming!" She witnessed a Buddhist mob catch a young Muslim man holding a Molotov cocktail and beat him to death there on the street. She had never seen such violence in her life.[13]

Neither had Tin Hlaing, the Muslim businessman mentioned earlier, who was then thirty-seven years old. He had over five hundred laborers working for him, including about a hundred Muslims. The day after Thida Htwe was killed, he saw activists from the (Buddhist) Arakan National Party at the central market. They were handing out leaflets that said, "Are we just going to stand for this?" When the violence began, he was told by the authorities to evacuate his Muslim workers to prevent trouble.[14] He was worried for his family and quickly returned to his home in the Muslim quarter, a densely packed neighborhood of approximately 30,000 people. He remembers Buddhists setting fire to buildings, and Muslims retaliating by throwing rocks.

At first Tin Hlaing didn't think much of what was happening. "In 2001 there had been a big fight," he told me. "Houses and shops were burned. Rocks were thrown. Troops fired into the crowds. Then it was finished. Over. Two weeks later everything was normal, as if nothing had happened, people meeting, greeting, buying and selling. So I didn't have the feeling that my life was about to change completely."

But this time, the violence intensified. It was a scorching hot and humid summer week, with temperatures over 100 degrees Fahrenheit, made worse by the fires all around. Every hour the fires came closer, and so Tin Hlaing and his family decided to go north, on foot. Soon they were in a crowd of thousands. He held tightly to the hands of his wife and child but in the crush lost sight of his parents and siblings. He and another university-educated Muslim man talked to police they passed along the way, pleading for their help. There was a Buddhist mob, several hundred strong, not far away, and twelve policemen in between. "People were crying, shouting. I could hear the police captain on his phone asking permission to shoot. I knelt down in front of him and begged him to help get what was now about 20,000 men, women, and children to safety. He then fired into the air and allowed us to walk to a village about an hour and a half away. We reached the village after dark. By then it was pouring with rain and we were all drenched, our feet covered in mud. People rested where they could, in the houses of villagers, under trees, in the open field. There was a little Buddhist village nearby. If we wanted, we could have attacked them. But no one did. That night, I was reunited with my parents and siblings."

On June 10, President Thein Sein declared a state of emergency in northern Arakan, "to restore security and stability," imposing martial law and giving the army temporary administrative control of the region. Five infantry battalions arrived in Sittwe and fanned out across the countryside to reinforce existing security forces. It took two more weeks to quell the riots. By the end of the month, as many as a hundred people had died and nearly 100,000 were displaced.

Burma was visited that week by António Guterres, then UN High Commissioner for Refugees (and from 2016 the UN's Secretary-General). He met with President Thein Sein. This was the same week that Aung San Suu Kyi was beginning her triumphal visit to Europe. The meeting didn't go well. International media reported that Thein Sein had told Guterres that the UN should intern all Rohingya and then ship them overseas.[15] It was the first indication, later etched in the minds of people abroad, that the government had taken a hardline anti-Muslim stance, already bordering on the genocidal.

It was partly a problem of translation. Thein Sein had said, "During the colonial period, many Bengalis came to Arakan to work. A portion chose to stay. Under Burmese law, anyone who is a third-generation descendant of these immigrants is entitled to Burmese citizenship. But there are also illegal immigrants who have come since colonial times and who are using the name 'Rohingya.' Their presence threatens stability. We cannot take responsibility for them. The UN should place them in refugee camps until they can be taken to a third country."

This wasn't a statement of universal brotherhood. But neither was it a call to expel all Muslims. Instead, the president was confirming that Muslims were entitled to citizenship, except for those who had illegally entered the country since 1948. In private, Burmese ministers admitted that, at most, 20 percent were illegal immigrants. The remarks by the president to Guterres were later taken down from his web page precisely because he had gone further in suggesting citizenship for Muslims in Arakan than any government leader had before. It was a potential opening for the UN to work with the new government on this now explosive issue. But it wasn't followed up.[16]

That same year, the Burmese government approached Noeleen Heyzer (the senior UN official who had hosted Joseph Stiglitz) to help devise an economic development strategy that would benefit both communities. Heyzer passed this request on to the UN headquarters in New York. Nothing happened.

AYE AYE SOE returned safely to her hometown in the south of Arakan. She realized that the recent violence had altered the political landscape. "If you asked people in early 2012 if they were interested in politics, they would say no. If you asked them if they were interested in *amyotha-ye* [nationalism or the nationalist cause], they would also have said no. But after the riots that changed. We have to ask who benefited from this." Within three months, the violence had come to her home too.

Beginning on the night of October 23, deadly clashes between Muslims and Buddhists broke out again, this time in and around Kyaukpyu. Some of the Muslims of the area are similar to Muslims in the north, nearer Bangladesh, speaking a dialect of Bengali and identifying themselves as Rohingya. But many Muslims in Kyaukpyu had a very different tale to tell, centuries old. In 1660, the Mughal prince Shah Shuja, having lost a contest for the imperial throne, fled with his family, harem, bodyguards, and vast treasure to the royal court at Arakan, hoping for asylum. It didn't work out well. According to the accounts of contemporary Dutch traders (who had come from New Amsterdam), Shah Shuja attempted to overthrow his host, the king of Arakan, who in turn killed him and slaughtered many of his entourage. But not all: hundreds of the mostly Afghan soldiers, mainly archers, who accompanied the prince were merged into the king's own forces. Their descendants were known as Kaman, from the

Persian word for "bow." It was this Muslim community, the Kaman, who lived in Kyaukpyu.

Unlike the Rohingya, whose identity is contested, the Kaman are acknowledged as an indigenous people, a *taing-yintha*, whose ancestors had lived in Burma since well before colonial times. In the villages around Kyaukpyu, they had lived alongside their Buddhist neighbors without problem for centuries, speaking the same dialect of Burmese.

Aye Aye Soe felt that the problem was not the Kaman villagers but "Bengali" troublemakers in the Muslim quarter of Kyaukpyu itself. She believes that it was they who first provoked the violence, leading to a response by the Buddhist Arakanese. "Within days there was all-out fighting, with Buddhists burning down Muslim buildings and Muslims shooting back with *jinglees* [slingshots]. I saw soldiers fire into the air. But there were not nearly enough soldiers or police to really crack down. I stayed most of the time in my house but could see the blazes in the distance. We were so scared. Our men took turns guarding the street. There were rumours all the time. "The *kala* are getting close!" "They're coming to get us!" We didn't sleep at all for days. Then we saw the Muslims leaving in their little boats. We were relieved to see them go."

One of the Muslims who left was a close childhood friend of Aye Aye Soe. "I felt sorry for her. She left by car. I know she cried when she left. She sent me a note saying that she had to leave without her things, only the clothes she was wearing. I wanted to help and so, with a couple of other friends, collected as much as we could, clothes and other essentials, and sent it to her secretly. If any Buddhist Arakanese had found out, they would have killed us. She went first to a displaced persons' camp, but because her family was well off they managed to get to Rangoon. From there she got a job in Qatar, where she is now. I haven't seen her since we left. We sometimes send each other a little greeting on Facebook."

At the Myanmar Peace Center, Kyaw Yin Hlaing had been tracking events closely. When I spoke to him in 2018, he said that the situation before 2010 had been a terrible one for most Muslims in the north. "The *Nasaka* [the state border police] were ruthless. It was like a caste system. The Muslims were the lower caste. But at that time they accepted it. A government official one day said to me, 'Let me show you what I can do,' and slapped a Muslim on the street. Before 2011, the Muslims felt they had to accept their status. But after the 2010 elections, in which they voted, and the political changes in 2011, they became more liberated in their minds. They hoped for international support. In 2012, when I spoke to people, almost no one referred to themselves as Rohingya. But in late 2012, everyone did."

The state was very weak. The dismantling of the intelligence services in 2004 meant that the state was nearly blind. Now the *Nasaka* border force disbanded too. The remaining security forces had no idea what was happening in Arakan, especially in the north. Under the new constitution, the army had to take a back seat as well. In their place were ordinary police with Second World War .303 rifles of dubious quality. Kyaw Yin Hlaing remembers, during the 2012 violence, an incident in which the chief judge of the state, U Kyauk, found himself with three police officers on the top floor of a building, surrounded by a Muslim mob. The judge told the police to fire into the crowd. The police officer in charge said he didn't have the authority. The judge shouted, "I'm the chief judge! I am giving you the authority. Fire!" One of the policemen finally pulled the trigger—but the gun didn't fire.

In 2013, violence flared again, this time outside Arakan. Whereas in Arakan, the clashes had involved rioters from both Buddhist and Muslim communities, now the violence was overwhelmingly anti-Muslim. Meiktila, a large town south of Mandalay, was the epicenter of the bloodshed, with as many as fifty people killed and another 12,000 displaced over a few days in March. In April, the violence spread to Okkan, near Rangoon, with dozens of Muslim shops burned to the ground. A month later, in Lashio, a trading hub far to the northeast, near

China, a mosque, a school, and a Muslim-owned cinema were destroyed by mobs wielding iron poles. The Muslims attacked in Lashio included many Panthay Muslims, the descendants of Turks and Mongols from Yunnan. In August, in a village near Shwebo, sword-carrying rioters singing the national anthem torched Muslim shops, stopping firefighters from fighting the blaze and even injuring a government minister who tried to intervene. Finally, in October, thugs killed five Muslims, including a ninety-four-year-old woman, in Sandoway, a palm-fringed coastal town on the Bay of Bengal.

The spark was different in each case: the violence in Meiktila started with an altercation between a Burmese couple and Muslim shop owners; in Okkan, after a Muslim woman allegedly bumped into a novice monk; in Lashio, after a Muslim man set a Buddhist woman on fire after a quarrel; and in Sandoway, after reports of the rape of a Buddhist woman by a Muslim man. The incidents were different but the dynamic was the same: rumors of a Muslim harming a Buddhist woman or a monk igniting mass anger and bloodshed.

The ferocity of the violence shocked many Burmese political figures. "I can't handle what I saw there," said Nilar Thein, a former political prisoner who had helped lead pro-democracy protests in 1988, who went to Meiktila to try to calm the situation. She described what she saw as "anarchic and unspeakable."[17] Some were certain that the violence had been instigated. Min Ko Naing, another 1988 protest leader, blamed "terrorists" who were "strangers and not local residents." He also blamed security forces for doing too little.[18]

In many places, Buddhist monks protected Muslims. In Lashio, for example, a Buddhist abbot named U Ponnanda sheltered 1,200 Muslims in his monastery. "I welcomed them on humanitarian grounds, and gave them food and shelter," he said, believing it was his duty as a Buddhist to protect the most vulnerable. "We were able to look after everyone, regardless of race and religion."[19]

In Meiktila, the abbot of a Buddhist monastery, U Vithuddha, gave refuge to over a thousand people, including eight hundred Muslims, during the height of the riots.[20] When news spread that he was sheltering Muslims, an angry crowd surrounded his monastery after midnight and demanded he turn them over. He believed there was only one genuinely Buddhist reaction to the situation. "If you really want them, you have to get through me," he told the mob. He reminded them of the Buddha's teaching of compassion. He felt strongly that ordinary people were not the problem. Buddhists and Muslims sheltering in his monastery were talking and sharing food. "There was an invisible hand," he said.

"This is the most complex situation I've ever seen in my life," a veteran UN mediator told me in 2013. He had served in a dozen conflict situations in Latin America, Africa, the Balkans, and Asia. There was the peace process involving the government (which in turn was divided between the president, his cabinet, the army, and parliament) and dozens of Ethnic Armed Organizations, with other insurgencies and militia sitting on the sidelines; the contest between the generals and ex-generals and Aung San Suu Kyi and the National League for Democracy, as well as dozens of other political parties and now hundreds of civil society organizations, all wanting a say in the future of the country; and the rising violence between Buddhists and Muslims, mainly in Arakan but spilling over into other parts of the country. And big powers—including China, the US, Japan, India, the UK, and a host of other governments—were jostling for influence.

At the heart of the problems was a state that still did not control its territory and a society divided on who belonged and who did not. Both were colonial legacies. In 1948, the British had left behind a weak state that collapsed within months into civil war. The peace process had started off well, but there was no real strategy for how a state could be knitted together. The old-fashioned way was for the central power simply to defeat its enemies on the battlefield. But that road to state-building—a military solution—was neither desired nor probably even possible. And questions around belonging were raising their heads just as a more open and democratic politics was trying to take root. This was no coincidence. In the absence of other ideologies or agendas, identity-based mobilization was an obvious way to gain political advantage. Troublemakers saw the value in setting communities against one another. But more than that, there was no vision of Burma as a genuinely multiracial, multicultural place.

Fear and intolerance were easy to kindle where there was a failure of the imagination. No history, other than nationalist mythology, had been taught in schools or universities for generations. Isolation bred insecurity. And the idea that race, ethnicity, and identity could be mutable, evolving, and contingent was nowhere to be found across the Burmese political spectrum. The peace process, in a way, only entrenched the notion that there were fixed ethnic groups around which everything else must be structured. International advisors did little to suggest a more useful approach.

By 2013, there was constant, upbeat talk of Burma's "transition." And the country was indeed changing, fast—though not necessarily toward either peace or democracy.

EIGHT

VIRTUAL TRANSITIONS

THE GOOD NEWS IN 2013 was that Burma's economy seemed to be headed in a brighter direction. Sanctions were rolled back and business confidence was sky-high. Prospective foreign investors crowded Rangoon's hotels. Real estate prices rose to stratospheric levels. The bad news was that Sofia and I had to find an apartment.

Until late 2011, we had commuted weekly from Bangkok. Beginning in 2012, we spent nearly all of our time in Rangoon, living in different hotels. But with the price of a room with reliable air-conditioning and Internet access spiraling to well over $150 a night, this became unsustainable.

Our choices on a decent but still limited budget were awful. A couple of years back, just as the country was beginning to show promise, I remember diplomats chatting at a reception about the need to avoid the worst of other "post-conflict" experiences, in which a deluge of expats led quickly to a bubble in rental prices, crowding out local residents, only later to collapse. Many governments were planning on setting up new embassies or expanding old ones. "We should consider a coordination mechanism," said one ambassador enthusiastically, while the others nodded.

What happened was the opposite, as foreign companies and embassies vied for the small supply of nice houses, to use both as offices and residences. A three- or four-bedroom house with a garden in a pleasant part of Rangoon might have rented for $1,000 a month in the late 2000s. By 2013, the same house cost $20,000 a month. Both UNICEF and the World Health Organization were reported to have spent nearly $1 million a year each (in rent!) on small compounds to use as their headquarters in Burma. Multilateral organizations such as the World Bank and the European Union began providing staff "housing allowances" of as much as $10,000 a month.[1] Renters were expected to pay a year's rent up front. For us, a house became out of the question.

The apartments, though, were dismal. The very few serviced apartments run by foreign firms were an exception, but they charged astronomical sums. So we were left looking at the apartments built by local developers during the days of the military regime, shoddy constructions with bizarre interior layouts: living rooms with no windows, bathroom tiles lining the corridor. Electricity was intermittent, the wiring dangerous, the water filthy, the furniture made of plastic covered in vinyl: all yours for the price of a similar-sized flat in Mayfair or the Upper East Side.

There was one other possibility: renovating a place in the old colonial downtown. We had visited the apartment of an Australian friend, Richard Horsey, and saw what was possible. The space, in a gritty but gorgeous 1920s construction, had been exquisitely remade, with teak floors, a 21st-century kitchen, and French windows overlooking the Edwardian-era Secretariat, once the hub of British rule. By sheer luck the apartment just upstairs was about to come on the market, for a fraction of the normal expat rent.

The building was once known as Soorti Mansions, and had a very special history. In 1927, the poet and future Nobel laureate Pablo Neruda lived here as the Chilean consul, during which time he had a torrid love affair with a Burmese woman named Josie Bliss, a "passionate and knowledgeable lover" who was, he wrote, "consumed by her overwhelming jealousy" and whose temper drove to her "savage paroxysms." They listened to Paul Robeson records together, in the sticky heat, the windows open to the pungent smells below. At night, he would sometimes awaken and see her brandishing a long, sharpened "native" knife, trying to decide whether or not to kill him. "When you die, she used to say to me, my fears will end." Neruda soon fled to Ceylon.[2]

The renovations over the coming months weren't easy, but in the end we had a fine-looking place with a Neruda connection to boot. Neruda had written a poem during his time in Rangoon titled "From My Windows on Dalhousie Street." Now they were our windows on Dalhousie Street. I began imagining that my experience could be replicated, that all of the old downtown could be remade, and that this remade downtown could be the centerpiece of an amazing new urban plan. Dreams soon came up against reality.

Around this time I set up the Yangon Heritage Trust. The mission was to save what was left of Rangoon's built heritage. Until the mid-1990s, Rangoon was a time capsule, not socially or politically, but in how it looked: dilapidated but with more or less the same layout and buildings as in the 1930s, beautiful edifices in an eclectic mix of architectural styles from the neoclassical New Law Courts to the art deco headquarters of Standard and Chartered. Then came the return of capitalism. Over a thousand prewar structures were demolished. Only a thousand were now left, mainly downtown. This square mile was not only Asia's last intact colonial-era landscape, but was also home to an unparalleled collection of sites belonging to all the world's major religions: Anglican and Roman Catholic cathedrals, Protestant churches of every imaginable denomination, an Armenian church, a Jewish synagogue, dozens of Hindu, Chinese, Sikh, and Parsi temples, Buddhist pagodas and monasteries, and dozens of mosques, both Sunni and Shia. It was a landscape with a bloody history of war, riots, revolution, colonialism, and anti-colonialism. It was for the

Burmese a physical connection to their past. And, except for the religious buildings themselves, it was being torn down.

I was already meeting ministers on a regular basis to discuss the latest VIP foreign visitor or the peace process then still in full swing. I added heritage protection to the agenda. "Never heard of the word 'heritage,' much less the idea of protecting these old buildings," said one minister. "What a crazy idea!" said another. I pulled together a team of dedicated architects, historians, and businesspeople who shared a desire to protect what was left.

After several high-level meetings and an international conference, to attract maximum media exposure, the government called a temporary halt to further demolitions. "It's good you intervened when you did, we were about to knock down the whole lot," said a top official. There was a buzz. City administrators began boasting to Western ambassadors about Rangoon's "heritage" buildings: "The famous poet Richard Kipling stayed in one!"

Soe Thane was an early advocate of our work. He was lobbied in turn by a slew of foreign dignitaries, in particular Australian prime minister Kevin Rudd. "All these foreigners always talk about your heritage buildings!" Soe Thane told me enthusiastically. One day, Soe Thane phoned me from Oslo to say he noticed historic plaques on buildings. "You should do the same thing. They will offer some protection, even before any new laws are in place." We did. Our "blue plaques" program has been a big success, with ministries, schools, and private associations such as the YWCA lobbying to be the next to receive the now coveted recognition.

I met with President Thein Sein to explain my views. I told the president that our built heritage was an asset, worth billions of dollars in the long run, which needed safeguarding. I agreed that Rangoon's priorities today were electricity and other basic infrastructure, but in fifteen or twenty years we would have all these things. At that point, we could be like any other Southeast Asian conurbation, a concrete jungle of skyscrapers, elevated highways, and shopping malls, or we could protect what was unique and beautiful and create a very special 21st-century cityscape. I gave him specific ideas about how initial renovation projects could be financed. I stressed the importance of involving the people who actually lived and worked downtown, and making sure they and not outside firms benefited first and foremost. I also stressed the importance of expanding green and public spaces. He was interested, and had many questions. He requested a plan. And he asked that I use the media to explain to the public what I had told him.

The Australian government sent experts in conservation who proved invaluable. In April 2014, I called on Prince Charles in London. We discussed many things, including Burmese history and elephant and tiger conservation. We also discussed the work of the Yangon Heritage Trust. He soon dispatched architects and urban planners from several of his charities.

In November 2014, I met Barack Obama. On the plane after his very brief first visit in 2012, he had looked out the window and said to his aide Ben Rhodes, "It's interesting how the place feels frozen in time. It reminds me of what Jakarta looked like when I lived there. Now it's just high-rises. They'd be smart to preserve some of what makes this part of the world different."[3] Now he was visiting Burma a second time, and in his motorcade came straight from the airport to the colonial-era Secretariat downtown. I was asked to show him around. For twenty-five minutes, the two of us walked around the courtyard and the chamber that once housed the Burmese parliament, as National Security Advisor Susan Rice and an assortment of Burmese ministers waited in the distance. We talked about mutual friends, Burmese politics and Burmese history, and the importance of urban planning. He repeated what he had said to Ben Rhodes on the plane. Over the next couple of years, his encouragement helped bring us support from experts in Chicago as well as several US foundations.

There was a deluge of goodwill and, within Burma, political support at the highest level. No one was really against what we were trying to do, which was to move beyond a halt in demolitions to the actual renovation of several derelict and largely empty government-owned buildings, as a first step toward a broader program of urban renewal. There were no major vested interests to counter us. The public was on our side. But the Yangon Heritage Trust faced a wall of inertia, the existing way of doing things, which was nearly impossible to overcome. The bureaucracy offered many avenues for corrupt bureaucrats to get rich. In the past, a direct order from the military dictator had produced results. For anything else, however, there was only a Dickensian labyrinth of dusty desks piled high with yellowing typed and handwritten forms, and an endless number of departments whose clearance was required for even the tiniest permission. Everyone's approval was needed, in triplicate, and anybody could hold things up for months if not years. A bribe could grease the wheels, but even a greasy wheel sometimes didn't turn. The bureaucracy, under the old junta, had evolved to simply be, not to get anything done.

I saw more clearly how weak the state was. It could crack down on a protest, lock up any number of dissidents, or keep rebel militias in check, but it had had few instruments to craft policies and bring about actual results. Its instincts were to avoid confrontation and allow society to go about its business, unless its own survival was at stake. My own Soorti Mansions building was a case in point. No one knew who owned it. The Indian family that had bought the land and built the building was long gone. A taxi driver who was a distant cousin claimed ownership, but had no papers. There was no strata law, so those who acted as owners of the twenty apartments also had no documents other than a receipt from the previous owner. Different people had different rights to different parts of Soorti Mansions, some simply because they had been there for a long time and couldn't easily be evicted. Downstairs was a shop that had been nationalized and taken over by a ministry. None of the higher-ups at that ministry had any idea that the space was still theirs.

The state didn't collect taxes on rental income or property. They didn't enforce regulations. It was up to the people living in the building to find a modus vivendi. The common areas were occasionally fixed up in a group effort, but more often they weren't. If there was an appeal to the government (for example, for permission to fix the roof), the first question was invariably: "Does everyone agree?" Things moved slowly, or not at all.

What was true of my building was true of the country. And into this dynamic came expectant investors from around the world. There were reasons to be hopeful. Thein Sein was a practical man, who wanted to see a rise in rural living standards. He also wanted massive foreign investment to kick-start industrial growth. He had aimed for an early end to Western sanctions, and achieved that by 2013. The same year, his finance minister, Win Shein, successfully renegotiated Burma's $10 billion foreign debt. Then followed the normalization of ties with the international financial institutions, including the World Bank and the Asian Development Bank. Until then, the government had been dependent on China, which charged far higher interest rates. The foreign exchange system was overhauled. There was even a new Burmese stock exchange, established in 2015.

Over these few years, Thein Sein and Soe Thane personally met with every major potential investor and corporate CEO who came, from the heads of Google and General Electric to Samsung and Mitsubishi. Global capitalists felt welcome. There was much talk of corporate social responsibility, ending corruption, ensuring high labor standards, and protecting the environment. The government entered into the Extractive Industries Transparency Initiative that Bono had championed.

In May 2013, the consulting firm McKinsey issued a breathtaking report, which stated that Burma had the ability to quadruple its GDP by 2030 if it could attract $650 billion in investment. Just under half of that, $320 billion, would be needed for infrastructure projects alone. McKinsey further predicted that Burma's consumer class would grow from 2.5 million people to 19 million, spending $35 billion a year within seventeen years. A Burmese translation was made required reading for cabinet ministers. It was mouthwatering stuff.[4]

By then, global capitalists were expecting only the best. Burma was being rebranded. A public relations company produced an ad for international television with the theme "Myanmar: Let the Journey Begin." And in June 2013, Naypyitaw hosted the annual East Asia Summit of the World Economic Forum. The Davos crowd came in droves, nine hundred in all from fifty-five countries, dark pinstripes and stilettos mingling with slippers and silk sarongs. There were complaints that the convention center only served regular coffee and not espresso, but otherwise the jamboree was a success, adding to the feeling that the country was now open for business. The BBC aired a special panel discussion from the convention center (built a few years before as a gift from the Chinese government), starring Aung San Suu Kyi and Soe Thane. I was invited to make a comment and said something about the challenges around identity, violent conflict, and low state capacity. No one seemed very bothered.

The single largest target of new investment was telecommunications. Under the junta, this was a tightly controlled state monopoly that provided exquisitely poor service at exorbitant rates. A phone call to a relative oversees could bankrupt the average middle-class family. Internet usage was less than 1 percent in 2011, one of the lowest in the world. Downloading an email took minutes if not hours. A SIM card cost the equivalent of over $1,000, more than a year's income for most people. In 2012, Thein Sein liberalized the phone market, opening up mobile networks to foreign companies. Several billion dollars in investment quickly flowed in. By 2014, the cost of SIM cards had fallen to $1. Telephone towers sprouted up even in the most remote areas. By 2015, over 40 million people who had never had a phone were enjoying Internet speeds that were among the fastest in Asia.

The businessmen of the old regime were kept happy as well. There were no new windfalls like the ones made in the mid-2000s from contracts to build Naypyitaw. Few wanted to be tarnished by any connection to illicit sectors, like drugs. The more forward-looking ones were sliding away from logging, mining, and any industry that reeked of the old days. In any case, there were now enormous profits to be made from Rangoon real estate. Businessmen, bureaucrats, and generals had snapped up the best property in town over the preceding decade and were either leasing it for previously unimaginable sums or constructing their own multi-star hotels, condominiums, and shopping centers.

For millions of ordinary people, the picture was more mixed. The growing urban middle class had more jobs and more ways to spend money. There was a boom in retail and entertainment: hundreds of new eateries, from Mexican to Turkish to Vietnamese, popped up across Rangoon, together with world-class malls offering food courts and multiplex cinemas. If you wanted an evening in, there was now Netflix, Burmese reality TV shows, and home delivery of everything from bento boxes to Burger King. A newer type of businessman (and woman) also emerged, not cronies attached to army elites but self-made entrepreneurs, many of them working in the fast-expanding tourism and IT sectors.

In the countryside, as well, people saw their incomes rise, more than 40 percent between 2011 and 2016, as new roads and affordable scooters connected villages to markets and cheaper solar panels provided electricity. Candles were becoming a thing of the past.[5] Villagers benefited as well from more affordable loans, the effect of government credit programs targeted at the poor. Farmers, buoyed by higher export prices, mechanized harvesting and turned to cash crops, like sesame and peanuts for sale to China.

Children's health was getting better. In just the two years between 2013 and 2015 the percentage of kids who were stunted decreased from 33 to 25 percent, and those moderately or severely underweight dropped from 25 to 14 percent. Income in rural areas also improved. In 2011, half of village households in one survey were making more than $50 a month; by 2015, that number had gone up to 85 percent.[6]

Burma was, however, by any estimation still a poor country. In Maubin, a fair-size town in the Irrawaddy delta about two hours' drive from Rangoon, only one house in ten had electricity or a water pump. Only half had a table. In Kanpetlet in the remote Chin Hills, 90 percent of homes had no bed.[7] And families whose land had been confiscated by the army under the old regime still had little hope of restitution. Corrupt officials and shady but connected businessmen had conspired to appropriate millions of acres since the early 1990s.[8] In 2012, a Farmland Investigation Commission was set up; it soon received over 12,000 complaints. But there was little sign that millions of acres of farmland would ever revert back to the poorest. Instead, a steady stream of landless poor trekked to slums around Rangoon. For now there was work in construction or in the garment sector, which was beginning again to take off. But it was a tenuous life at best. A generation before, losing a city job meant a return to subsistence farming back home. Now that safety net was gone.

One option for the poor was the jade mines of Hpakant. "I went hoping to save enough to give my wife and kids a better life," Mra Tun told me. "Instead, I discovered hell."[9] Mra Tun was an Arakanese Buddhist born not far from Bangladesh. Local authorities had confiscated his five acres for a development project in the late 2000s. Destitute, he did what thousands of other Arakanese villagers were doing and scraped together enough money for the long bus ride to Hpakant, on the other side of the country, in the Kachin Hills near China. Hpakant is the world's only source of imperial jade, carat for carat more valuable than diamonds.

Estimates of the value of Burmese jade exports in the early 2010s run from a few billion dollars a year to $30 billion in 2014, the peak year of production. Mining was done on an industrial scale, with hundreds of digging machines, including giant Komatsu PC2000s, carving out vast canyons across the 5,000-acre site. Only a small part of the profits from this trade found its way into government coffers. The rest slithered into the hands of the transnational mix of companies who mined, polished, and then sold the jade to an insatiable Chinese market.[10]

Like the other poor people attracted to Hpakant, Mra Tun became a scavenger. Every day, the big machines tipped waste soil over man-made cliffs, and every day, in 100-degree heat or under relentless monsoon rains, masses of emaciated men combed through the muddy heaps with their bare hands, hoping to find tiny fragments of treasure. To keep from collapsing from exhaustion they shot themselves up with heroin, available for 1,000 kyats (about $1) a shot, sharing needles. Women, also poor migrants and also high on heroin, offered sex in the little hovels crowded together across the moonlike landscape. Mra Tun never found the piece of jade he hoped might save him and his family from poverty. He was in Hpakant in November 2015 when a landslide killed more than two hundred scavengers. No one was ever held to account.[11]

THE ECONOMY WAS a strange beast. On the surface, Burma in the early 2010s looked to some like a new frontier market, emerging from long years of hibernation, and set to receive global capitalism with open arms. Scratch the surface and even the casual observer might realize that— unlike, say, Vietnam twenty years before—Burma was already enmeshed in its own strain of capitalism, more than a generation in the making, with markets stronger than state agencies, and a legion of shadowy businessmen keen to protect their turf. Dig deeper, and outsiders might see that just a few hours' drive from Rangoon or Mandalay were territories beyond any state control, inhabited by a patchwork of armies and armed groups, illegal and illicit trades, and a Chinese frontier over which even Beijing's sway was tenuous at best.

The Thein Sein government had moved fast and decisively to improve the economy. The results were plain to see. Inequalities, however, remained as deep as ever. And there was no real conversation about the future shape of the economy. To the extent that there was a vision, it was to move from the anarchic capitalism of the past two decades to a more garden-variety state capitalism, following other Asian examples and focusing on export-oriented industrialization.

And any genuine effort to restructure the economy faced monumental obstacles. Office-holders and cronies had fine-tuned venal relationships. Many stood ready to frustrate further change. State-owned firms, most suffering heavy losses, employed tens of thousands of poorly skilled and virtually idle workers. The army, through its own conglomerates and massive landholdings, still enjoyed a fat piece of the pie. Budgets were bloated and billions of dollars in public funds disappeared into the bureaucratic labyrinth. Few paid taxes, including on property. In 2012, two new land laws were passed, with the stated aim of rationalizing an extremely messy land tenure system; but depending on how the laws are implemented, they may well entrench a status quo that concentrates millions of acres in the hands of those with access to state power, leaving millions of people with nothing.

At the same time, the shadow of the country's illicit industries loomed ever larger. By 2015, the northern and eastern Shan Hills had become the global epicenter for the production of meth tablets, as well as the higher-value crystal meth, or ice. Militia allied to the Burmese army were deeply involved. So, too, was the biggest rebel force, the United Wa State Army. Ice was exported to fast-expanding markets in Australia, New Zealand, and Japan, where an increasing number of housewives are among the new addicts. As with jade, no one knows the total value of the trade, though United Nations estimates run into the tens of billions of dollars a year.

All along the Chinese border were casinos in the hands of various insurgent armies and militia. They catered exclusively to Chinese customers, many of whom had been lured from cities across China with free transport and a week's luxury accommodation. In all these places the staff spoke Chinese, Chinese currency was used, and Chinese phones could even be used with no roaming charges. Some customers lost the equivalent of hundreds of thousands of dollars in a few days. Anyone who couldn't pay up would be held and even tortured until their relatives wired the money demanded. "To travel there is to be doomed," said one gambler.[12]

Casinos were one way to make money. Robbing casinos was another. In March 2017, armed men belonging to the Myanmar National Democratic Alliance Army forced their way into the Fulilight Casino in Laukkai and rounded up three hundred staff members. In the pitched gun battle that followed between the thieves and both government troops and government-allied militia, over a hundred people were killed or wounded, including forty civilians. Using twenty trucks they had lined up outside the casino, the attackers made off with no less than $73 million in cash, burning the money they couldn't take.

And wildlife trafficking to China was now reaching epic proportions. Tigers, bears, elephants, and pangolins from Burma were being smuggled whole or in parts for bogus medicinal use or to be served as dishes in exotic restaurants. The National Democratic Alliance Army, another (similarly named) rebel group based at Mongla, near Laos, was becoming a world hub for illegal wildlife trading, acting as a transshipment point for ivory and rhino horns in particular from Africa to China.

Over the past two decades, the biggest of Burma's rebel armies, the United Wa State Army, had made weighty investments in China, Hong Kong, Macau, and Thailand. They also owned major businesses in Burma itself, including Yangon Airways. But after a crackdown on money laundering in 2015, the Wa Army found a new partner in the King's Roman Casino on the Laos side of the Laos–Burma border. A colossal structure with water fountains, mock Italian Renaissance frescos, a health spa and, of course, hundreds of gambling tables, the casino is part of a Special Economic Zone run by China-born businssman Zhao Wei. In 2018, the US government placed Zhao Wei under sanctions for alleged ties to "drug trafficking, money laundering, child prostitution, bribery, and human and wildlife trafficking," all facilitated through the casino.[13]

There were also strange new Chinese connections. The Yucheng Group was a Chinese financial company owned by a thirty-something-year-old entrepreneur named Ding Ning. Its most famous product was something called EZuBao, a Ponzi scheme which swindled more than $7.5 billion from nearly a million private investors. Before its collapse, the Yucheng Group was also deeply involved in Burma. It supported the Kokang militia as well as several other insurgent armies along the Chinese border. In 2015, it announced plans to set up a Yucheng Southeast Asia Free Trade Zone in the territory controlled by the United Wa State Army, promising 40 billion yuan (around $4 billion) in investment. Ding Ning and his Yucheng Group were likely planning to use Burma's already well-established money-laundering operations to launder their own Ponzi scheme gains. Ding Ning is today in jail, but no one knows what happened to the $7.5 billion. Most suspect that wherever the money is, it got there via Burma.[14]

These sums, from narcotics, casinos, wildlife trafficking, and cross-border organized crime, are staggering. There's no good estimate of how much money has actually been made or where it's been kept. But even if only a fraction of the tens of billions of dollars involved wound up in Burma, the money would be shaping incentives across the political landscape. And it probably is.

Let's assume for a minute, though, that all these problems could be miraculously solved, replaced by responsible investment, steady growth, less inequality, and even peace for all. Burma would then follow a path similar to many other countries in Asia, moving from the export of primary commodities to manufactured goods, and benefiting from a new consumerist middle class. Across the region, the default outcome is plain to see: relentless environmental destruction and congested cities, compensated for only by the opportunity for lots of shopping. Is this really the only future possible?

Burma is one of the richest countries in the world in terms of its biodiversity. In the past few years alone, more than forty new animal species were discovered in the country. Despite the ravages of the past two decades, the country still commands breathtaking natural landscapes and is home to the last free-flowing rivers as well as the largest population by far of wild elephants in Asia. It is also a country rich in unique cultural traditions, from forms of meditation to the art, cuisine, and folklore of dozens of different ethnic communities. In 2015, Burma was ranked the most generous nation in the world, measured in part by how often people helped strangers or volunteered for charities. That same year, torrential rains led to severe floods that displaced a million people. UN officials organizing the relief effort say they had never seen anything like the community-based efforts across Burma to raise money and deliver assistance. Yet none of these things are valued when the future of the economy is under discussion.

Neither has there been much discussion of climate change. Burma is set to become one of the five countries in the world most negatively impacted by climate change. By the mid-2000s, the monsoons, whose regularity set the seasons and are critical for farming, were becoming unpredictable. Tens if not hundreds of thousands of people from the arid middle of the country, where a few monsoon storms at the right time each year are essential for a good crop, were already leaving, because of repeated drought, in search of jobs in the cities or in Thailand. In 2015, extreme rain and the long-term effects of deforestation combined to produce the epic floods just mentioned. Other extreme climate events, like Cyclone Nargis, will without question become more common. Extreme heat will make vast swaths of the interior uninhabitable within decades. And if current predictions are even close to accurate, rising sea levels will submerge most of the coastline, including parts of Rangoon, within a generation.

By 2015, Rangoon was already becoming a less livable place. Liber-alization and rising incomes led to a deluge of new cars, from 50,000 to 400,000, on the same colonial-era roads. For poor people, a thirty-minute commute by bus became a three-hour commute each way. Sidewalks were ripped up to make way for vehicle traffic, making walking impossible. Disease-ridden slums grew up around the city, as did adjacent high-end gated communities. The Yangon Heritage Trust tried to promote ideas around livability, urban planning, and the protection of public and green spaces, not least to offset future floods, but the momentum was on the side of growth at all costs.

Even those who were clearly better off were increasingly anxious, fearing being left behind. In the absence of a good conversation on issues of equality and the economy to come, there was little resistance to those who peddled an alternative set of conversations around race and identity. Those conversations would now steal the limelight.

IN 1914, THE FOSSIL of a small mammal was discovered northwest of Mandalay. It was later found to be the remains of an anthropoid primate, and the oldest of its kind. By the early 2000s, scientists concluded that this Eocene creature might well be of a genus ancestral to later, more human-like species. That tantalizing fact was enough to spur speculation in Burma that the country might be the actual cradle of mankind. Scientists had said nothing of the sort, but imaginations ran in a resolutely nativist direction. By 2015 Burmese scholars were suggesting an uninterrupted lineage from the little primate, through recently discovered Neolithic sites and Bronze Age civilizations, right down to the last kingdom of Mandalay. British colonialism was, in this story, the only interregnum in the proud descent of the Burmese *taing-yintha*, the indigenous races, through the ages.

The old junta and a nexus of antiquarians, scholars, and bureaucrats under the military regime had nurtured a view of the past that was now conventional wisdom. There was no challenge to the *taing-yintha* idea. Fitting a prehistoric monkey into the picture was not difficult.

By 2015, there was also a new pride in the country. For generations, people had seen only a decline of their status in the world. A trigger for the 1988 protests had been the labeling of Burma by the UN as a "least developed country." In the late 2000s, the idea that countries once far poorer, such as Cambodia and Bangladesh, were edging ahead was seen as deeply shameful. Now things seemed to be turning around, in all spheres. In 2013, Myanmar had hosted its first big international sports tournament, the South East Asia Games, with great pageantry; after years of doing abysmally poorly, it came second in gold medals. Tens of thousands packed the stadiums, waving the new flag and singing the national anthem.

This newfound pride also had a racial hue. In Burmese films and in the growing advertising and beauty industries, all the faces were of a type. Walk down the street in Rangoon and you will see people who could pass for anything from Siberian to Mediterranean to Polynesian, together with the faces of people whose ancestors came from every part of the Indian subcontinent. But in beauty pageants and on the giant billboards sprouting up everywhere, the only faces on display were a paler version of what many considered a "pure Burmese." There was influence from elsewhere in the region, especially Korea, with Burma being one of the very first foreign countries to embrace K-pop, together with Korean soap operas and Korea's light-skinned East Asian aesthetics. In the 1950s, many Burmese watched Bollywood films and an "Indian-like," or *kala-sin*, look was often prized; not anymore.

At the same time, rapid change brought about fears that a traditional way of life was under attack. The ending of military dictatorship was almost universally welcomed, but there was concern that new elites—people whose values were not those of the conservative, largely rural or small-town Buddhist majority, people who mixed their Burmese with English words that most couldn't understand—were coming to the fore, together with foreign companies and foreign influences.

Then came the violence in Arakan in 2012. I remember the strong emotions of many Burmese in Rangoon who believed their kinsmen were being slaughtered. The Muslims in Arakan were seen as *kala*. In the eyes of the Burmese Buddhist majority, they were indistinguishable from the "Indians" of Bangladesh. That they are usually of dark complexion, the men often bearded and some Rohingya women veiled, only added to the impression that they were alien and dangerous. So these currents intermingled: racial pride, fears of tradition under threat, and fear of the Muslim *kala*.

There was also Facebook. For most Burmese, the Internet means just Facebook, and by late 2013 more than half of all adults were regularly using the social network. By mid-2014, Facebook had become the principal if not the only way to reach a mass audience for Burmese media organizations, government agencies, celebrities, and political figures of all stripes. In many ways, Facebook added enormously to the transparency of political life. Nearly everyone, including the military commander-in-chief, posted their comings and goings. But it gave rise, as well, to a sudden coarseness in public discourse. One member of parliament told me that more than a few colleagues, after a hard day's work and dinner at home, downed a couple of whiskeys before logging in to Facebook, ready to post comments. Facebook also made easier the mobilization of violence.

On July 14, 2014, a Facebook post alleged that the Indian Muslim owner of the Sun Teashop in Mandalay had raped one of his Burmese Buddhist employees. Within hours, a furious mob gathered. Police attempted to disperse the mob, at one point firing rubber bullets, but they were not successful, and by dusk bands of rioters, many on motorbikes and armed with machetes, were setting fire to cars and buildings. A curfew was imposed. It was barely a year after the Meiktila riots, and the government was keen to quell the violence as quickly as possible.

The president's office made an urgent overnight attempt to contact

Facebook.[15] Having no direct connection, the senior official in the office, Zaw Htay, reached out to an acquaintance, Chris Tun, who worked at Deloitte and had contact with several tech companies. "They started to panic and they did not know what to do," said Tun in an interview with Reuters. After hours of trying to reach a human at Facebook, the government decided to temporarily block access to the site. This seemed to have an effect, as the violence quickly abated. The next morning, Chris Tun woke up to several emails from Facebook, concerned that their site seemed to be down in Burma. Facebook at the time had only a single Burmese-language speaker, who was tasked with monitoring all 18 million new users.

The Rohingya issue was seen in a very particular light. Until the 2010s, few people outside Arakan thought at all about the Muslims along the Bangladesh border. But the communal riots of 2012 focused attention and riveted the sympathy of the Burmese Buddhist majority squarely on one side. The idea that most of the Muslims of northern Arakan were either recent illegal arrivals, or at best Britsh-era immigrants, was accepted without question.

Few if any in the rest of Burma had ever heard the term "Rohingya" before. The British had not used the term, and neither had the military regime. Many Burmese saw the name as part of a drive to force acceptance of illegal immigrants from Bangladesh not only as Burmese citizens but as *taing-yintha*, an indigenous race. They insisted on calling the Muslims in northern Arakan "Bengali" (if not "*kala*") instead. The more that outside activists, governments, and media insisted on using the term "Rohingya," the more many non-Muslims in Burma suspected an international conspiracy.

Countless images of Al-Qaeda and Islamic State atrocities elsewhere were shared over Facebook. Stories circulated that Al-Qaeda cells were already at work near Rangoon. People were scared of an imminent attack. Maps were posted on social media which showed the spread of

Islam over the centuries, with only Burma now standing between 160 million Muslims in Bangladesh on one side and 250 million Muslims in Malaysia and Indonesia on the other. For nationalists across the country, the Bangladesh border was increasingly referred to as *anauk-taga*, "the western gate." The plight of the Rohingya and this dread of global Islamicist movements converged.

In early 2014, a new nationalist organization commonly known as Mabatha arose as a significant force.[16] The word is a Burmese acronym for its full name, which translates as Association for the Protection of Race and Religion. Race, or *amyo-tha*, meant the Burmese race. Religion, or *thathana*, meant Buddhism. At the core of Mabatha's worldview was a dissatisfaction with modernization as it had been experienced in Burma and a feeling that corrupt elites were running roughshod over ordinary people and the values most dear to them. Women, many pushing for greater women's rights, were a big component of Mabatha's growing constituency. Led by Buddhist monks, Mabatha members believed that at the root of recent conflicts were the tensions caused by the taking of young Burmese women as second wives by older Muslim men.

Mabatha championed four new laws formally called the laws to "protect race and religion." The word used in Burmese, *saungshauk*, actually means something closer to "taking care," as in taking care of your parents in old age. The first outlawed polygamy and made extramarital cohabitation a criminal offense (the first of only a few arrests, after the laws were passed in 2015, would actually be a small-town Burmese Buddhist man who cheated on his wife with a mistress in Rangoon). The second required anyone wanting to change religion to first undergo an interview and then study the new religion for at least ninety days before receiving permission to convert. The third stipulated that a Buddhist woman wanting to marry a non-Buddhist man needed parental consent if she was under twenty. The fourth and most controversial allowed the government to impose family planning requirements in geographic regions where population rates were considered abnormally high (meaning the Rohingya areas of Arakan).

In a meeting with one of Aung San Suu Kyi's chief aides in February 2014, U Wirathu, a firebrand monk and member of Mabatha, asked why the National League for Democracy would oppose these laws when it claimed to be on the side of "the people." Many Buddhist nationalists applauded the NLD aim of ending military rule and returning power to "the people." They saw the protection of "the people," meaning the Burmese Buddhist "race," as integral to the same agenda. The monk said, "We would put Aung San Suu Kyi's bronze statue on a pedestal and worship her forever" if she supported the laws.[17]

In Burmese, the word for "National" in the name of the National League for Democracy is *amyo-tha*. It's the same as the word for "race." "Race" and "nation" are synonymous, and for some "democracy" should mean nothing more or less than the supremacy of the race-based nation. In Arakan, Buddhist women told Western and Burmese researchers that their number-one fear was being raped by Muslim men.[18]

Into this explosive environment came the first nationwide census in over thirty years, conceived and carried out in close collaboration with the United Nations Population Fund.[19] In a country were nearly everyone I know has parents or grandparents from different communities, all responders were asked to list their ethnicity. That the government had not thought to use the census as an opportunity to encourage a more fluid notion of identity was not surprising. That the UN did not consider this at all was inexcusable.

The key issue then became whether "Rohingya" should be one of the categories offered. The immigration minister, Khin Yi, who was in charge of the census, first said that people would be free to self-identify as they wished. This prospect—that Muslims in Arakan could list themselves as "Rohingya"—rang alarm bells across Arakanese nationalist circles. Feelings were at a fever pitch. In February 2014, the charity Doctors Without Borders was told by the government to suspend all work in Burma, on the grounds that it was biased in favor of the Rohingya community. That impoverished Arakanese Buddhists received little or nothing from international agencies was not entirely true, but it was universally believed. A month later, large protests against allowing Muslims to identify themselves as they pleased in the census swept towns across Arakan. When the government refused to budge, Arakanese nationalists called for a boycott of the census. And after a Western aid official removed a Buddhist flag from the front of an office in Sittwe, aid agencies across the town were attacked, prompting the evacuation of over three hundred aid workers. Tensions were already running high against a foreign aid community believed to have taken sides. Vital humanitarian assistance was interrupted.

On the eve of the census, the government gave way to mounting pressure and announced that Rohingya would not, after all, be permitted to list themselves as such, only as "Bengalis." The boycott was lifted.

In January 2014, the UN High Commissioner for Human Rights, Navi Pillay, called for an immediate investigation after receiving "credible information" that "at least 40 Rohingya Muslim men, women and children" had been killed by police in the little village of Ducheeyartan.[20] This massacre was allegedly carried out as a reprisal for the murder of a policeman days before. The government enquiry that followed found that no one had been killed, and Western human rights researchers and diplomats quietly admitted that the story had been made up.[21] The UN, though, never acknowledged this. The suspicion grew on Burmese social media, as well as in Naypyitaw, that Rohingya leaders and their supporters abroad were becoming adept at manufacturing "fake news."

Also that January, three Burmese-born members of the Pakistani Taliban were arrested in Bangladesh. Bangladeshi police charged them with planning to "launch activities" in Arakan using their experience in "high-powered explosives." Pakistani Taliban were then urging their followers to take revenge for violence against Rohingya and "Kill in the Path of God."[22] In the minds of many Arakanese Buddhists, fear mingled with conspiracy theories.

Meanwhile, life for Rohingya were getting bleaker by the day. Nu Nu Khin, a Rohingya educated at Sittwe University, had been a government worker in Maungdaw until 2012. She and other Muslims were summarily dismissed.[23] In the middle of Sittwe itself, Aung Mingala, the largely Muslim quarter, was surrounded by barbed wire, its several hundred inhabitants unable to leave without a pass. Anyone with even a passing knowledge of European history in the 1930s would find it difficult not to draw analogies. Mosques were closed or torn down. Rohingya now had at best limited access to essential public services and no access to higher learning. Approximately 100,000 people were trapped in "internally displaced persons" camps around Sittwe or elsewhere in Arakan. Schools in the camps were abysmal, and a trip to the hospital required permission. Many died before permission was received. Access by humanitarian aid groups was also restricted, leading to rising malnutrition as well as death from water-borne illnesses.

Rohingya women were at the very bottom of the heap, suffering the abuses of their own male-dominated society in addition to those of officialdom and other ethnic communities. Stateless, denied access to education or even the most elementary health care, they also had little understanding of family planning. Many married extremely young, aged fourteen or fifteen, and had several children by their early twenties. Often, a Rohingya woman or girl was the second or even third wife of a husband who had a limited ability to care for her, eking out an existence on the equivalent of a dollar or two a day, sometimes abandoning her in a desperate search for a job overseas.[24]

In February, the president signed a bill giving Muslims in Arakan holding temporary white ID cards (as opposed to the pink ID cards held by citizens) the right to vote. Parliament had originally rejected a bill giving voting rights to temporary card-holders, but reversed its decision at the request of the president. In Sittwe, mass protests soon followed.

One of the protest organizers was Nyo Aye. Then in her mid-fifties, she had been active in politics all her life. "Growing up, I had absolutely no problem with our Muslim neighbors," she says. "We played sports together in school and visited each other at home. The only difference was in dietary restrictions. I remember once I accidentally offered a pork dish to a Muslim friend, thinking it was mutton. I still feel bad about it."[25]

As a teenager, she took part in demonstrations over the rising price of rice. "Then it was Buddhists and Muslims together protesting against the military regime." And during the 1988 uprising, she took a leading role. "We wanted democracy, a return of power to the people," she explained to me. She had read many books on political theory: Marx, Engels, various works on socialism. "I didn't necessarily want either a capitalist or socialist system. I wanted power transferred from the army to the people's elected representatives." When the army cracked down, she was caught up in the arrests. "I've never told anyone what happened to me in prison. I still don't want to think about it. I haven't even told my husband, though he asks me sometimes because I used to wake up in the night."

Nyo Aye was a member of the National League for Democracy for nearly a quarter century, facing constant threats from the army regime as a result. She says everything changed in 2012, with the communal violence in Sittwe. When I met her in 2018, she reflected on this period: "We have to ask how is it that at exactly at that moment in our politics, when we were starting to return power to the people, that so much paranoia was spread, and then the first killings happened?" Like so many others in Arakan, both Buddhist and Muslim, she suspected dark forces at work, but didn't say exactly who they were. "We were just about to collect 300,000 signatures against the Chinese pipeline," she told me. "We had 200,000 already."

Yet she was unequivocal in her belief, shared with nearly every Burmese I've ever met, that illegal immigration from Bangladesh was real, and a threat. "In the 1990s and early 2000s, a person from Bangladesh could pay 5,000 kyats [then about $10] and cross the border without a problem," she said. The two million Arakanese Buddhists felt squeezed between the Burmese military on one side and Bangladesh's teeming population on the other. In 2015, she was adamant that Muslims holding temporary ID cards shouldn't be allowed to vote. Demonstrations spread from Sittwe to towns around Arakan, and then to Rangoon. Within days, the government buckled under pressure and canceled the cards altogether. A million Rohingya would have no say in the upcoming elections.

Over that spring, 25,000 people from both Bangladesh and Arakan took to the high seas in flimsy boats in the hope of reaching promised jobs in Malaysia. Smuggling routes had existed for years. The smugglers, who were mainly Thai, routinely kept migrants at camps in the jungle, extorted money from relatives back home, and killed those whose families couldn't pay. When mass graves were discovered in the south of Thailand in May 2015, Thai authorities finally cracked down, leaving thousands temporarily stranded in the Andaman Sea. Hundreds died before they could be rescued by the Burmese or other navies. Bangladeshi prime minister Sheikh Hasina called the Bangladeshi migrants "mentally sick" for attempting to find jobs overseas and hurting the country's image.[26] For most of the world, however, the crisis highlighted the plight of the Rohingya.

For the Rohingya, especially young Rohingya men, the crackdown meant the end of the hope of a new life overseas. They had just one hope left: the election of a government led by Aung San Suu Kyi.

BURMA IN 2015 faced a bewildering array of challenges. The country was enjoying far greater political freedom, including over the Internet, than at any time in over half a century. Hundreds of thousands of people were part of new civil society organizations, mobilized around issues from environmental protection to women's rights. But in general, this freedom, rather than giving rise to progressive agendas, was reviving older anxieties around race, religion, and national identity. There was still optimism, though, that the country was finally turning a corner.

The coming elections could cement democratic progress. But at this point, elite politics unraveled.

Burma's constitution was not a democratic constitution. The armed forces enjoyed considerable autonomy. They controlled the key ministries of defense, border affairs, and home affairs, as well as a quarter of the seats in parliament. The commander-in-chief, Senior General Min Aung Hlaing, had to be managed by the president with care.

The cabinet, too, had to be managed with care. This wasn't Thein Sein's cabinet. Than Shwe, the old dictator, had chosen every one of its members before the junta was dissolved. Ministers couldn't be easily fired. There were rivalries. Some were termed "hardliners," as opposed to the reformist clique around Thein Sein. But in reality, the dynamics were as much as anything the result of personality clashes. Government ministers were nearly all ex-generals who had served with one another for decades, some since their teenage years at the academy. They knew one another's strengths and weaknesses well. There were deep friendships and deeper animosities.

Soe Thane and Aung Min had promised a sunny upland of peace and prosperity driven by Western investment. They had set the agenda from 2011 to 2014. But now their political clout was ebbing, in part because of incessant inter-ministerial turf wars and the inability or unwillingness of the president to always side with his "coordinating ministers."

The bigger cleavage was between the president and parliamentary speaker Shwe Mann, and by extension between the executive and legislative branches of government. The Burmese constitution resembles the American one, in that parliament, like Congress, is meant to counterbalance an otherwise strong presidency. The ex-generals in parliament demanded "checks and balances." In other words, they believed themselves no less important than their former army colleagues now running ministries. Shwe Mann, who had wanted to be president and was still ambitious, built up the power of the speakership. He also grouped around him leading businessmen, several also members of parliament, who were of a protectionist bent, and were wary of Soe Thane's efforts to maximize foreign competition. He also built a surprisingly close relationship with Aung San Suu Kyi.

Aung San Suu Kyi and her newly elected NLD members of parliament had taken their seats in April 2012. No one knew exactly what to expect. Thein Sein was advised to offer her a cabinet position, perhaps as minister of health or education. But this never happened. Shwe Mann, however, immediately gave her the chairmanship of a new parliamentary committee (on the "rule of law and stability"). He also tried hard to make her feel at home in her new Naypyitaw surroundings, treating her as a partner, gaining her confidence. There was good personal chemistry, something Aung San Suu Kyi never had with Thein Sein.

Aung San Suu Kyi herself was very clear about what she wanted: a free and fair election and the chance to be president of Burma. For her to become president was impossible under the current constitution, as the clause listing qualifications for the presidency explicitly states that no one with immediate family who were foreign citizens could be chosen. Aung San Suu Kyi's two sons, Alexander and Kim, living overseas, were both foreign citizens. Neither she nor her party liked the current constitution. If it were up to them they would have scrapped it and written a new one with clear civilian control of the armed forces. But at this point, what mattered most was to change the presidential qualification clause, so that Aung San Suu Kyi could lead the government after winning at the polls.

In 2014, Aung San Suu Kyi called for a dialogue involving herself, Shwe Mann, the president, and the commander-in-chief of the army. The country was clearly headed toward a political impasse. Though the president finally relented and meetings were held in late 2014 and 2015, they were far from the open dialogue Aung San Suu Kyi had envisaged. Instead, they were stiff affairs modeled on international conferences, involving not just the four key figures but leaders of lesser political parties as well, with everyone sitting far apart and speaking into microphones. They led nowhere.

By June 2016, all attempts to revise the constitution had fallen through. In welcoming Thein Sein's reforms in 2011, Aung San Suu Kyi had thought that the army would eventually allow the constitution to be amended. She felt betrayed. "People are now crystal clear about who they have to support," she said.[27]

Shwe Mann was siding openly with Aung San Suu Kyi. The ruling party—the ex-generals of the Union Solidarity and Development Party—was essentially riven down the middle, with some on Thein Sein's side and the others on Shwe Mann's. The two factions were barely on speaking terms. When the USDP picked candidates for the elections, things came to a head. Shwe Mann's allies in command of the party's central office blocked Soe Thane and Aung Min from running, forcing them to stand as independents. There were disagreements too with the army, who had their own list of generals they wanted to retire and run in the elections under the USDP banner.

On the night of August 12, President Thein Sein, with the tacit backing of the army commander-in-chief, forced the resignation of Shwe Mann and his top lieutenants from the party leadership, physically taking over the party headquarters. This was, though, only an internal party purge, aimed at preventing a Shwe Mann–Aung San Suu Kyi coalition from assuming power. Shwe Mann remained parliamentary speaker. The next morning, he posted a photograph on Facebook showing himself back at work.

At a time when the country needed strong collective leadership, the country's top political figures were split. It was, in a way, a consequence of the move toward democracy and the more competitive political space that had indeed been established.

In September 2015, Thein Sein signed the four "race and religion protection" bills into law. Mabatha, the monk-led nationalist organization, had mobilized millions of people to sign a petition in support of them. The new laws were heavily criticized by Rangoon-based and often Western-funded civil society groups, making Mabatha members feel even more strongly that their values were under threat.[28] Though the NLD remained largely silent, Mabatha threw its support behind the USDP.

The Nationwide Ceasefire Agreement, now nearly three years in the making, was also signed before the end of Thein Sein's term. Some on the ethnic minority side had injected a late demand for the idea of a federal army to be included, meaning that in future each state would keep its own separate armed forces. This was hotly rejected by the Burmese military. The final draft negotiated by the government and a slew of Ethnic Armed Organizations was completed in March 2015. It included lots of tediously crafted political language, weak ceasefire arrangements, and a follow-on process whose complexity rivaled anything I had seen at the UN. There was now intense debate about who could and should sign the accord. Some ethnic leaders speculated that an Aung San Suu Kyi government might give them a better deal. Why give these ex-generals a last-minute boost before the elections? The government wanted as many as possible to sign, other than a few of the smaller forces against whom there was still active fighting.

China influenced what happened next. Beijing was unhappy with Thein Sein, having seen his government suspend the Myitsone dam project and then rush to embrace Western suitors. All their ideas for new, big infrastructure projects were stalled. They felt disrespected. The Chinese government was widely believed to have told the armed organizations along the common border, including the biggest ones like the Kachin Independence Army and the United Wa State Army, not to sign.[29] They didn't.

In the end, fewer than half the insurgent armies came to the signing ceremony in October 2015. In order to avoid giving the government a pre-electoral boost, Aung San Suu Kyi didn't attend either, sending an aide instead. Lian Sakhong, one of the ethnic leaders who had negotiated the accord, believed that the past few years had been a wasted opportunity. "There was a window. Thein Sein was open and willing to negotiate a deal. But we were divided among ourselves and couldn't agree on a strategy until it was too late." He was right.

For me, these were disappointing times. I spent a lot of time at the Myanmar Peace Center and on the Beyond Ceasefires Initiative, but it was clear that fresh, outside-the-box thinking was both more needed than ever and nowhere in sight. I proposed discussions on underlying economic and identity-related issues. There was interest, but the peace process had by now become so complex that a focus on anything other than the nuts and bolts of the process itself seemed impossible. I worked as well on Rangoon conservation and urban planning efforts. There had been considerable success, but by 2015 we were hitting a brick wall. Here, too, the problem wasn't lack of interest or support; the problem was the lack of ability to analyze and imagine different futures. I spoke to one minister about turning the industrial waterfront into a promenade. He politely agreed, but nothing happened. When I saw him a few months later, he had just returned from his first trip to Europe. "Now I understand what you mean," he said. "Before, I had no idea what you were talking about." But he was just one of many who had to be convinced. As a member of the National Economic and Social Advisory Council, I was also still an advisor to the president, but after the first year the council met extremely infrequently and had by 2015 become moribund. I knew that people in the government were suspicious of me, as someone who had lived most of his life overseas. My advice was still welcome but, more often than not, it simply drifted into a bureaucratic abyss.

ON NOVEMBER 8, 2015, 22 million Burmese voters, nearly 70 percent of those eligible to vote, went to the polls to choose a government, in the first free and fair election since 1960. Over the past months, the USDP, the NLD, and dozens of other mainly ethnic minority parties had canvassed hard throughout the country. Mabatha campaigned for the USDP, using a vast network of monks. But the momentum was on the other side. Wherever Aung San Suu Kyi went, she drew enormous and enthusiastic crowds. Election day in Rangoon was beautiful and sunny. Offices were closed and, with few cars on the streets, walking became pleasurable again. I remember families queuing up early at the little polling station downstairs in our building, everyone smiling. I saw Ko Ni, the NLD constitutional lawyer who lived around the corner, approaching the booth with his wife. They too were smiling. "We must hope the future will be better," he said.

The result would be a decisive win for the National League for Democracy. Everyone I asked who voted for the NLD said the same thing: they wanted to show their hatred of past military rule as well as their love and respect for the sacrifices made by Aung San Suu Kyi and other members of her party. They also said they wanted a brighter economic future for themselves and their children. Issues of race and religion played little part in their choice. This was the view in most urban areas. In the countryside, it was different. Many had no idea what they were voting for. An NLD candidate told me that at least one-third of his rural constituency had no understanding of what an election was. Others were swayed by Buddhist monks who were members of Mabatha or the government's track record, which in many areas had included real improvements in daily life. Here the polls were closer, but the size of the NLD's margin in Rangoon and other cities ensured an impressive overall victory: the party won no fewer than 86 percent of the seats up for grabs and 57 percent of the popular vote, against 28 percent for Thein Sein's USDP. The NLD did not win in Arakan, which voted decisively for an Arakanese Buddhist party, but they won in many other ethnic minority areas, including strife-torn Kachin state.

In general, people had voted for a better tomorrow and had rejected an ethno-nationalist turn. The entire world—including China and America, Europe, India, and Japan—stood ready to help. Burma seemed on the brink of its best opportunity in decades to unite around a new agenda for peace and development, and a more equal society. Politics and the weight of history, though, would get in the way.

NINE

UNFINISHED NATION

THE MONTHS FOLLOWING the November 2015 election were a period of intense uncertainty. Under Burma's constitution, the president is chosen by parliament. He or she then appoints the rest of the government, including the chief ministers of the fourteen states and regions. The National League for Democracy had won a big enough landslide that even despite the army's hold on a quarter of the seats in parliament, they still had a majority. At least in theory, they could choose the next head of state without relying on either the army's votes or those of another political party. This was a scenario few, if any, had predicted.

The ex-generals in the old government were crestfallen. Some blamed reformists around the president for making possible Aung San Suu Kyi's reemergence from what they believed was her enfeebled position in 2010. Many had harsher words for Shwe Mann, whose partnership with Aung San Suu Kyi they saw as treacherous. Soe Thane managed to bag a seat in parliament as an independent, representing a constituency in the remote Kayah Hills on the Thai border. Aung Min tried the same tactic and lost.

What next? No one knew. Within twenty-four hours, the USDP leadership admitted defeat. But would the old guard really allow Aung San Suu Kyi to be president? In 1990, when the NLD won a similar landslide, the army first prevaricated and then essentially ignored the results. For the next twenty years, they looked upon the NLD as their implacable foe.

On December 4, 2015, Aung San Suu Kyi met with former Senior General Than Shwe at his newly built residence in Naypyitaw. Than Shwe had, as he planned, made the transition from dictator to comfortable retiree. He had not been part of the picture for five years. There was no media coverage of the meeting and no official press release. Instead, Than Shwe's twenty-four-year-old grandson posted a photo on his Facebook page that evening of a single 5,000-kyat banknote (about $5) signed (at different times) by Aung San Suu Kyi, Thein Sein, and his grandfather, together with a brief account of what had taken place. The meeting had lasted more than two hours, he wrote. At the end, Than Shwe said, according to his grandson, "It is the truth that she will become the future leader of the country."[1] No one knew exactly what that meant, but the old man seemed to be giving his blessing for a government headed by Aung San Suu Kyi.

How could this happen? Under the constitution, she was barred from the presidency as her sons were foreign citizens. She met around the same time with the army chief, Min Aung Hlaing, who made clear that this would not be changed. Constitutional amendments could be blocked by a quarter of the seats in parliament, which essentially gave the army a veto.

Resigned to not being president for the time being, Aung San Suu Kyi selected an old school friend, Htin Kyaw, for the role. Over six feet tall, the courtly Htin Kyaw, the son of a renowned poet, was a retired bureaucrat who had trained as a computer scientist in London in the early 1970s. He had no desire for high office and was assured by Aung San Suu Kyi that his presidency would last only a matter of months, while she found a way to convince the army to amend the constitution.

In the meantime, she left no doubt who would wield power, telling the BBC's Fergal Keane that she would make "all decisions" and would be "a rose by any other name."[2]

Indeed, Aung San Suu Kyi would make all decisions on behalf of what became a ceremonial presidency. But she would also have to contend with the armed forces commander-in-chief, Senior General Min Aung Hlaing. Min Aung Hlaing was ten years her junior. Born in the far south, in the seaside town of Tavoy, he had grown up in a middle-class family in Rangoon, where his father served as a government civil engineer. He attended one of the best schools in the country and then studied law at Rangoon University. But in his early twenties he decided on a military career, left university for the Defense Academy, became an officer, and quickly climbed through the ranks.

By 2009, he was a major general and part of a new breed of more educated officers. That same year, he spearheaded the army's successful blitz against the Kokang militia. In 2010, he became the first head of the armed forces under the new constitution. For a few years he took a back-seat role; President Thein Sein and many of the new ministers had been far senior to him in the military hierarchy. Then he started giving press conferences and interviews, including to opposition media, and even to the *Washington Post*. He also had his own Facebook page and Twitter account, posting sometimes several times a day about his visits around the country and frequent trips abroad.

He positioned himself as the guardian of the constitutional order. He also made it clear that he wanted his military transformed from the light-infantry counterinsurgency force it had been since inception into what he termed a "standard armed forces," with state-of-the-art land, sea, and air capacities, defending the country's borders. A bespectacled man with a ready smile, he was genial, almost self-effacing with visitors, in a way that belied his steely convictions. He was a staunch nationalist, clear in his own reading of Burmese history and clear in his belief that the army had a historic nation-building role to play. He would now have to work together with the daughter of the army's founder, Aung San Suu Kyi.

It was a rocky start. From the NLD's point of view, the desire of the people for Aung San Suu Kyi to lead them had been conclusively proven. The commander-in-chief's unwillingness to allow the constitution to be amended was a sign of bad faith. From the army's point of view, simply allowing their long-term (and, in their minds, Western-backed) foe to take charge of the government was a big risk and a big compromise. They believed they should be congratulated for allowing the NLD to chose whomever they wanted as president, other than Aung San Suu Kyi, not criticized for standing in the way of any further constitutional change.

But if the ex-generals were getting ready to cede the stage, at least some in the National League for Democracy had difficulty believing that power would really soon be theirs. One newly elected NLD member of parliament said to me that they had no idea what would come next, and that "we were even worried that we might all be arrested that first day in parliament." A senior NLD official, a medical doctor, suggested to me at the time that at least a quarter of his colleagues, former political prisoners, might be suffering from post-traumatic stress disorder. There had been little preparation for this moment, no policies waiting to be implemented, no real strategy for how to manage a future government.

The UK government, for its part, was happy in the expectation that it was now on the inside track. For decades, London had taken the hardest line against the old junta, driving European Union sanctions, showing solidarity with Aung San Suu Kyi above all else. Even with Thein Sein's government they had held back, hoping for the day when Aung San Suu Kyi herself would be in charge.

The British saw themselves in a mentoring role. In 2012, they worried that Aung San Suu Kyi was not building enough of a team, and so, when she visited the Foreign Office in London that year, they had deliberately walked her past offices filled with staff before meeting foreign secretary William Hague "so she could be shown he did not work alone."[3]

The UK government was now effusive in its offers of help. There was even talk of new NLD ministers going first to London "for training." A young British diplomat was seconded to be Aung San Suu Kyi's assistant, and Jonathan Powell, former chief of staff to Tony Blair, was made her new peace process advisor.

On March 30, Thein Sein formally handed over the presidency to Htin Kyaw. It was the high point of Burma's democratic transition: the first peaceful transfer of power to an elected government since 1960. Thein Sein moved to a farm nearby. He said that the years he had spent in the presidential mansion were "the hardest time in my life," and that his wife and daughters, who had often wept at the constant media attacks on the now departing head of state, called it "the hot house."[4]

In the week that followed, the NLD-dominated parliament passed a law to create the entirely new position of State Counsellor for Aung San Suu Kyi. The post would allow her both to direct the government and to steer the NLD in parliament. When the army raised objections, on the grounds that the bill was unconstitutional, her party simply overrode them. The entire bloc of army officers in parliament stood up in protest during the vote. In an ironic twist of fate, one of the army officers present accused the NLD of "bullying."[5] Shwe Mann, seen as a turncoat by many other generals and ex-generals, was appointed head of a special parliamentary commission, even though he had lost his own seat in the elections. When the army objected to this as well, they were overridden again.

Aung San Suu Kyi also took on several ministerial portfolios, initially becoming minister for foreign affairs, education, electric power, and energy. The rest of her cabinet of twenty-one were all men. It was the oldest cabinet in Burmese history, with an average age older than Aung San Suu Kyi, who was seventy-one. Many new ministers were NLD stalwarts, earnest and well-intentioned men, but with little experience in managing much at all. A few were ex-generals who had served in parliament, in the faction of Shwe Mann, rather than under Thein Sein. Others were bureaucrats brought out of retirement. The new minister for finance and planning, Kyaw Win, was quickly revealed as having bought a fake PhD from a Pakistani website.[6] The media made a racket, but he was appointed all the same.

At the same time, Aung San Suu Kyi dismantled the ecosystem of advisors and think tanks that had surrounded Thein Sein and had constantly fed him and his ministers new ideas. This included the Myanmar Peace Center. The hundred or so young staff, many of whom had returned from abroad, were dismissed. The antipathy toward Thein Sein in recent years had been strong, and these institutions were viewed by the NLD as increasingly partisan. It was an unfortunate perspective: though several at the top had clearly aligned themselves with Thein Sein, the vast majority of staff, especially the younger ones, were fervent supporters of democratic change and came from the most liberal fringes of Burmese society. They would have gladly worked under an Aung San Suu Kyi government.

Harder to understand was the absence of any outreach to the hundreds of civil society organizations, activists, and exiles who been waiting for this moment and who wanted nothing more than to lend a hand. One young staffer at the Myanmar Peace Center told me that many of his friends had been divided: some had joined the Peace Center while others refused, saying they didn't want to serve until the NLD came to power. None would have the chance.

Aung San Suu Kyi spoke again and again during these months about the importance of "national reconciliation." For her, this chiefly meant reconciliation between the NLD and the army. Her overriding aim now was constitutional change. For that, she needed the commander-in-chief of the army on board. From her first entry into politics in 1988, she had emphasized at every opportunity that she loved the army, that the army was her father's creation, and that she wanted more than anything to see it stronger and more respected than ever. And for that, she wanted the army beholden to an elected president, which would in the first instance be her.

In several of his interviews, the commander-in-chief had said that the army would indeed agree to constitutional change, but only once the country's myriad armed conflicts were no more. With peace, the army's safeguarding role would diminish. And so Aung San Suu Kyi's priority became peace.

In February 1947, her father, General Aung San, had attended a special conference in the little highland town of Panglong, convened by the hereditary chiefs, the Shan *sawbwas* of the eastern uplands, to discuss Burma's post-colonial future. The British wanted these chiefs and other representatives of the "Frontier Areas" to agree on a way forward before handing over power to Aung San. After a couple of days of discussion and compromise, a deal was struck: there would be a new "Union of Burma," including both the lowlands and uplands, the uplands continuing to enjoy the autonomy they had under the British as well as equality as citizens of the new republic. It was not to be; within months, the country collapsed into civil war. But the dream of Panglong was there for some, not least Aung San Suu Kyi, who saw the event as one of her father's great triumphs.

So she began thinking of a "21st-century Panglong," a new conference, this time not of hereditary chiefs but of all the leaders of the myriad Ethnic Armed Organizations. They would hammer out a new compromise, setting the foundations for the "federal" and "democratic" constitution to come. She told visiting foreign ministers that this could be done quickly, within months. In the meantime, though, the old Myanmar Peace Center, the secretariat established under Aung Min, was dissolved. Aung Min offered help, but this was rebuffed. In his place, Aung San Suu Kyi appointed her personal physician, Dr. Tin Myo Win, to be chief negotiator. Among some of the ethnic minority leaders, there was optimism.

They hoped the incoming government could skillfully mediate between them and the army.

The army leadership also began to think that Aung San Suu Kyi might be just the right person to be in charge. Because of her, the American, European, Chinese, Indian, and Japanese governments were all eager to please. The army's relations with the West looked set to improve. In mid-July, Aung San Suu Kyi expressed a desire to visit the Defense Services Museum in Naypyitaw, a gargantuan complex that told the history of the country from the Stone Age to the present day from the army's point of view. The commander-in-chief could well have sent any senior officer to greet her at the museum, but instead chose to escort her himself. A week later, he attended the commemoration in Rangoon of the anniversary of her father's assassination, and took part the same day at a religious service at her home.

BURMA'S DEMOCRATIC TRANSITION seemed to be settling into its final chapter. Washington planned not only for close ties with the new government but for ties with the army as well. After all, at a time when the Arab Spring had turned into multiple nightmares and even Thailand next door was under a new military junta, the Burmese generals had been true to their word and had allowed their erstwhile foes to take office after free and fair elections.

Hillary Clinton was particularly excited. She was then running to be Obama's successor as president of the United States. Ben Rhodes, then deputy national security advisor, was alone with her backstage after the Democratic Convention in August that year, and mentioned that he had just been in Burma. At that point Clinton "came alive, peppering me with questions." She asked about Aung San Suu Kyi, her relations with the military, the peace process, and the situation in Arakan. They talked about the United Wa State Army and the Kokang militia. "She has to worry about the Chinese in all this, doesn't she?" Clinton asked. This was just minutes after she accepted the Democratic nomination for the presidency. Barack Obama then came into the room and asked, "What are you guys talking about?" "Burma," was the reply. Obama cared deeply about Burma too, but at that point he gave Rhodes a look that could only mean, "Are you crazy?"[7]

At the same time, the Chinese government was planning a comeback. They had carefully cultivated ties with Aung San Suu Kyi, welcoming her to Beijing the year before even though she was then still only the opposition leader. As soon as her new government was in office, China's foreign minister, Wang Yi, sped to Burma to be the first foreign dignitary to pay his respects. In August, the Chinese Communist Party's head of international relations, Song Tao, arrived to meet with all the most powerful figures in the country: Aung San Suu Kyi, the army commander-in-chief, ex-president Thein Sein, Shwe Mann, and even the old dictator Than Shwe. The Chinese were covering their bets, moving methodically.

On August 19, in Beijing, Aung San Suu Kyi met with Chinese president Xi Jinping, who "praised her efforts to follow in the footsteps of older generations." As a princeling himself, the son of a senior revolutionary leader, he was curious about Aung San Suu Kyi and respected her as the daughter of a nation's founder. Both stressed their *paukpaw* friendship. *Paukphaw* literally means "born together" and implies a blood affinity. There was a shared belief that the Chinese and the Burmese were racially akin.[8]

By then, the Chinese government felt confident enough that Aung San Suu Kyi was going to be good for Sino-Burmese relations that they gave her a special gift. The "21st-century Panglong" that Aung San Suu Kyi had convened was coming up in a couple of weeks' time, and the big insurgent armies on the Chinese border were not sure if they wanted to turn up. The Chinese made sure they did, packing their leaders into a plane and flying them to Naypyitaw themselves.[9]

The conference attracted hundreds of ethnic minority delegates, including high-ranking figures from nearly all the armed organizations. It didn't, however, produce any concrete results, so it was re-billed as the start of a series of conferences. There were days of speeches, for the most part light on substance or strategy. The UN Secretary-General, Ban Ki-moon, blandly said, "There is a long road ahead, but the path is very promising." There was little discussion of the nature of capitalism as it had developed in Burma, of the booming illicit economies, or even of issues related to race and belonging. Instead, most delegates—there were nearly a thousand in all—took existing ethnic categories as given and sought a formula by which they could all live side by side in a new "federal" system of government. The plight of the Muslims in northern Arakan was not mentioned, as they were beyond the pale of included ethnicities. The word "Rohingya" was not uttered.

More ominously, though, the conference roused the suspicions of the army. They saw Aung San Suu Kyi relying on British assistants and advisors, and they worried that the peace process would be used to corner them, forcing them to accept sweeping constitutional changes. Worse, from their viewpoint, would be a peace agreement that didn't include their number one goal: the disarmament of all the rival armed forces.

At the same time, the revolutionary dynamic that some on the military side might have feared from the new government was nowhere in sight. If anything, change was creeping along too slowly. Other than the conference, not much had happened since the handover of power six months before.

The old president, Thein Sein, had used his external advisors, quasi-government bodies such as the Myanmar Peace Center and an assortment of think tanks, in part to circumvent the old bureaucracy. Having dismantled these institutions, and with no grand strategy for reforming the public sector, the incoming administration was becoming dependent on the same bureaucrats, most ex-military men, who had been around since the days of the old dictatorship. In several ministries, there was one new man, the minister, usually a septuagenarian NLD loyalist with no government experience, trying to preside over thousands of long-serving civil servants, adept at managing red tape, many with their hands deep in the till. Parliamentary questions and answers were televised live, and ministers found themselves entirely reliant on their underlings for the answers needed to avoid public embarassment. By late 2017, the NLD was caught up in the vortex of Naypyitaw.

Many were disappointed by the lack of dynamism, including local and foreign businesspeople. They expected the NLD, as a "pro-democracy" movement, to be resolutely pro-market. But the new government was unsure of its economic agenda. Most in government advocated liberalization and a welcoming of foreign investment. At the same time, senior bureaucrats were keen to hang on to their micromanaging authority. Every department wanted to have a say in every project. What talk there was of economic reform centered on improving business conditions, creating more efficient markets, and making marginal improvements to education and health services. Debate often focused on whether or not to protect domestic businesses from global competition.

There was no diagnosis of the failures of capitalism in Burma over the past quarter century. No one advocated higher taxes or a redistribution of wealth or land. No one suggested writing off the crushing debts facing poor people or creating a new welfare state through sweeping increases in social spending. A radical, urgent plan to help ordinary people and reduce inequality was nowhere in sight.

Over these months, I met several ministers as well as the chief ministers of Rangoon and Mandalay to offer my assistance. All were eager to do the right thing, yet it was plain to see how difficult it would be for them to get anything done. In business circles and in the political class, there were rumblings, but over the summer of 2016, the millions of people who had voted for the NLD were still more than satisfied. Sure, the government was slow, but this was the first elected civilian government in fifty years; "Give them a chance!" many people posted on Facebook. NLD members had been battered and bruised, many literally, for decades. They needed time to understand how things worked and who was who. NLD supporters worried that there were conspiracies all around. They feared especially that issues around the Rohingya, nationalism, and the "protection of race and religion" would be used to weaken them politically.

Up to this point, Aung San Suu Kyi had said little about the Rohingya, or Buddhist–Muslim relations more generally. The NLD had been criticized by liberal voices in Burma for not having included a single Muslim candidate on its parliamentary election roster. There were no Muslims in government either. But Aung San Suu Kyi realized the importance of finding a lasting solution to the crisis in Arakan, and at the end of August 2016 she appointed former UN Secretary-General Kofi Annan to head a new advisory commission. It was a bold move. Kofi Annan was not someone who could be manipulated. He would place the rights of all people front and center of whatever recommendations he made. The army was critical of the appointment, saying that foreigners should not be included. The Arakanese Buddhist politicians were even more critical; from the start, they said they would boycott the work of the commission. There was a furious debate in parliament, but the NLD's majority overrode all objections. Then came a new round of violence that changed everything.

ATAULLAH ABU AMMAR JUNUNI was born sometime in the 1960s in Karachi, Pakistan, to a Rohingya immigrant father and a Pakistani mother. Fluent in both Arabic and the Rohingya dialect, he grew up in Saudi Arabia, receiving an Islamic *madrassa* education, before going on to military training in Pakistan or Afghanistan. After the 2012 communal violence in Arakan, he and twenty or so other Rohingya exiles in Saudi

Arabia set up what became known as the Arakan Rohingya Salvation Army, or ARSA.[10]

There have long been Muslim insurgencies in Arakan. The first was the so-called Mujahedeen, which seized control of northern Arakan during the transition from colonial rule in 1948, hoping to join the area to the new East Pakistan. When Pakistan rejected any such annexation, the goal shifted to a separate Muslim "homeland" within Burma. It wasn't until 1954, with an army counteroffensive called Operation Monsoon, that Rangoon was able to retake control. In the 1970s and 1980s, there were a series of other insurgencies, including the Rohingya Solidarity Organization, inspired in part by the rise of Islamist groups around the world.

In 2013, Ataullah began recruiting local men in the areas of Arakan closest to Bangladesh. They were not in short supply: many young men, especially, were both angry and desperate after the events of recent years and believed an armed insurrection, however unlikely to suceed, might be the only choice left. The Burmese army's intelligence capabilities in the area were extremely weak. Nevertheless, secrecy was of the utmost importance. Several suspected informants were killed. The group used WhatsApp, the encrypted messaging app. As many Rohingya are illiterate, soundfiles were used to communicate information.

The aim was to seize control of Maungdaw township, the slice of land bordering Bangladesh. If they could take the hills just to the east as well, they could defend the terrirtory from an army counterattack. ARSA could then claim to be an Ethnic Armed Organization deserving of a place at the peace table. But things went awry. In early September 2016, before they were ready for their first operation, two of their members were arrested after informers tipped off the local police. They were released after heavy bribes, of more than 30 million kyats (around $30,000), were paid. Ataullah knew that he needed to act fast.

In the early morning of October 9, an ARSA-led force of several hundred Rohingya men, armed mainly with homemade weapons, attacked three police posts, hacking nine policemen to death and capturing sixty-two firearms and around 10,000 rounds of ammunition. Two days later, the group posted a video on YouTube claiming responsibility.

The army leadership was caught off-guard. The generals, feeling humiliated, were incensed. They were also sensitive to criticism. Myo Yan Naing Thein, the head of a prominent NLD-affiliated think tank, criticized the army commander-in-chief, blaming the attacks on his "negligence." The think tank director was soon arrested under a draconian new anti-defamation law and sentenced to six months in prison.[11]

In the weeks and months that followed, the army conducted a classic counterinsurgency operation, sealing off the area, burning down villages, displacing villagers, and trying to dislodge rebels from any possible popular base of support. This is what the army had done ever since its first counterinsurgency operation, Operation Flush in 1947, which was conducted together with the British Army a few months before independence. Access by humanitarian aid organizations was also cut off. Non-Muslims began to be armed as militia, a longtime demand by Arakanese Buddhists that until now been had denied.

In one incident, the army moved into a predominantly Muslim village and found itself confronting not only ARSA rebels but hundreds of other men and boys attacking them with whatever they could use as weapons. ARSA was in this way different from other rebel groups, like the Kachin or Wa: they wore no uniforms and aimed to provoke a more general uprising. In the incident, a lieutenant colonel was shot dead and troops were forced to retreat before calling in helicopter gunships for support.

Thousands of Muslim civilians were now crossing the border into Bangladesh, bringing with them harrowing tales, including of widespread sexual violence committed by the army as part of its crackdown. "Refugee accounts paint a horrific picture of an army that is out of control and rampaging through Rohingya villages," said Brad Adams, Asia chief for the New York–based Human Rights Watch.[12]

IN LATE JANUARY 2017, Debbie Aung Din (who had met George Bush in the weeks after Cyclone Nargis) organized a special trip to the Malukus in Indonesia, where Christians and Muslims had learned to live together again after years of bloody intercommunal violence. She took with her the government's information minister, Pe Myint, as well as both Muslim and Buddhist leaders from Arakan, senior army officers, and members of the NLD. Later, she told me she felt the trip had exceeded expectations. "They began discussing practical next steps. Everyone was energized." One of the key participants was Ko Ni, an NLD Muslim lawyer who had been pushing hard for constitutional change. We lived in the same apartment building in Rangoon, and I had last seen him on election day.

Debbie Aung Din described what happened next: "When our plane landed at Yangon airport the VIPs—the minister, two deputy ministers, and army generals—walked toward the VIP lounge. The rest of us went to get our bags and then walked out the main exit. We all said goodbye. Ko Ni was met by his family, and I remember seeing him pick up his little grandchild and carry her across the taxi lane to wait for his car. Just then I heard an incredible bang. The next thing I knew, I saw him collapsed in a pool of blood. People were shouting "U Ko Ni!" I could see the assassin running down toward the car park with his gun held up in the air, being chased by a group."

Ko Ni, a leading figure in the NLD and a constitutional advisor to the government, had been murdered in the most public of places. A taxi driver who led the chase was killed as well. The gunman was apprehended, and a former army officer alleged to have hired him was arrested. But no one knows exactly who was behind the plot.

The assassination marked a watershed. In the hours and days afterward, there was much debate about motive. Was Ko Ni killed because he was a Muslim of Indian descent, or because he was the leading voice for constitutional change? Whatever the motive, the effect was clear: the NLD, already fearing plots against them, was sent reeling. For months, there had been growing paranoia that the army establishment, the ex-generals, the USDP, the bureaucrats, everyone was scheming against them. Now their paranoia seemed justified. If Ko Ni could be killed, who was next? I was at Ko Ni's burial on the outskirts of Rangoon, together with several leading NLD figures and thousands of Rangoon Muslims. Aung San Suu Kyi neither attended nor made any statement for several days. Caution now dominated.

BY FEBRUARY 2017, over 70,000 Rohingya were seeking refuge in Bangladesh. That same month, the UN alleged widespread abuses amounting to "crimes against humanity" and called for an international inquiry. The army rejected all allegations, but subsequently sacked the local police commander for "poor performance." The Rohingya situation was now dominating international and especially Western images of Burma. Kofi Annan's commission continued with its work. The government responded to foreign calls for an inquiry or any other action by saying that they would need to wait for the commission's recommendations.

No one believed the crisis was in any way over. Over the spring and summer of 2017, at least thirty-three Rohingya civilians were killed by ARSA, mainly suspected police informers or village officials seen as government collaborators. In one village, a Rohingya man who denied to reporters (on a staged media visit) that army abuses had taken place was found beheaded the next day.[13] The government of India had recently passed on intelligence to the Burmese government alleging links between Rohingya militants and the Pakistani terrorist group Lashkar-e-Taiba.[14] In July, Al-Qaeda's Bangladesh offshoot Ansar al-Islam urged Muslim youths of Bangladesh to join the fight.[15]

The army's principal demand was for the president to convene the

National Defense and Security Council. The council was a constitutional body that brought together top members of the executive and legislative branches of government with leaders of the armed forces. Under the previous government, Thein Sein had regularly chaired the body, to discuss and decide security issues. During the communal riots in 2012 in 2013 and during the Kokang fighting in 2015, he used the council to declare a local state of emergency, giving the army wide-ranging powers.

According to the constitution, the president, in extreme circumstances and "in consultation" with the council, could temporarily hand over power to the commander-in-chief. This was the scenario the NLD dreaded most, a constitutional coup d'état. So Aung San Suu Kyi resolutely refused to convene such a meeting, perhaps worried that doing so might confer enhanced legitimacy on the council. Meanwhile, the army was increasingly adamant that they be given the proper authority to act.

In July, the old ruling party, the Union Solidarity and Development Party, met in Rangoon with thirteen smaller parties and called for the National Defense and Security Council to be convened, along with a declaration of a local state of emergency and the toughest possible response to ARSA. As the public cry for action increased, the security forces stepped up arrests of suspected ARSA militants.

In the West, there was escalating criticism of the Burmese army and government. The crisis was portrayed first and foremost as a human rights and humanitarian disaster, the tens of thousands of refugees in Bangladesh adding to the sense of urgency. UN agencies warned that up to 80,000 Rohingya children still in the country were suffering from severe malnutrition, the result of a breakdown in local markets as well as restrictions on aid access. But for the army commander-in-chief, the priority was to show that he was not being weak in the face of what in Burma was portrayed as an unprecedented terrorist threat.

In early August, there were growing reports of ARSA killings. These now included the murder of non-Muslim civilians in the area. Arakanese

Buddhist politicians flew to Naypyitaw and appealed to the army chief for increased protection. Within days, the military sent significant reinforcements to the area, including three battalions of their elite 33rd and 99th Light Infantry Divisions.

One morning that week, the traffic near my apartment building was unusually light. A taxi driver told me many parents had kept their children home because of rumors of an impending Islamic attack. In the Philippines, the Battle of Marawi was then in full swing. Militants allied with the Islamic State of Iraq and the Levant (ISIL) had seized the port city of Marawi in late May, leading to months of intense fighting with the Philippines army. Public opinion in Burma saw ARSA not as a ragtag outfit trying to defend the rights of an oppressed minority but as militants who were the local leading edge of a global Islamic threat.

On August 24, Kofi Annan submitted his report in person to both Aung San Suu Kyi and the army commander-in-chief. The former Secretary-General warned that "unless concerted action—led by the government and aided by all sectors of the government and society—is taken soon, we risk the return of another cycle of violence and radicalization, which will further deepen the chronic poverty that afflicts Rakhine State." He offered an approach that integrated security concerns, human rights, and the long-term development of the region.[16] Aung San Suu Kyi embraced the recommendations and promised their full implementation.

A few hours later, just after midnight on August 25, 2017, ARSA launched simultaneous assaults on thirty police posts as well as an army base across three townships in northern Arakan. Each assault involved hundreds of Rohingya men, a few armed with guns and explosives and the rest with machetes and homemade weapons. Ten policemen were killed, as well as a soldier and an immigration officer. The government said seventy-seven attackers were killed and one captured. ARSA tweeted: "This is a legitimate step for us to defend the world's persecuted people and liberate the oppressed people from the hands of the oppressors!"

At around 8 a.m. that morning, ARSA fighters entered a small Hindu village, rounded up all sixty-nine men, women, and children—people of Indian descent who were neither Rohingya nor Arakanese—killed most and abducted the rest. The forty-six Hindus of a neighboring settlement were abducted as well. To this day their whereabouts are unknown.[17] ARSA also attacked Arakanese Buddhist villages and the villages of the small Mro and Daingnet minority. Over WhatsApp, ARSA sent out the message: "Burn down all Rakhine villages, one by one. . . . Attack their village from all sides so that every corner of the village will start burning. Do not spare even a single village—all Mro villages, all Daingnet villages—set fire to all of them."[18]

Burmese social media was alive with fear and anger that all of northern Arakan was about to be overrun by "Islamic terrorists." "Maungdaw and Buthidaung have fallen," said one former senior official to me that afternoon, referring to the two townships closest to Bangladesh. That was far from the case. But the stories of atrocities against non-Muslims were circulating widely within hours, fanning calls for the army to do anything it took to wipe out the enemy at the "western gate."

The army's response was merciless. "We received an order to burn down the entire village if there is any disturbance. If you villagers aren't living peacefully, we will destroy everything." This was part of an audio recording of a Burmese military officer, taken during a phone conversation with a Rohingya man from Inn Din village, Maungdaw township, in late August 2017. Within days, the village was razed to the ground.[19] Brutal fighting continued through the first days of September, leaving hundreds if not thousands dead.

According to the United Nations, Amnesty International, and other international human rights organizations, there were large-scale massacres in at least three Rohingya villages, perpetrated by the Burmese military, targeting mainly men but with women and children also being killed. These massacres took place in the villages from which ARSA had attacked. In at least four other villages, but likely several more, security forces opened fire indiscriminately, killing people as they fled and then burning down their homes. As many as seventy people may have been killed in each instance. These were also villages linked to ARSA, suggesting a collective punishment for the rebel attacks. In a much larger number of villages, the vast majority of people fled after hearing of violence nearby, before the army and Arakanese militia arrived. Over the coming months, the army or newly armed Arakanese Buddhist militia burned down scores of villages, or the Muslim parts of mixed villages, either after people left or to force them to leave.[20]

The total number of people killed in the weeks after August 25 is difficult to know, as no independent assessments or forensic teams have been allowed into the area. The French aid organization Médecins Sans Frontières estimated in December 2017 that at least 6,700 Rohingya men, women, and children were killed, mainly by gunshot wounds. This estimate was based on interviews with refugees in Bangladesh.[21] Amnesty and other human rights groups have attempted to corroborate this figure with satellite imagery, and say the estimate is approximately correct.[22] But without a proper investigation, no one can say for sure.

The worst incident was probably at the riverside village of Tula Toli. It was from there that ARSA had attacked government troops and also burned down a Mro village, killing six people. By August 30, the army had gained the upper hand and, together with militia, moved into the village, forcing hundreds to flee onto a peninsula to the east. Most couldn't swim, so they were trapped. The men and older boys were separated from the rest before being executed. Some women and children were hit in the gunfire as well. No one knows exactly how many people were killed, but estimates run into the hundreds.[23]

Two days before, about five miles to the south, the army had arrived at the coastal village of Inn Din and, together with Arakanese militia, began torching Muslim homes, forcing Rohingya to flee into the nearby hills. On

September 1, hundreds of people who had fled were caught by soldiers on the beach, looking for food and a means of escape to Bangladesh. Ten of the men were detained, interrogated, and then executed as suspected militants the next morning.[24]

The reaction in the West and the Islamic world was devastating. In New York, American UN ambassador Nikki Haley called what was happening a "brutal, sustained campaign to cleanse the country of an ethnic minority," while UN Secretary-General António Guterres described it as a "human rights nightmare."[25] Turkish president Recep Tayyip Erdogan claimed that genocide was taking place against the Rohingya minority. In Grozny, Chechnya, tens of thousands rallied in support of the Rohingya in front of the city's main mosque. In Jakarta, days of protests including members of the extremist Islamic Defenders Front brought traffic to a standstill. Across Pakistan, demonstrators demanding action against the Burmese government clashed with police. Al-Qaeda warned that Myanmar would face "punishment for its crimes."[26]

By mid-September, as many as 400,000 refugees, nearly all of them Muslim, had crossed the border into Bangladesh, many having walked for days without food or rest. It was the biggest single flight of refugees in modern times. Aung San Suu Kyi's staunchest supporters in the West were dismayed that she had not demanded an end to the violence. In a public letter sent on September 7, Archibishop Desmond Tutu, calling her "my dearly beloved sister," wrote, "It is incongruous for a symbol of righteousness to lead such a country. If the political price of your ascension to the highest office in Myanmar is your silence, the price is surely too steep."[27]

On September 19, Aung San Suu Kyi broke her silence and, in a televised address to diplomats in Naypyitaw, questioned the narrative taking shape overseas. No military operations had taken place in the last two weeks, she stated. And most of the Muslim population of Arakan had not fled, which suggested that the situation wasn't as severe as some were making out. She also said that those who had left for Bangladesh would be welcome back. Overseas, few were satisfied by this response. A wave of even more intense international criticism followed.

In late September, St. Hugh's College, Oxford, replaced Aung San Suu Kyi's portrait with a classical Japanese painting entitled *Morning Glory*. A couple of months later, the cities of Oxford and Dublin stripped her of the awards they had given her in 2012. Bob Geldof, who had sung for her that year, said, "We should not have any truck with this woman . . . it's ridiculous, but she's sort of let us Dubliners down, she's let Ireland down, because we thought she was wonderful. But we've been duped."[28]

The views inside Burma were not only different but diametrically opposed. The vast majority believed that ARSA was not only a real and present danger to the country but had inflicted terrible suffering on non-Muslim communities in Arakan. Burmese Facebook pages teemed with photographs of Arakanese Buddhists and Hindus who had been killed. Radio stations broadcast interviews with weeping survivors of ARSA attacks. Most cheered the army's offensive to wipe out ARSA. Aye Aye Soe, whose hometown, Kyaukphyu, had been the scene of communal violence five years before, remembers people saying, "Why couldn't the army have protected us like that back in 2012?"[29] Few believed the stories of atrocities told by the Rohingya refugees in Bangladesh. "Everyone has a smartphone these days, why aren't there any photos or videos?" I heard many argue. Others queried why Western governments could not produce any satelllite images of mass graves, when they had been able to do so in Kosovo nearly twenty years before. At worst, people said, the army campaign was no different from other counterinsurgency operations that had been going on for decades.

Over September and October, the army commander-in-chief, General Min Aung Hlaing, delivered a series of uncompromising speeches, promising to do his duty and finish the "unfinished business of 1942"—meaning the twin threats of "Bengali" immigration and Muslim insurrection. On

Facebook, his following soared. There were loud calls for a wall to be built to prevent renewed "Islamic" aggression from across the Bangladesh border. Both Aung San Suu Kyi's government and the army promised to make this happen and asked leading businessmen to help foot the bill.

Because so few believed the allegations of army massacres, there was also mounting anger at what was seen as extreme Western bias. Regional governments were largely supportive. Just days after the fighting began, Indian prime minister Narendra Modi, on a visit to Burma, refused to denounce the crackdown, instead saying, "We share your concerns about extremist violence in Rakhine State and especially the violence against security forces." In late October, thousands rallied in downtown Rangoon in support of the army and against "international pressure."

On social media, the Burmese conjectured that the West's unwillingness to even acknowlege the violence committed by ARSA was part of a Saudi–Western plot to destabilize Arakan and force the country to accept hundreds of thousands of new "Bengali" settlers. For what purpose, no one could say. Burmese cartoons showed UN officials, their pockets stuffed with cash, unlocking the "western gate" for jihadi militants while bearded men in Arab dress looked on approvingly.

Discussing the Rohingya crisis with the *Washington Post* in November, Aung San Suu Kyi said, "The whole thing is a rigmarole."[30]

By year's end, there were over 700,000 newly arrived Rohingya in Bangladesh, the vast majority at the sprawling Kutapalong camp, the largest single refugee site in the world. More than half were children, thousands of them traumatized by the violence they had witnessed. The Burmese government wanted to counter increasingly strident international claims of "ethnic cleansing," but they were wary of opening themselves up to criticism at home, where few accepted the UN's figures. So they entered into a bilateral agreement with the Bangladesh government, promising to take back all who could give evidence of past residence. It wasn't clear what evidence might be accepted, and it was even less clear whether actual citizenship for those who had left would be any more likely if they returned than it had been before. In any case, with over a hundred thousand Rohingya left behind in Arakan still languishing in camps, aid restricted, few journalists allowed into the area, and an adamant refusal to permit international investigation, there seemed little possibility that the refugees themselves would want to return anytime soon.

If they did, they would be coming back to a changed landscape. Over late 2017, dozens of burned-down villages were bulldozed. New roads were built as well, to better connect northern Arakan with the rest of the state. Many on the Burmese side, believing that the strip along the Bangladesh border had long been a locus for illegal entry, crime, and more recently militant violence, argued that it should be kept "Bengali-free" and be given a beefed-up security infrastructure. Rohingya returnees, after undergoing a "verification process," would be resettled farther inland.

In December, two Reuters journalists, Wa Lone and Kyaw Soe Oo, were arrested while carrying documents that had just been given to them by police officers, in what was widely viewed as a set-up. Both men had been investigating the execution of Rohingya men at Inn Din village. The military subsequently conducted its own inquiry, uncovered the bodies of the ten men, and sentenced seven of their own to ten years' hard labor. The Reuters journalists were nonetheless prosecuted for violation of the Official Secrets Act, setting off an international furor.

With the new year, the situation became more convoluted still. On the evening of January 16, 2018, police opened fire on Arakanese Buddhist demonstrators in Mrauk-U, a large town not far from Sittwe which was also the capital of the old Arakanese kingdom, its sublime 16th-century temples and the remains of palace walls and moats a reminder to Arakanese nationalists of past sovereignty. The demonstrators were demanding the right to commemorate an upcoming anniversary of the fall of the kingdom to Burmese invaders in 1785. Seven were shot dead, and twenty police were reported injured in clashes with the crowd. Two days later, the leading Arakanese politician and member of parliament Aye Maung was arrested for sedition. Prosecutors alleged that at a literature festival earlier in the month, he had made comments that were supportive of the Arakan Army. This was a new rebel outfit, set up far to the north at the Kachin Independence Army's headquarters on the China border. Its leader, Twan Mrat Naing, was a charismatic thirty-something erstwhile tour guide, who now promised self-determination for the Arakanese (Buddhist) people. Using the hashtag #ArakanDream2020, he and his followers posted increasingly assertive statements on Twitter while also uploading slick videos of their military prowess, including versions in English, on YouTube. Recruits included the desperately poor Arakanese migrants who had been working in the jade mines. During 2018, the Arakan Army, now several thousand strong, moved at least a thousand troops south and began battling government forces in the hills just north of the area where the recent Rohingya violence had taken place.

Aye Maung and his Arakan National Party had trounced both the NLD and the USDP in state elections—the only party to defeat the NLD anywhere. They dominated the state legislature. But under the constitution, the president appoints the chief minister of every state. The Arakan National Party had hoped that, in the spirit of democracy, Aung San Suu Kyi would appoint one of their own. When she didn't even reach out to them, they felt humiliated. Many, especially young Arakanese, gravitated toward the Arakan Army.

The conflict in Arakan in 2018 was not simply between Muslims and Buddhists, or between the Burmese state and the Rohingya. Forgotten in many outside perspectives is the central place of the Arakanese Buddhists, many of whom consider themselves heirs to a once independent Arakan, and who see both the Burmese to the east and the "Bengalis" to the west as existential threats to their future.

By April, Facebook founder Mark Zuckerberg was getting ensnared in the Burma debacle. That month, he was called before the US Senate to answer questions about his company's use of personal data. He was also grilled on Facebook's possible role in stoking communal violence in Burma. He said that what had happened was a "terrible tragedy, and we need to do more."[31] Speaking to the news site Vox, he later said that Facebook was indeed actively monitoring Burmese posts and in one case had moved quickly to stop incitements to violence. Burmese human rights groups critical of Facebook's lackadaisical approach responded immediately, saying that it was they who had discovered the posts, alerted Facebook, and then waited days for Facebook to respond. Zuckerberg apologized and promised again "to hire more Burmese speakers." He made no mention of hiring speakers of Burma's many other languages.

In August, the UN's Independent International Fact-Finding Mission on Myanmar released its initial report. This investigation was mandated by the global body's Human Rights Council in the aftermath of the 2017 violence and refugee exodus. From the start, the Burmese government refused to cooperate. Investigative teams were not allowed inside the country to collect evidence and so relied primarily on the reports of Rohingya refugees.[32] Their conclusions were stark. At a press conference in New York, one of the mission's members, Radhika Coomaraswamy, argued that "the horrors inflicted on Rohingya men, women and children during the August 2017 operations, including their indiscriminate killing, rise to the level of both war crimes and crimes against humanity." Other mission members called for "top military commanders in Myanmar to be investigated and prosecuted for the gravest crimes under international law, including genocide." In addition, they said that Aung San Suu Kyi had "not used her de facto position as head of government nor her moral authority to stem or prevent the unfolding events."[33]

A day later, the UN Security Council met in open session. Western representatives issued damning statements. Nikki Haley spoke of the "stomach-churning" accounts in the State Department's own report. At the UK's invitation, the actress Cate Blanchett, who had just visited the refugee camps in Bangladesh, pleaded for more assistance. "Please let's not fail them again," she said.

The following week, the International Criminal Court ruled that it had jurisdiction over the crime against humanity of deportation allegedly committed against the Rohingya, opening the door to possible future prosecution. Even though Burma wasn't a signatory to the Rome Convention, the court said that it had jurisdiction because "an element of the crime" took place in Bangladesh.[34] A few days later, responding to an ICC investigation into possible American war crimes in Afghanistan, US National Security Advisor John Bolton launched an excoriating attack on the court, calling it illegitimate and threatening sanctions. "We will let the ICC die on its own. After all, for all intents and purposes, the ICC is already dead," said the longtime foe of international institutions.[35] His remarks were shared widely on Burmese social media.

But the move that received the most attention in Burma was the shutting down of the army commander-in-chief's Facebook page, which was followed by millions of people.[36] Just as the UN's human rights report was being released, Facebook took down eighteen accounts, an Instagram account, and dozens of linked pages, including the army's official pages. Facebook had learned the day before that it was going to be named by the UN as having contributed to the rise of hate speech in Burma, panicked, and chose the most obvious targets.

As Western opprobrium mounted and the United Nations heaped on the pressure, China stepped into the breach. In the early 2010s, Beijing had watched as the military junta it had supported for decades first mutated into a quasi-democratic government and then embraced Western suitors without even a nod in their direction. They felt that an Aung San Suu Kyi government might give them a fresh start, and they were right. Since her time in opposition, Aung San Suu Kyi had said consistently that she wanted good relations with Burma's northern neighbor. She knew that China, with its influence over all the rebel groups along the common border, was indispensable for the success of any peace process. And now China offered vital protection at the UN, blocking (with Russia) any move toward harsh Security Council action.

In December 2017, as international media coverage of the Rohingya crisis reached fever pitch, Aung San Suu Kyi called on Xi Jinping and other top Chinese leaders. She was accompanied by a team of ministers, including the ministers of energy and construction as well as the chief minister of Mandalay. The week before, the army commander-in-chief had visited as well, meeting Xi on what was his eighth visit and touring extensively arround the country. Burma was already a partner in China's Belt Road Initiative, a set of global insfracture projects, valued at over a trillion dollars, designed to place China squarely at the center of a new world economic order. Talks now turned to a "Chinese–Myanmar economic corridor": massive Chinese investments in Burma, including fulfillment of the long-held dream of a multi-billion-dollar deep-sea port in Arakan and a rail network connecting the port to Mandalay and then the Chinese hinterland.[37]

The Chinese had long assumed that they would be Burma's primary economic and strategic partner. The past few years had disrupted their plans. Now was the time to get things back on track. The Chinese foreign ministry went on a charm offensive, inviting hundreds of Burmese from across the political spectrum (including me) to visit on study tours and to attend conferences. While Western embassies discussed punitive measures, China's energetic ambassador in Rangoon, Hong Liang, hosted lavish banquets for the country's business elite. China's top party officials, ministers, and senior officers of the People's Liberation Army visited Naypyitaw almost weekly. The proposed projects would not only connect China across Burma to the sea; they would also fasten Burma even more tightly to Chinese markets. In September 2018, Burmese and Chinese ministers signed an agreement to move ahead.

By early 2019, Burma was facing a wall of challenges. Near the Bangladesh border, the Arakan Army, moving south from their hilltop bases into the plains below, attacked police stations and military convoys. Fresh counterinsurgency operations then displaced thousands of Arakanese Buddhist civilians. Tensions between Arakanese nationalists and their Burmese counterparts approached a boiling point as insults were traded over social media. Meanwhile, the plight of both Rohingya refugees in Bangladesh and the half million remaining in Arakan showed scant signs of improvement. Over the preceding year, relations between Burma and the West had cooled dramatically, with the US, Canada, and the European Union all considering a fresh round of sanctions.

Hopes for a lasting peace had also dimmed. Fighting flared across the north and northeast of the country, not only between government and rebel forces but now among the Ethnic Armed Organizations as well. On secluded hillsides, troops of the Restoration Council of the Shan State battled both the Taang National Liberation Front and their ostensible brethren in the Shan State Army North. In Lashio, near China, fighting between rival militias could be heard on the outskirts of town. At least 100,000 people were living in displaced persons' camps in the Shan and Kachin states, many with little access to outside assistance.

The "21st-century Panglong" conference and its follow-up meetings had delivered little. The problem wasn't just the process itself but the idea that a single mechanism could address so many different challenges, from combating discrimination against minorities, to decentralizing government, to ending the long-running conflicts between different armed factions, some tied tightly to illicit trade. As profits from methamphetamine production skyrocketed, funds for arming militias became more plentiful.

There was also rising internal criticism of the government, in the media and from civil society organizations, for its perceived authoritarian style and unwillingness to listen to dissenting views. Aung San Suu Kyi rarely if ever met with local media, and had little contact with civil society organizations. She had selected as her key aides bureaucrats, diplomats, and retired army officers, all from the days of the military junta. Whereas the ex-generals of the previous government had needed to prove their democratic credentials, Aung San Suu Kyi and the NLD, having won an election landslide, believed legitimacy was already on their side.

Another serious challenge was the economy. Growth slowed, business confidence tanked, foreign investment ground to a halt, and tourism dropped to levels not seen in years. The overinflated real estate market buckled into recession. By 2019, top companies were increasingly and in some cases desperately strapped for cash. The central bank had imposed stringent new regulations to bring Burma in line with international standards. The banking system was a mess. Businessmen had borrowed hundreds of millions of dollars as overdrafts, with no real intention of repayment. Now the loans were being called in and dozens of the largest companies were teetering on the edge of bankruptcy.[38]

Businessmen blamed the government for poor management and the lack of a clear economic agenda. What many wanted was a kind of state capitalism, with a cozy relationship between leading political figures and the private sector at its core. With others, there was simply a hankering for the old days, when officially licensed riches were there for the taking. The government itself seemed torn between the neoliberal prescriptions of experts, both local and international, bureaucratic desires to micromanage the economy, and the old left-wing instincts of many in the NLD rank and file. There were good people on the government's economic team, but decision-making was slow and there was little coordination across ministries.

For ordinary people, the picture was mixed. Over the past three years, the garment sector had boomed and rice exports to China had soared, benefiting rural families across the country. At the same time, the situation of Burmese workers in Thailand improved considerably, the result of changes made under the past government to legalize migration and facilitate remittances. Over a billion dollars a year were now being channeled back to poor villages. All these things, however, provided nothing approaching real security. In early 2019 China was looking to impose new quotas on rice imports, the garment sector was under threat from possible European Union sanctions, and populist feelings in Thailand were increasingly hostile toward migrant workers.

The underlying problem, as always, was that there was little idea of what life for ordinary people could or should be like in ten or twenty years' time. And this wasn't an economy that had been doing reasonably well and needed only a gentle steer: a deeply exploitative colonial economy had been followed by war and a disastrous socialist experiment. Capitalism was then resuscitated in the 1990s by a hodgepodge of illicit industries. It was an incredibly unequal economy that was in danger of being overwhelmed by two unmanageable forces: the disastrous effects of climate change and the rise of China next door.

On all sides of Burmese politics, there was little vision of the future.

EPILOGUE

AUNG SAN SUU KYI had long given up her Rangoon lakeside villa and was living in Naypyitaw in a modest, recently built house, decorated with paintings by local artists and glass coffee tables she had designed herself, together with her beloved golden retriever, Taichito, a gift from her son Kim.[1] She had few close friends or confidants, and as a teetotaler no one with whom she enjoyed a drink at the end of the day. She hadn't lived anything approaching a normal life for thirty years, having gone straight from Oxford housewife into the maelstrom of Burmese politics, then house arrest and the trauma of separation from her family, near death at the hands of the regime, a sudden new political opening, trips around the world, endless adulation, and finally the crisis of the Rohingya. She was, however, close where she had wanted to be for three decades.

In 2019, Burma was a kind of democracy. She had won an election and was for all effective purposes the head of government. She chaired the cabinet and nearly all important committees. Her image dominated state media, and at every public function she attended, from Buddhist ceremonies to diplomatic receptions, she was in the top spot. Power was centralized in her office, and no other figure stood even close in terms of either popularity or decision-making authority. Though the constitutional set-up meant that the armed forces enjoyed near-absolute autonomy, and that the three security ministers were appointees of the commander-in-chief, the chain of command led to a president who was effectively a deputy of Aung San Suu Kyi. All non-military issues, from the government budget to health and education to foreign policy, were in her hands alone.

It was a power she used sparingly. There were no clear-cut policy aims or timetables that had to be met, few changes in government personnel, and little intervention in the day-to-day work of her ministers. There was also little in the way of succession planning. She appointed a new president, Win Myint, and the Mandalay chief minister, Zaw Myint Maung, both former long-serving political prisoners, as her deputies in the party, but both were only a few years younger than she was.

Instead, Aung San Suu Kyi presided over the country, offering up a life story and an example for others to follow, one steeped in nationalism, self-sacrifice, and a gritty determination to stand firm in the face of any opposition. Her rule was never about government solving people's problems. Her instincts were deeply conservative. Personal responsibility was paramount. In August 2018, in front of a gathering of over a thousand students and teachers at Rangoon University, she held a nearly two-hour-long discussion with a select group of young graduates. The topic she chose wasn't the economy, the peace process, or even the future of democracy, but literature, her love at Oxford; a central question she posed to the young graduates was whether, in a novel, plot or character was more important.

Three years before, when the National League for Democracy won its landslide election victory, some Burmese analysts had guessed that its government wouldn't last: differences with the generals would come to a head and there would be an army takeover. But nothing of the sort happened. There was mutual distrust, and at times rising tension. But at the end of the day, the former political prisoners and their erstwhile captors had found a way to work together. At a talk in Singapore, Aung San Suu Kyi said that relations with the military "were not that bad" and that the generals in her cabinet were "rather sweet."[2]

In January 2019, the General Administration Department, or GAD, was transferred from the Home Ministry to the Cabinet Office. The GAD was no ordinary department: its 40,000 or so staff were the entire administration of the country, down to the district and township level. They had reported via the home minister, a serving general, to the commander-in-chief as well as the president. Now the military link was severed. It was a big victory for Aung San Suu Kyi's hope of moving the army away from civilian functions. It was a step toward her dream of fulfilling her father's legacy and leaving behind an armed forces subordinate to an elected leader. In February 2019 the NLD-dominated parliament set up a new committee to explore options for constitutional reform. After initial opposition, the army agreed to take part.

In a way, the tissue graft of the NLD onto the old establishment, as created and nurtured by the former dictator Than Shwe, had held. There was no rejection. For the army, the NLD in 2019 seemed decidedly less threatening than it had been even a few years before, and far removed from its revolutionary origins. Both Aung San Suu Kyi and the generals perhaps also sensed in one another similar nationalist leanings, grounded in the same myths around the country's fall to colonial domination and its resurrection in the 1940s. Both prized discipline and the idea of service to "the people." A commitment to "free markets" was also unquestioned. There was a shared Naypyitaw view of the world.

And despite a darkening environment for the media, including the imprisonment of Reuters journalists (released under an amnesty in May 2019) and the draconian use of anti-defamation and colonial-era security laws, Burma was undoubtedly a far freer place than the Burma of a decade before. No one then, in their wildest imaginations, would have guessed that Aung San Suu Kyi would within years lead a government chosen in a free and fair election.

The next general election was scheduled for late 2020, and there was every reason to believe that the NLD would win again. Constitutional change with an end to the army's role in politics might still be long years away. But if the story was just about moving toward a form of democracy—or, even more, if it was just about the coming to power of Aung San Suu Kyi—it was going reasonably well.

Other stories, though, were now commanding the stage. As relations with the West cooled, Sino-Burmese relations were moving into ever higher gear. In early 2019, plans were finally being drawn up for a railway that would connect Rangoon and Mandalay to Shanghai and Beijing. More than two thousand years before, a mission from the Han emperor had tried unsuccessfully to find a passage via Burma to the sea; a millennia-old Chinese dream was coming true. But it wasn't just an issue of government-to-government ties. Chinese companies saw Burma as a cheap market, a place where quick profits could be made, and Chinese tourists began to outnumber Western ones. As China's economy advanced, the sheer force of gravity was becoming impossible for Burma to resist.

India, too, attempted to increase its influence, promising through its Act East policy to connect its northeastern states to Burma. These were the very states—Assam and Manipur—whose conquest in the 1820s by Burmese kings had helped trigger the first Anglo-Burmese War. The British were now nowhere in sight, but Burma was being drawn into a new rivalry between emerging Asian superpowers. Diplomatic instincts were to be friendly with everyone, but friendliness alone would do little to prepare for a future in which Burma became a crossroads between the hinterlands of the world's two biggest nations.

It would be one thing if these tectonic shifts were taking place in an otherwise stable landscape. But Burma in 2019 was a place where core issues around race and identity were not only unsettled but were heating up, with civil society groups, political parties, businesses, militia, and armed organizations all mobilized around ethnic identities to a degree unprecedented in the country's history.

The latest and worst round of violence in Arakan had begun in 2016, with ARSA's attacks on the police and army. The scale and ferocity of the response shocked the world. But what happened was far more than a matter of insurgency and counterinsurgency. At the heart of the crisis are issues of blood and belonging that first consigned Rohingya-speaking Muslims to a second-class status and then ostracized them from the emerging democracy.

And far away from the international gaze are a host of other violent conflicts, between the Burman-dominated state army and militias, big and small, claiming to speak on behalf of a bewildering array of ethnic communities. Millions of lives are at stake in remote highlands where identity politics, moneymaking, and a basic instinct for protection intertwine.

The peace process that began in 2011 attempted to stop all fighting. So far, it hasn't worked. If anything, this period of attempted talks has led to more violent conflict and the emergence of more armed factions than ever before. Part of the problem is that the situation is seen as a "war" requiring "peace," as if a previously orderly society had fragmented into civil conflict and needed only to be repaired. But Burma was never whole. And it's not a coincidence that nearly all the fighting since the 1950s has been in what the British termed the "Frontier Areas": rugged hills and distant valleys that had always been a patchwork of authority and had never before come under the sway of a single state.

The core strategy of the state since independence—of seeing Burma as a collection of peoples with the Burmese language and culture at the core—has failed, and will continue to fail. The government and army may well agree on a formula for constitutional devolution, one that might even be acceptable to many Ethnic Armed Organizations. But to think that was ever the main issue would be a tragic mistake.

Race and identity have been at the heart of Burmese politics since the start of modern Burmese politics a hundred years ago. Colonialism and the immigration of millions of people from India brought on an identity crisis that has not yet been resolved. Any brighter future will depend on Burma crafting a new and more inclusive identity, one not tied to race and one not based on a notion of uniting fixed ethnic categories. The British were correct in analyzing Burma as a zone of "racial instability." Accepting this, seeing it as a strength rather than a weakness, finding new sources of national identity, separate from notions of ethnicity, and embarking on an aggressive agenda to end discrimination in all its forms, are elements of a conversation that's been almost entirely absent.

IT'S EASY TO SEE IDENTITY as the driving story today, in Burma as everywhere, and it's tempting to view the past few years as a democracy experiment gone awry because of a resurgence of ethno-nationalism. But that would be to overlook an even bigger story, one more hidden, which is the story of Burmese capitalism. It's been the missing element in the thinking of nearly all observers, though not ordinary people, who are prospering or becoming impoverished, living and dying, as a result of markets that are bound by few restraints.

In the late 1980s, left-wing ideologies collapsed and there was a move toward capitalism under the harshest of dictatorships, without debate. Cronyism and racketeering thrived, and in the shadow of rotting state institutions grew powerful networks focused entirely on moneymaking. At the apex are men and women who collude and conspire across every racial and religious divide.

After 2011, the assumption was that the economy needed only reform, in the direction of a cleaner, greener capitalism more integrated with global markets. There was an unstated ambition to transition from the anarchic, plundering capitalism of the dictatorship toward a fast-industrializing state capitalism, one powered by global investment. And today, neoliberalism, a faith in free markets and a disdain for state-led development, is held out as the only alternative to the corrupt and crony-driven capitalism of the past. There is much talk of Burma's democracy transition but next to no discussion around its transition from one strain of capitalism to another.

Democracy can mean many things, but in Burma it has meant primarily a form of competitive politics, organized around political parties and regular elections. It's been an elite-level substitute for the junta over a state that is scarcely functioning and that doesn't even control significant patches of the country.

And democratic change so far has at the very least been insufficient. At worst it has legitimized inequalities and unleashed a maelstrom of identity-based conflicts for which society was ill-prepared.

The sequencing has been misjudged. It's hard to imagine any meaningful progress toward democracy with existing levels of inequality. To a far greater extent than even twenty years ago, the rich and poor in Burma today live entirely different lives.

The focus should have been on radical measures to fight discrimination, enabling a robust and free media, building new and inclusive state institutions, including for taxation, policing, and justice, and creating a welfare state on which all citizens could depend. Instead, the focus has been on injecting a new layer of partisan competition on an already fractious landscape. The result has been a coarsening of public debate and a polarized political class.

At a time when democracy and markets are increasingly seen in the West as unable to cope with issues of inequality, identity, and climate change, they have become Burma's only prescription for the future. Twentieth-century solutions are being offered as the default answers to the country's 21st-century challenges.

The critical questions are not discussed. Burma will before long bear the brunt of rising sea levels, unbearably hot summers, and more-frequent extreme weather, including cyclones like Nargis. China and India's gargantuan economies next door may be friends or foes. With automation and a changing pattern of global consumption, the world may soon have no need for Burma's cheap labor or even its natural resources: the ladder of export-oriented growth so successfully climbed by other Asian countries may soon be a ladder to nowhere. So what economic future is possible? What economy can overtake the pull of methamphetamine production and other illicit industries, withstand climate change, and make possible free and dignified lives for tens of millions of people? As importantly, if given a real choice, what kind of life would Burmese people want to live: the lives of other Asian consumers, or something different?

In the meantime, the plight of the poor in Burma continues to be ignored with impunity. Western sanctions, which included aid cut-offs, destroyed the lives of millions, but on this there has been no quest for accountability. Sanctions during the 1990s and 2000s did nothing to compel the generals in a liberal direction and, if anything, have made any transition to a better future more difficult. Yet they may be returning. Over 2019, the European Union will likely decide whether or not to revoke trade privileges, a move that would collapse the garment industry and throw more than 500,000 otherwise destitute young women out of work.

Since colonial times, whatever has happened in Burma, the ordinary people have consistently wound up the losers.

The warning signs are flashing. The two most combustible elements on the Burmese political landscape remain race and inequality. They are now being mixed together with immature democratic institutions, a blind faith in free markets, multibillion-dollar illicit industries, and an uplands awash in weapons. We risk a failed state in the heart of Asia.

Burma is running out of time. The country needs a radical agenda to fight inequality and prepare for the climate emergency to come. It needs as well a new story that embraces its diversity, celebrates its natural environment, and aspires to a new way of life. Perhaps most of all, Burma needs a new project of the imagination.

ACKNOWLEDGMENTS

THIS BOOK IS BASED in part on my experiences over the nearly twelve years (2007–2019) that I've lived and worked in Rangoon. Everything I've done during this time would not have been possible without the advice and help of people from all walks of life, Burmese and foreign, who are too numerous to name but whose friendship has been invaluable. My conversations with them and our mutual efforts to try to improve things—some failures, others quietly successful—have been my education on Burma.

This book is based as well on more than forty interviews conducted over 2017–18. The names of those interviewed are all in the references except for those, primarily serving and past government officials, who have asked to remain anonymous. I'm grateful to Esther Htusan, Ohnmar Ei Ei Chaw, and Susanne Kempel for helping to arrange several of the interviews.

My special thanks go to my editor, Alane Salierno Mason at Norton, for her patient attention and all-important guidance, since the very earliest days of this book's conception and writing. I'm especially grateful as well to Chiki Sarkar and Nandini Mehta at Juggernaut and Will Atkinson at Atlantic Books for all their sage advice and enthusiastic support. Thank you, too, to my agent Clare Alexander whose counsel has, as always, been indispensable.

My son Thurayn read drafts during our trips around Burma together this past year, providing unique insights and suggestions.

My deepest thanks go to my wife, Sofia, who has been with me in Rangoon through all these turbulent, often bewildering years. So much of my work has been in partnership with her. Without her steadfast support, encouragement, and good humor, this book and much else would not have been possible.

NOTES

ONE: NEW WORLD

1. Richard Eaton, *The Rise of Islam and the Bengal Frontier, 1204–1760* (Berkeley: University of California Press, 1996).

2. Erik Klementi, "Tambora 1815: Just How Big Was The Eruption?," *Wired*, October 4, 2015.

3. Robert Kelly, "Blast from the Past: The eruption of Mount Tambora killed thousands, plunged much of the world into a frightful chill and offers lessons for today," *Smithsonian Magazine*, July 2002.

4. C. C. Gao, Y. J. Gao, Q. Zhang, et al., "2017: Climatic Aftermath of the 1815 Tambora Eruption in China," *Journal of Meteorological Research* 31, no. 1 (2017): 28–38.

5. J. N. Hays, *Epidemics and Pandemics: Their Impacts on Human History* (Santa Barbara, CA: ABC-CLIO, 2005), chapter 22.

6. Thant Myint-U, *The Making of Modern Burma* (Cambridge, UK: Cambridge University Press, 2012), 100.

7. Quoted in Dorothy Woodman, *The Making of Burma* (London: Cresset Press, 1962), 64.

8. Government of India, Home Department, October 19, 1886, quoted in *History of the Third Burmese War* (1885, 1886, 1887), Period One (Calcutta: Superintendent of Government Printing, Government of India, 1887).

9. Mira Kamdar, *Motiba's Tattoos: A Granddaughter's Journey into her Indian Family's Past* (New York: PublicAffairs, 2000), 123.

10. J. S. Furnivall, *Colonial Policy and Practice: A Comparative Study of Burma and Netherlands India* (New York: New York University Press, 1956), 304–5; see also Lee Hock Guan, "Furnivall's plural society and Leach's political systems of highland Burma," Institute of Southeast Asian Studies, October 7, 2018.

11. Furnivall, *Colonial Policy and Practice*, 310–12.

12. George Orwell, "How a Nation is Exploited: The British Empire in Burma," *Le Progrès Civique*, May 4, 1929.

13. Thomas Callan Hodson, "Analysis of the 1931 Census of India," (New Delhi: Government of India Press, 1937).

14. Census of India, 1931, vol. 11: "Burma, Part One (Report)" (Office of the Superintendent of Government Printing, Burma), chap. 1, "Caste tribe race." Available at: http://www .burmalibrary.org/show.php?cat=3540&lo=&sl=.

15. Census of India, 1911, vol. 9: "Indigenous Races of Burma" (Office of the Superintendent of Government Printing, Burma), section 269. Available at: http://www.burmalibrary.org/ show.php?cat=3540&lo=&sl=.

16. Mitra Sharafi, "Bella's Case: Parsi Identity and the Law in Colonial Rangoon, Bombay and London, 1887–1925," (PhD dissertation, Princeton University, 2006), 309.

17. Census of India, 1901, vol. 12, "Burma, Part One (Report)" (Office of the Superintendent of Government Printing, Burma), 169. Available at: http://www.burmalibrary.org/show .php?cat=3540&lo=&sl=.

18. Rudyard Kipling, *From Sea to Sea* (New York: Doubleday, 1913), 202.

19. Census of India, 1921, vol. 10: "Burma, Part One (Report)" (Office of the Superintendent of Government Printing, Burma), 207. Available at: http://www.burmalibrary.org/show .php?cat=3540&lo=&sl=.

20. Census of India, 1911, vol. 9, "Burma, Part One (Report)" (Office of the Superintendent of Government Printing, Burma), 241. Available at: http://www.burmalibrary.org/show .php?cat=3540&lo=&sl=.

21. Quoted in Henry Yule, *A Narrative of the Mission to the Court of Ava in 1855* (Oxford: Oxford University Press, 1968), 107.

22. Anne Thackeray Ritchie, *Lord Amherst and the British Advance Eastwards to Burma* (Oxford: Clarendon Press, 1909), 25.

TWO: CHANGING LANES

1. Nick Cheeseman, "How in Myanmar 'National Races' Came to Surpass Citizenship and Exclude Rohingya," *Journal of Contemporary Asia* 47, no. 3 (2017).

2. Aung San Suu Kyi, "Socio-Political Currents in Burmese Literature, 1910–1940," in *Burma and Japan: Basic Studies on their Cultural and Social Structure* (Tokyo: Tokyo University School of Foreign Studies, Burma Research Group, 1987), 65–83.

3. Aung San Suu Kyi, "Intellectual Life in Burma Under Colonialism," in *Freedom from Fear, and Other Writings* (New York: Penguin, 2010), 104.

4. Nilanjana Sengupta, "Why Suu Kyi Favours Jean Valjean over Ulysses," *The Straits Times*, December 13, 2015.

5. Aung San Suu Kyi, "The True Meaning of Boh," in *Freedom from Fear*, 191.

6. Aung San Suu Kyi, "The True Meaning of Boh."

7. Arab Press Service Organization, March 14, 1992, quoted in Minorities at Risk Project, "Chronology for Rohingya (Arakanese) in Burma, Minorities at Risk," http://www.mar .umd.edu/chronology.asp?groupId=77501.

8. Bertil Lintner, *The Rise and Fall of the Communist Party of Burma* (Ithaca, NY: Cornell University Press, 1990), 90–91.

9. Inter-Press News Agency, "Burma—Human Rights: Divestment Campaign Gets Boost from Pepsi," April 24, 1996.

10. Michael Hirsh, "Making it in Mandalay," *Newsweek*, June 18, 1995.

11. Aung San Suu Kyi, "Please Use Your Liberty to Promote Ours," *New York Times*, February 4, 1997.

12. Thomas Fuller, "Profits of Drug Trade Drive Economic Boom in Myanmar," *New York Times*, June 5, 2015.

13. Fuller, "Profits of Drug Trade."

THREE: DRIFTING TO DYSTOPIA

1. Moe Moe Myint Aung, author interview, August 21, 2018.

2. Charles Petrie, "End of Mission Report: UN Resident and Humanitarian Coordinator, UNDP Resident Representative for Myanmar, 2003–2007."

3. https://wikileaks.org/plusd/cables/03RANGOON53_a.html.

4. Hannah Beech, "Laura Bush's Burmese Crusade," *Time*, September 5, 2007; Laura Bush, "Stop the Terror in Burma," *Wall Street Journal*, October 10, 2007; Laura Bush, *Spoken from the Heart* (New York: Scribner, 2010), 393.

5. Francis Fukuyama, "The End of History?," *The National Interest* 16 (1989): 3–18.

6. Agence France Presse, "US Lawmakers Send Myanmar Sanctions Bill to White House for Signing," July 17, 2004.

7. Jennifer Steinhauer, "Myanmar's Leader Has a Longtime Champion in Mitch McConnell," *New York Times*, September 14, 2016.

8. Human Rights Watch, "Crackdown on Burmese Muslims," briefing paper, July 2002.

9. "A Darker Shade of Bleak," *Economist*, October 21, 2004.

10. Organization for Economic Co-operation and Development, "Aid (ODA) disbursements to countries and regions," 2005. Available at https://stats.oecd.org/Index.aspx?DataSetCode=Table2A.

11. World Health Organization, "World Health Report 2000," http://www.who.int/whr/2000/en/.

12. Htet Aung, "Freed HIV/AIDS Activist Calls for Government Cooperation," *The Irrawaddy*, July 3, 2007.

13. Maung Than, author interview, August 20, 2018.

14. Razali Ismail, "Meetings with Aung San Suu Kyi," *The Irrawaddy*, April 2007.

15. Jane Perlez, "Myanmar Is Left in Dark, an Energy-Rich Orphan," *New York Times*, November 17, 2006.

16. Ko Ko Gyi, author interview, August 22, 2018.

FOUR: TEMPEST

1. Herman M. Fritz et al., "Cyclone Nargis Storm Surge Flooding in Myanmar's Ayeyarwaddy Delta," in Yassine Charabi, ed., *Indian Ocean Tropical Cyclones and Climate Change* (London: Springer, 2010), 297.

2. ASEAN and United Nations, "Comprehensive Assessment of Cyclone Nargis Impact Provides Clearer Picture of Relief and Recovery Needs," joint press release, July 21, 2008.
3. Thein Sein, author interview, August 2, 2018.
4. Simon Montlake, "Burma (Myanmar): An Unbending Junta Still Blocks Aid," *Christian Science Monitor*, May 12, 2008.
5. Seth Mydans, "Myanmar Seizes U.N. Food for Cyclone Victims and Blocks Foreign Experts," *New York Times*, May 10, 2008.
6. Global Policy Forum, "The Responsibility to Protect and Its Application," May 9, 2008; Timothy Garton Ash, "We Have a Responsibility to Protect the People of Burma. But How?", *Guardian*, May 22, 2008.
7. Scott Marciel (deputy assistant secretary of state for East Asia and the Pacific), "Burma in the Aftermath of Cyclone Nargis: Death, Displacement, and Humanitarian Aid," statement before the Subcommittee on Asia, the Pacific, and the Global Environment, House Committee on Foreign Affairs, May 20, 2008. Available at: https://2001-2009.state.gov/p/eap/rls/rm/2008/05/105017.htm.
8. Kyaw Thu, author interview, September 3, 2018.
9. Soe Thane, author interview, March 1, 2017.
10. Farik Zolkepli, "Asean task force to channel aid to Myanmar," *The Star*, May 19, 2008.
11. "Myanmar Agrees to Allow 'All Aid Workers': UN Chief," *Sydney Morning Herald*, May 23, 2008.
12. "At Donors' Meeting, Ban Ki-Moon Says Myanmar Relief Effort to Last at Least Six Months," *UN News*, May 25, 2008.
13. Irin News, "ODA Shrinks Post-Nargis," January 24, 2011.
14. Irin News, "Myanmar: Shelter Issues and Land Rights Frustrate Resettlement," June 9, 2010.
15. Kyaw Thu, author interview, September 3, 2018.
16. Noeleen Heyzer, author interview, April 19, 2018.
17. Noeleen Heyzer, author interview, April 19, 2018.

FIVE: FIGHTING CHANCE

1. Thant Myint-U, *The Making of Modern Burma*, 29.
2. Michael Wines, "China Fails to Prevent Myanmar's Ethnic Clashes," *New York Times*, September 3, 2009.
3. Ja Nan Lahtaw, author interview, August 28, 2018.
4. Glenn Kessler, "Shift Possible on Burma Policy," *Washington Post*, February 19, 2009.
5. Josh Rogin, "Webb Fires Back at Critics of his Burmese Outreach," *Foreign Policy*, September 18, 2009.
6. Jim Webb, "We Cannot Afford to Ignore Myanmar," *New York Times*, August 25, 2009.
7. Thant Myint-U, testimony before the East Asia Subcommittee of the Senate Foreign Relations Committee, September 30, 2009, https://www.foreign.senate.gov/imo/media/doc/Myint-UTestimony090930p.pdf.
8. Tin Maung Thann, author interview, February 28, 2017.
9. Tin Hlaing, author interview, August 10, 2018.

10. "Myanmese Envoy Says Rohingya Ugly as Ogres," *South China Morning Post*, February 11, 2009.

11. Jack Davies, "Aung San Suu Kyi Release Brings Joy, Tears—and New Hope for Burma," *Guardian*, November 13, 2010.

12. John Simpson, "Aung San Suu Kyi Aims for Peaceful Revolution," BBC News, November 15, 2010.

13. U Myint, "Second Development Partnership: Roundtable and Development Forum, Naypyitaw, 15 December 2009," press briefing, January 9, 2010.

SIX: ALIGNMENT

1. Simon Montlake, "McCain Visits Burma, but Will Calls for Change Backfire?" *Christian Science Monitor*, June 7, 2011.

2. Joshua Hammer, "A Free Woman: Can Aung San Suu Kyi Unite a Badly Weakened Opposition?," *New Yorker*, January 24, 2011.

3. Aung Min, author interview, December 22, 2016.

4. Hla Maung Shwe, author interview, February 23, 2018.

5. Wai Moe, "Suu Kyi Satisfied with Thein Sein Talks," *The Irrawaddy*, August 20, 2011.

6. Thein Sein, author interview, August 2, 2018.

7. Thein Sein, author interview, August 2, 2018.

8. Rachel Harvey, "Burma Dam: Why Myitsone Plan Is Being Halted," BBC News, September 30, 2011.

9. "'Save The Irrawaddy' Campaign Gains Momentum," *The Irrawaddy*, September 2, 2011.

10. Hannah Beech, "In a Rare Reversal, Burma's Government Listens to Its People and Suspends a Dam," *New York Times*, September 30, 2011.

11. Aung Hla Tun, "Myanmar Govt Shelves $3.6 Bln Mega Dam – Officials," Reuters, October 1, 2011.

12. Waiyan Moethone Thann, author interview, December 8, 2017.

13. Ben Rhodes, *The World as It Is: A Memoir of the Obama White House* (New York: Random House, 2018), 167.

14. Steve Lee Meyers, "Clinton Says U.S. Will Relax Some Restrictions on Myanmar," *New York Times*, December 1, 2011.

15. William Wan, "Clinton, Suu Kyi Discuss Burma's Road to Democracy," *Washington Post*, December 2, 2011.

16. Agence France Presse, "Norway Lifts Economic Sanctions Against Burma," April 16, 2012.

17. Aung Kyi, author interview, July 1, 2018.

18. Ye Htut, author interview, January 9, 2018.

19. Soc Thane, author interview, April 3, 2017.

20. Hannah Beech, "The Lady Abroad: On First Foreign Tour, Aung San Suu Kyi Enchants and Lectures," *Time*, June 1, 2012.

21. "Aung San Suu Kyi Receives Honorary Degree," *University of Oxford News*, June 20, 2012.

22. "Aung San Suu Kyi Awarded US Congressional Medal," *Guardian*, September 20, 2012.

23. "Burma's Aung San Suu Kyi Given US Congressional Medal," BBC News, September 19, 2012.
24. Rhodes, *The World as It Is*, 243.
25. Rhodes, *The World as It Is*, 193.
26. Rhodes, *The World as It Is*, 193.
27. David Eimer, "Barack Obama Warned: Don't Be Lured by Burma 'Mirage of Success,'" *Daily Telegraph*, November 19, 2012.

SEVEN: BLOOD AND BELONGING

1. Aung Min, author interview, December 22, 2016.
2. Aung Min, author interview, December 22, 2016.
3. Aung Min, author interview, December 22, 2016.
4. Aung Min, author interview, December 22, 2016.
5. International Crisis Group, "A Tentative Peace in Myanmar's Kachin Conflict," update, June 12, 2013.
6. Bertil Lintner, "Myanmar Airstrikes Reopen Ethnic Wounds," *Al Jazeera*, January 10, 2013.
7. Lian Sakhong, author interview, September 3, 2018.
8. Lian Sakhong, author interview, September 3, 2018.
9. Yun Sun, "China and the Myanmar Peace Process," US Institute for Peace, March 2017, 13.
10. Ankit Panda, "After Myanmar Bombing, China Deploys Jets, Warns of 'Resolute Measures,'" *The Diplomat*, March 15, 2015.
11. United Nations Office for the Coordination of Humanitarian Assistance, *Humanitarian Bulletin* 7, Myanmar issue, November–December 2015.
12. United Nations High Commisioner for Refugees, "Villagers Still Fleeing Homes in Myanmar's Rakhine State," update, October 4, 2012.
13. Aye Aye Soe, author interview, August 10, 2018.
14. Tin Hlaing, author interview, August 10, 2018.
15. "Call to Put Rohingya in Refugee Camps," Radio Free Asia, July 12, 2012.
16. President's Office, statement, July 12, 2012, http://www.networkmyanmar.org/ESW/Files/Thein-Sein-Guterres.pdf (with unofficial translation).
17. Thomas Fuller, "Myanmar Troops Sent to City Torn by Sectarian Rioting," *New York Times*, March 22, 2013.
18. "Meiktila Violence Work of 'Well-Trained Terrorists,'" *Myanmar Times*, April 1, 2013.
19. Tun Khaing, "The True Face of Buddhism," *Frontier*, May 12, 2017.
20. Kyaw Phone Kyaw, "The Healing of Meiktila," *Frontier*, April 21, 2016.

EIGHT: VIRTUAL TRANSITIONS

1. Kyaw Hsu Mon and Simon Lewis, "Rangoon Rental Costs in the Spotlight After UNICEF Outcry," *The Irrawaddy*, May 30, 2014.
2. Adam Feinstein, *Pablo Neruda: A Passion for Life* (New York: Bloomsbury, 2004), 53–67.
3. Rhodes, *The World as It Is*, 193.
4. McKinsey Global Institute, "Myanmar's Moment: Unique Opportunities, Major Challenges," May 30, 2013.

5. World Bank, *Myanmar Living Conditions Survey 2017*, June 2018.

6. Myanmar Livelihoods and Food Security Trust Fund (LIFT), *Household Survey*, 2015, vii–viii.

7. *Livelihoods and Food Security in Rural Myanmar: Survey Findings*, report of a joint Australia-Myanmar project funded through the Australian Research Council, 2016.

8. Htet Naing Zaw, "Gov't Committee to Settle All Land Grab Cases in Six Months," *The Irrawaddy*, July 1, 2016.

9. Mra Tun, author interview, August 21, 2018.

10. See Yan Naung Oak, "Even with New Data, Valuing Myanmar's Jade Industry Remains a Challenge," *Open Data*, Natural Resource Governance Institute, http://openjadedata .org/Stories/how_much_jade_worth.html.

11. Shibani Mahtani, "Myanmar Mine Disaster Highlights Challenge to Suu Kyi," *Wall Street Journal*, November 23, 2015; David Scott Mathieson, "Dispatches: Greed and Death in Burma's Jade Mines," Human Rights Watch, December 15, 2015.

12. Huang Jingjing, "Myanmar Border Town Is an Attraction and Trap for Chinese Gamblers," *Global Times*, December 19, 2016.

13. US Treasury Department, "Treasury Sanctions the Zhao Wei Transnational Criminal Organization," press release, January 30, 2018. Zhao denies the allegations: https:// calvinayre.com/2018/02/06/casino/laos-king-romans-casino-co-owner-decries -transnational-criminal-tag/.

14. Sun, "China and the Myanmar Peace Process," 8–9.

15. Timothy McLaughlin, "How Facebook's Rise Fuelled Chaos and Confusion in Myanmar," *Wired*, June 7, 2018.

16. International Crisis Group, "Buddhism and State Power in Myanmar," September 5, 2017.

17. Aung Kyaw Min, "Religion looms large over poll as NLD, Ma Ba Tha trade words," *Myanmar Times*, July 31, 2015.

18. Matthew J. Walton, Melyn McKay, and Ma Khin Mar Mar Kyi, "Why Are Women Supporting Myanmar's 'Religious Protection Laws'?," September 9, 2015.

19. Transnational Institute, "Ethnicity Without Meaning, Data Without Context: The 2014 Census, Identity and Citizenship in Burma/Myanmar," Burma update, February 13, 2014; International Crisis Group, "Counting the Costs: Myanmar's Problematic Census," update briefing, May 15, 2014.

20. United Nations Office of the High Commissioner for Human Rights, "Pillay Calls for Killings in Northern Rakhine to Be Investigated," January 23, 2014.

21. David Scott Mathieson, "Burma's Lost Rapport on Rights Protection," *Tea Circle Oxford*, April 2, 2018.

22. "Pakistani Taliban Attempts to Recruit Rohingyas to Kill Myanmar's Rulers," *Sydney Morning Herald*, June 19, 2015.

23. Nu Nu Khin, author interview, December 12, 2018.

24. Thin Thin Lei, "Sexism, Racism, Poor Education Condemn Rohingya Women in Western Myanmar," Thompson Reuters Foundation, July 9, 2014.

25. Nyo Aye, author interview, August 10, 2018.

26. "Bangladesh PM Says Illegal Migrants Taint National Image," BBC News, May 24, 2015.

27. Ngeginpao Kipgen, "Leaders Face Constitutional Challenges," *Bangkok Post*, July 2, 2015.

28. Richard Horsey, "New Religious Legislation in Myanmar," prepared for the Conflict Prevention and Peace Forum, Social Science Research Council, February 13, 2015.

29. Sui-Lee Wee, "Myanmar Official Accuses China of Meddling in Rebel Peace Talks," Reuters, October 9, 2015; Sun, "China and the Myanmar Peace Process."

NINE: UNFINISHED NATION

1. Aung Hla Tun, "Myanmar's Ex-Dictator Sees Suu Kyi as Country's 'Future Leader': Relative," Reuters, December 5, 2015.

2. Fergal Keane, "Myanmar Election: Aung San Suu Kyi Positions Herself for Victory," BBC News, November 10, 2015.

3. Hannah Ellis-Peterson, "From Peace Icon to Pariah: Aung San Suu Kyi's Fall from Grace," *Guardian*, November 23, 2018.

4. Thein Sein, author interview, August 2, 2018.

5. Htoo Thant, "'State Counsellor' Bill Approved Despite Military Voting Boycott," *Myanmar Times*, April 5, 2016.

6. "Myanmar Finance Minister Nominee Kyaw Win Has Fake Degree," BBC News, March 23, 2016.

7. Rhodes, *The World as It Is*, 389–90.

8. China Ministry of Foreign Affairs, "Xi Jinping Meets with State Counsellor Aung San Suu Kyi of Myanmar," press release, August 19, 2016.

9. Jane Perlez, "China Helps Aung San Suu Kyi with Peace Talks in Myanmar," *New York Times*, August 20, 2016.

10. International Crisis Group, "Myanmar: A New Muslim Insurgency in Rakhine State," December 15, 2016; International Crisis Group, "Myanmar Tips into New Crisis after Rakhine State Attacks," August 27, 2017.

11. Su Myat Mon and Steve Gleason, "NLD Official Gets Six Month Sentence in Latest Telco Law Case," *Frontier*, April 7, 2017.

12. Human Rights Watch, "Burma: Rohingya Recount Killings, Rape, and Arson," December 21, 2016.

13. Kayleigh Long, "Rohingya Insurgency Takes Lethal Form in Myanmar," *Asia Times*, June 20, 2017.

14. Prashant Jha, "Lashkar Militants Inciting Rohingya Refugees, India Warns Myanmar," *Hindustan Times*, Feburary 7, 2017.

15. Probir Kumar Sakar, "Wider Support for Rohingya Terrorists Hints at Further Attacks," *Dhaka Tribune*, July 3, 2017.

16. Advisory Commission on Rakhine State, "Towards a Peaceful, Fair and Prosperous Future for the People of Rakhine," final report, http://www.rakhinecommission.org/the-final-report/.

17. Amnesty International, "Briefing: Attacks by the Arakan Rohingya Salvation Army (ARSA) on Hindus in Northern Rakhine State," May 10, 2018.

18. Amnesty International, "'We Will Destroy Everything': Military Responsibility for Crimes Against Humanity in Rakhine State," June 27, 2018, 47.

19. Amnesty International, "'We Will Destroy Everything,'" 1.

20. Associated Press, "'Everything Is Gone': Satellite Images in Myanmar Show Dozens of Rohingya Villages Bulldozed," Feburary 24, 2018.

21. Médecins Sans Frontières, "MSF Surveys Estimate that at Least 6,700 Rohingya Were Killed during the Attacks in Myanmar," December 12, 2017.

22. Amnesty International, "'We Will Destroy Everything,'" 59–61.

23. Amnesty International, "'We Will Destroy Everything,'" 72; Human Rights Watch, "Burma: Methodical Massacre at Rohingya Village," December 19, 2017.

24. Wa Lone, Kyaw Soe Oo, Simon Lewis, and Antoni Slodkowski, "How Myanmar Forces Burned, Looted and Killed in a Remote Village," Reuters Special Report, Feburary 8, 2018.

25. Rick Gladstone and Megan Specia, "Pressure Rises at U.N. on Myanmar Over Rohingya Crisis," *New York Times*, September 28, 2017.

26. Reuters, "Al Qaeda Warns Myanmar of 'Punishment' over Rohingya," September 13, 2017.

27. Naaman Zhou and Michael Safi, "Desmond Tutu Condemns Aung San Suu Kyi: 'Silence is too high a price,'" *Guardian*, September 8, 2017.

28. "He Admits Giving It Up Is 'a PR Stunt', but What Happens Now to Bob Geldof's Freedom of Dublin?," *The Journal*, November 13, 2017.

29. Aye Aye Soe, author interview, August 10, 2018.

30. Joe Freeman and Annie Gowen, "Burma's Aung San Suu Kyi Under Fire as Alleged Military Abuse Follows Militant Attack," *Washington Post*, November 4, 2018.

31. Tim McLaughlin, "How Facebook's Rise Fueled Chaos and Confusion in Myanmar," *Wired*, June 7, 2018.

32. United Nations Human Rights Council, "Report of Independent International Fact-Finding Mission on Myanmar," August 27, 2018.

33. UN News, Myanmar Military Leaders Must Face Genocide Charges – UN report," August 27, 2018.

34. Toby Sterling, "International Criminal Court Says It Has Jurisdiction over Alleged Crimes Against Rohingya," Reuters, September 6, 2018.

35. Owen Bowcott, "John Bolton Threatens War Crimes Court with Sanctions in Virulent Attack," *Guardian*, September 10, 2018.

36. Agence France Presse, "Facebook Bans Min Aung Hlaing, Army Top Brass after UN Genocide Allegations," August 27, 2018.

37. Zhang Hui, "FM Proposes China–Myanmar Economic Corridor," *Global Times*, November 20, 2017.

38. Kyaw Lin Htoon, "Tough Money: Central Bank Steers Painful Reforms," *Frontier*, May 7, 2018.

EPILOGUE

1. Pe Thet Htet Khin, "Daw Aung San Suu Kyi's Fetching Friend," *The Irrawaddy*, May 17, 2017.

2. John Geddie and Fathin Ungku, "Myanmar's Suu Kyi Says Relations with Military 'Not That Bad,'" Reuters, August 21, 2018.

INDEX